President Lyndon Johnson and Soviet communism

GW00702161

Published in our
centenary year
~ **2004** ~
MANCHESTER
UNIVERSITY
PRESS

President Lyndon Johnson and Soviet communism

JOHN DUMBRELL

MANCHESTER UNIVERSITY PRESS

MANCHESTER AND NEW YORK

distributed exclusively in the USA by Palgrave

The right of John Dumbrell to be identified as the author of this work has been asserted by him in accordance with the Copyright, Designs and Patents Act 1988.

Published by Manchester University Press
Oxford Road, Manchester M13 9NR, UK
and Room 400, 175 Fifth Avenue, New York, NY 10010, USA
www.manchesteruniversitypress.co.uk

Distributed exclusively in the USA by
Palgrave, 175 Fifth Avenue, New York,
NY 10010, USA

Distributed exclusively in Canada by
UBC Press, University of British Columbia, 2029 West Mall,
Vancouver, BC, Canada V6T 1Z2

British Library Cataloguing-in-Publication Data
A catalogue record for this book is available from the British Library

Library of Congress Cataloging-in-Publication Data applied for

ISBN 0 7190 6263 2 *hardback*
0 7190 6264 0 *paperback*

First published 2004

13 12 11 10 09 08 07 06 05 04   10 9 8 7 6 5 4 3 2 1

Typeset in Sabon with Syntax
by SNP Best-set Typesetter Ltd., Hong Kong
Printed in Great Britain
by Biddles Ltd., King's Lynn

Contents

Acknowledgements

The writing of this book was made possible by the granting of a research leave award by the Arts and Humanities Research Board. I wish to thank the AHRB for their support and for their refreshingly unbureaucratic approach to encouraging research. I am also very grateful to the staff at the Lyndon B. Johnson Presidential Library in Austin, Texas, where much of the research was conducted. Thanks also to Alison Welsby of Manchester University Press, to Jenny Dobbing and to colleagues in the department of American Studies at Keele University. The book is dedicated to all past, present and future members of the department.

Note on sources

The essential reference point for students of US foreign policy in the 1960s is the *Foreign Relations of the United States* series, abbreviated in the chapter notes as *FRUS*. The Lyndon Johnson Presidential Library in Austin, Texas, has an abundance of relevant documents. The National Security File (NSF) is the prime source, especially the Country File (CF) for the Soviet Union. Many other files, and also the Oral History collection, contain valuable primary material. Additional research was undertaken at the National Archives ('Archives II') at College Park, Maryland. Various standard published sources, notably the *Public Papers of the Presidents of the United States* (PPPUS) were consulted. Useful material was also found on the National Security Archive (NSA) and Woodrow Wilson Center Cold War International History Project (CWIHP) websites.

Introduction

Civil rights, Great Society, Vietnam: these words, correctly, dominate our understanding of the Presidency of Lyndon Baines Johnson. Popular memory identifies Johnson as the President who sponsored historic and successful civil rights laws, and who advanced a wider and very ambitious, if ultimately flawed, programme of domestic reform. It also recalls him as a loser of the Vietnam War. One recent study concludes that LBJ ended up 'losing the war and his Great Society'.[1]

As the years have gone by, numerous commentators have tried to extend some sympathetic understanding to Johnson's dilemmas in making decisions on the war. Very few seriously defend his actual handling of it. On the domestic side, most commentators have been prepared to give credit to Johnson at least for the hell of good intentions. In 1999, John Kenneth Galbraith – President Kennedy's Ambassador to India, an early adviser to the Johnson Administration and later a leading liberal intellectual critic of the war – praised LBJ as second 'only to [Franklin] Roosevelt, and in some respects more so, . . . the most effective advocate of humane social change in the United States in this century'.[2] For Irving Bernstein, Johnson 'has been charged with what went wrong and has not been credited with what went right'.[3]

Various defenders of Johnson's foreign policy have sought to include his non-Vietnam War policy as part of 'what went right'. For Walt Rostow (National Security Adviser to Johnson, 1966–69), there 'was a great deal more to Johnson's foreign policy than his determination to honor the Southeast Asia Treaty without triggering a larger war'. LBJ also stabilised the North Atlantic Treaty Organisation following France's 1967 defection. He followed sensible regional policies in the Caribbean, the Middle East, Africa, Latin America and Asia (Rostow credited LBJ for promoting 'regional coherence' in the latter three areas, especially in Asia with his work to create the Asian Development Bank and the Association of Southeast Asian Nations (ASEAN)). LBJ, according to Rostow, also fulfilled his 'responsibility to the human race to minimise the risk of nuclear war', not least by moving to normalise relations with the Soviet Union.[4] For Dean Rusk (Secretary of State under Presidents Kennedy and Johnson), Soviet policy successes in particular needed to be considered alongside Vietnam War issues. Historians should 'take a broader view' and give due weight to the consular and civil air agreements with the Soviet Union, the Nonproliferation Treaty, the Outer Space Treaty, the East–West trade bill, the commencement of the arms control process with the USSR and 'many other initiatives aimed at building the peace'.[5] For LBJ himself, the state of US–Soviet relations bequeathed to President Nixon in 1969 was hugely superior to that which President Eisenhower handed to Kennedy in 1961. In his memoir, *The Vantage Point*, Johnson observed that, in 1961, US 'relations with the Soviet Union were about as unpromising as they had ever been', following the Soviet shooting down of the American U-2 plane and the collapse of the Paris summit. Eight years of Democratic occupation of the White House transformed all this. According to LBJ, the 1968 signing of the Nuclear Nonproliferation Treaty was 'the most significant step we had yet taken to reduce the possibility of nuclear war'.[6]

Part of the intention behind the following chapters is to take seriously the contention of leading foreign players from the Johnson Administration that its non-Vietnam policies in general, and its Soviet policy in particular, deserve reappraisal. This book should also be seen as a contribution to the 'beyond Vietnam' Johnson historiography which has emerged in recent years.[7] It does seek to question the common opinion, expressed for example by Deborah Welch Larson: 'Johnson was too preoccupied with Vietnam to make a sustained effort to improve US–Soviet relations'.[8] That LBJ was preoccupied with the war is not in question. The most cursory examination of the primary record shows a President who was increasingly mired in the detailed management of a conflict which was slipping far beyond his control. Preoccupation with the war did not leave the Johnson Administration much time, energy nor opportunity for sustained diplomatic initiatives. Yet important progress towards détente with Moscow was made in these years, and this progress deserves serious attention.

The following chapters do not ignore the Vietnam War. That would be absurd. US–Soviet relations and American perceptions of the 'Soviet threat' were closely intertwined with America's conduct of the war, and two fairly long chapters of this book are devoted to Vietnam. The war profoundly affected both bilateral US–Soviet relations and superpower competition in other regions of the world. In a sense, the ending of the Cold War enables us to also put the Vietnam War into its international historical context. Much recent Vietnam War scholarship has embraced the global dimension to the conflict, and several parts of the following discussion are written in the same spirit.[9] *President Lyndon Johnson and Soviet Communism* is intended as a contribution to Johnson scholarship, to the wider contextual history of the Vietnam War, and as a contribution to the study of the Cold War itself. Lest my ambitions seem too grandiose, however, it should be stressed that, although I draw on secondary literature on the Soviet Union, this is primarily a book about *American* foreign policy. Few scholars have either the skill or the archival access to write genuinely international history. The author of this book certainly does not make any such claim. It is also worth emphasising that China is discussed in this book only in so far as developments in that country affected US–Soviet relations. There clearly is scope for a parallel, book-long, study of Sino-American relations under LBJ.

The first chapter is devoted to scene-setting: to considering the personalities, attitudes and working practices of LBJ and his key Soviet policy advisers; to commenting on how Congress and public opinion affected America's Soviet policy in this era; to raising questions about the nature of the Cold War conflict itself, as inherited from JFK by Johnson and as passed on by him to President Nixon; and to considering the central concept of 'détente'. Chapter 2 offers a chronological summary of bilateral US–Soviet relations, placing particular emphasis upon developing American perceptions of the character and shape of Soviet communism. Chapters 3 to 7 cover a series of particular topics and episodes. Selectivity is unavoidable here. Given the centrality of the US–Soviet rivalry, not only to American foreign policy but also to general international relations in the 1960s, a comprehensive account of all its aspects would rapidly become indistinguishable from some doomed attempt to achieve 'total history'. Chapters 3 to 7, therefore, do not attempt to be comprehensive. Chapter 3 deals with the superpowers' nuclear relationship. Chapters 4 and 5 discuss US–Soviet relations as they related to the Vietnam War. Chapter 6 considers the extraordinary case of Cuba, a Sovietised outpost in the Caribbean. And Chapter 7 deals with the two major crises for superpower relations which developed in LBJ's final years as President: the 1967 Six Day War in the Middle East, and the 1968 Soviet invasion of Czechoslovakia. Chapter 8 offers some general conclusions on LBJ's foreign policy leadership, on the coherence of his Soviet policy and on the nature of the Cold War in the 1960s.

Notes

1 J. W. Helsing, *Johnson's War, Johnson's Great Society* (Westport, Praeger, 2000), p. 256.
2 Quoted in J. A. Califano, book review, *Political Science Quarterly*, 116:2 (2001) 320.
3 I. Bernstein, *Guns or Butter: The Presidency of Lyndon Johnson* (New York, Oxford University Press, 1994), p. 5.
4 K. W. Thompson (ed.), *The Johnson Presidency: Twenty Intimate Perspectives of Lyndon B. Johnson* (Lanham, University Press of America, 1986), pp. 234–5.
5 D. Rusk, *As I Saw It: A Secretary of State's Memoirs* (London, Tauris, 1991), p. 282.
6 L. B. Johnson, *The Vantage Point: Perspectives of the Presidency 1963–1969* (London, Weidenfeld and Nicolson, 1971), pp. 551, 462.
7 See R. A. Divine (ed.), *The Johnson Years, Volume 3: LBJ at Home and Abroad* (Lawrence, Kansas University Press, 1994); D. B. Kunz (ed.), *The Diplomacy of the Crucial Decade* (New York, Columbia University Press, 1994); W. I. Cohen and N. B. Tucker (eds.), *Lyndon Johnson Confronts the World: American Foreign Policy, 1963–1968* (New York, Cambridge University

Press, 1994); H. W. Brands, *The Wages of Globalism: Lyndon Johnson and the Limits of American Power* (New York, Oxford University Press, 1995); H. W. Brands (ed.), *The Foreign Policies of Lyndon Johnson: Beyond Vietnam* (College Station, Texas A and M University Press, 1999); T. A. Schwartz, *Lyndon Johnson and Europe: In the Shadow of Vietnam* (Cambridge, Massachusetts, Harvard University Press, 2003).

8 D. W. Larson, *Anatomy of Mistrust: US–Soviet Relations during the Cold War* (Ithaca, Cornell University Press, 1997), p. 35.

9 See K. Ruane, 'Putting America in its place? Recent writing on the Vietnam wars', *Journal of Contemporary History*, 37:1 (2002) 115–28.

1

Lyndon Johnson and Soviet communism

LBJ

The successful exercise of power requires knowing when, how and how much
to delegate authority. No President can be his own Secretary of State, nor even
his own National Security Adviser. Johnson's Secretary of State, Dean Rusk,
estimated that, under his direction, the State Department sent out around one
thousand cables every day. Of these, the President usually saw one or two.[1]
LBJ was an unusually hard working Chief Executive. Indeed, one of his major
problems as President was his inability ever to relax. Yet even Johnson was
human. An account of his policy towards the Soviet Union cannot help but
be an account of his *Administration's* policy towards that country. Despite
this, I intend in this book wherever possible and appropriate, to draw attention to LBJ's own contribution to policy, and to the President's personal understanding of events. This was a very 'personal Presidency'[2] and Johnson's
personality was both extraordinary and imposing.

Most accounts of Johnson's personality emphasise a collection of striking
qualities, some apparently contradictory. The qualities include intense physicality, intelligence, driving wilful ambition, coarseness, concern for the poor
and excluded – above all, extreme emotional and personal complexity.
Rivalled in terms of self-torturing complexity only by Richard Nixon, LBJ in
many ways is the 'problem child' among recent US Presidents.[3]

Johnson's physicality is famed in many, much repeated anecdotes. The
'Johnson Treatment', meted out to political opponents and allies alike, amounted to actual physical intimidation. According to Larry O'Brien, head of the
legislative liaison operation inherited by Johnson in 1963, LBJ leaned 'so close
to you ... that your eye-classes bumped'.[4] Marianne Means, a White House
press correspondent, recalled LBJ as projecting 'a sense of perpetual motion':

> When he entered a room he didn't walk in, he hurtled. His body literally tilted
> forward at a 75-degree angle, head preceding feet, as though his brain moved more
> rapidly than his body. When he watched the television news, he watched all three
> networks at once. When he held meetings, he shuffled papers and talked on the tele-
> phone and listened to his advisers practically simultaneously.[5]

In 1967, Johnson expressed the desire to meet the Soviet leader Aleksei Kosygin in order, in the words of White House aide Jack Valenti, to 'touch and feel and smell another human being'.[6]

Johnson, according to Dean Rusk, was a 'very intelligent man' with an 'almost volcanic' personality. His intelligence 'was hidden from some people, particularly on the northeastern seaboard, by his southern accent and his corn-pone stories'.[7] LBJ read his briefing papers conscientiously; he retired at the close of a long working day with large packages of 'night reading'. His intelligence was, arguably, practical and problem-solving, rather than innovative or speculative. He was happy to leave academic reading and inquiry to 'the Harvards' – his own, semi-abusive term for the former university professors inherited from the Kennedy Administration. One of the very few books which LBJ studied – he read it 'over and over again' according to press secretary George Reedy – was The Rich and Poor Nations, published in 1959 and written by the British economist Barbara Ward. Johnson, like JFK, was strongly attracted by Ward's argument that the West should steal communism's thunder in the developing world by investing there, turning peasants into consumers.[8]

Johnson's ambition was massive. The awareness of his own mortality, intensified in the wake of his 1955 heart attack and sustained by the frequent physical ailments that afflicted him as President, underscored his self-promotive energy. His self-doubts were also enormous in scale and contributed to the restless and intense unhappiness he seems to have experienced as the nation's leader. Close associates certainly on occasions doubted his sanity.[9] His extraordinary combination of vulnerability, ego, energy and frustration also reinforced a tendency to dither over important decisions, or to seek a temporary, or 'middle way', solution to difficulties. Anatoly Dobrynin, Soviet Ambassador to the US, later recorded the views of close LBJ friend Abe Fortas on the President's approach to difficult decisions: 'Johnson instinctively avoided matters that demanded long and complicated decision-making, as well as those with grave and unforeseen consequences; he often tried to put them off'.[10] Johnson detested making decisions which could have major military implications. 'I'm not temperamentally equipped to be Commander-in-Chief', he told his wife in 1965.[11] Lady Bird Johnson declared that she was 'probably the only living person who would attest, believe, swear' that her husband 'never wanted to be President'.[12]

Johnson's private doubts, anxieties and frustrations often found expression in coarseness and personal invective. His coarseness was sometimes associated, in George Reedy's phrase, with a 'special delight in humiliating those who had cast in their lot with him'.[13] A conspicuous victim was Vice President Hubert Humphrey, whose balls LBJ claimed to be carrying around in his pocket.[14] Johnson vowed that if he could get Kosygin to Washington to settle the Vietnam War in 1967, he would take the Soviet leader to 'Garfinkels'

show window and publicly kiss his ass'.[15] LBJ's coarseness sometimes rose
to inspired levels of imagination and articulateness. Many of his associates
discerned a tension between cruelty, rooted in personal insecurity, and
what Reedy called a genuine personal commitment to 'uplift for the poor and
downtrodden'.[16]

Johnson's volcanic personality imposed itself upon his Administration, and
upon the conduct of his policy towards the Soviet Union, but not upon the
nation as a whole. Those who worked for him were constantly aware – if not
in actual terror – of the imperious and unpredictable wielder of the Oval Office
telephone. Yet, as Dean Rusk recalled, LBJ was a poor mass communicator and
'wooden before the cameras'.[17] A consummate persuader of individuals and
small groups, all Johnson seemed to do with mass audiences was 'talk Texas'.[18]

George Ball, European specialist at the State Department in the early
Johnson years and internal dissenter on Vietnam policy, guessed that 'LBJ suffered not from an inadequate education but from the belief that he had one'.[19]
In the realm of foreign affairs, Johnson's emotional complexity tended to
manifest itself in extreme sensitivity to charges that he was ignorant and un-
committed. In January 1964, he complained to pressman Walker Stone about
reports that he had neglected recent nationalist tensions in the Panama Canal
Zone. LBJ declared: 'On the Panama thing, I spent three fourths of my time
on foreign policy. I added it up this morning'.[20] Johnson was more committed to, and knowledgeable about, domestic than international politics. Lady
Bird's 1965 comment seemed also to capture her husband's attitude: 'From my
small viewpoint, it just looks like the problems of the world are so much more
insoluble than those of the United States. We can work on these here and make
a dent – a rather wonderful dent'.[21] In foreign policy, because of his own
limitations and because of the high stakes, there was always a special risk of
failure. Johnson frequently found himself trapped between the fear of failure
and the fear of appearing ignorant and irresolute.

This is not to suggest that Johnson was a foreign policy ignoramus. His
Congressional and Vice Presidential career – he visited 25 countries (not
Russia) as John Kennedy's deputy – gave him a sound grounding. LBJ entered
the White House with a far more impressive foreign affairs track record than
did later Presidents like Ronald Reagan and George W. Bush. Members of his
Administration varied in their verdicts on LBJ's foreign policy expertise. For
the loyal Rusk, Johnson was 'extraordinarily well informed about foreign
affairs'. According to Benjamin Read of the State Department, the President
was 'quite limited in terms of depth and breadth' on foreign affairs. Eugene
Rostow, brought into the State Department in 1966, conceded that Johnson
'knows the world is round'.[22] LBJ certainly did not have any especially close
or original understanding of Soviet communism. His attitudes towards the
USSR are best summarised in the context of a brief discussion of his pre-
Presidential career.

Various commentators have traced a kind of 'Alamo syndrome' in LBJ's foreign policy attitudes – a kind of excessive preoccupation with testing and what journalist Hugh Sidey called 'the chemistry of courage' – to his Texan origins.[23] Johnson's false claims to personal glory in World War Two, paralleled by his invention in 1966 of a great-great-grandfather who perished at the Alamo, have become well known in recent years. His early political career was as secretary to Texas Democratic Congressman Richard Kleberg, prior to his own election to the House of Representatives in 1937. He imbibed a tradition of radical Texas populism, and later recalled some of his associates from the 1930s as 'bomb throwers' – 'some of them about halfway to Moscow'.[24] Any sympathy for Bolshevism, however, was soon subordinated to the needs of political ambition. LBJ worked alongside politicos like Welly Hopkins and Roy Miller to smear liberal opponents of Kleberg as 'communist'. Johnson's New Dealism – he was appointed Texas Director of Franklin Roosevelt's National Youth Administration in 1935 – was not without its ironies. Kleberg certainly saw the New Deal as a stalking horse for communist dictatorship.[25]

Johnson's advancing career soon became associated with the emerging military-industrial complex, particularly as represented by Texan defence contractors Brown and Root. Like most of his generation of political leaders, Johnson was later profoundly affected in his views of Soviet power by the appeasement of European dictators in the late 1930s. As a young Congressman in this period, Johnson worked quietly with Austin businessman Jim Novy to help Jewish refugees from Nazi Germany. The lessons of the later 1930s seemed clear: be militarily prepared, and stand up to bullies. In February 1965, President Johnson reported to Senator Everett Dirksen on advice given him by former President Eisenhower on how to deal with communists: 'we know, from Munich on, that when you give, the dictators feed on raw meat'.[26] As President, LBJ made frequent references to his determination to be 'no Chamberlain umbrella man'. He continually recycled the following maxim: 'If you let a bully come in your front yard, he'll be on your porch the next day and the day after that he'll rape your wife in your own bed'.[27] A trip to war devastated Europe, as head of a House subcommittee on naval preparedness, reinforced fears of communist advancement. (It also confirmed his suspicions that US military chiefs were not immune to corruption.)[28]

As Congressman and Senator, of course, LBJ was himself a conduit, siphoning defence contracting funds to Texan backers. George Brown, of Brown and Root, later recalled that LBJ's support for 'good government' was designed 'to keep from having a socialist form of government'.[29] In the late 1940s, LBJ, especially in his successful 1948 Senate campaign, inveighed against 'labour bosses'. In 1947, he told a Texas audience that communism threatened the American system: 'We must apply to Dictator Stalin the same doctrine that we should have applied to the Kaiser and to Hitler'.[30] Some of Johnson's language in this early Cold War era was blood-curdling. During the 1948 race, he dedicated himself to fighting 'the surging blood-red tide of communism'. In 1951, he described the Korean conflict as 'the first battle of a greater struggle' between freedom and communism. The US should tell Russia: 'either you stop starting little fires around the world or else we will be willing to throw our might against your war-making capacity . . . We are ready to face a showdown'. Korea was 'only a detail in the communist design for world conquest', devised by 'the mad masters of the Kremlin'. In early 1952, he announced that the 'war in Korea is a war of Soviet Russia': 'If *any*where in the world . . . communism trespasses on the soil of the free world, we should unleash all the power at our command upon the vitals of the Soviet Union'.[31]

Most of the 'red meat' statements were either delivered to Texas audiences or written for LBJ's constituent newsletter. Johnson's Washington language tended towards greater circumspection. His attacks on Leland Olds, a liberal and former radical journalist who was rejected as a Federal Power Commissioner in 1949, were proto-McCarthyist. (LBJ did not go so far as to charge Olds, whose reconfirmation was opposed by Texan oil interests, with being 'a Communist'. However, Johnson did define the issue before the Senate as whether 'we have a Commissioner or a commissar'.)[32] His attitude towards Senator Joe McCarthy himself was cautious. LBJ did support the anti-communist 'loyalty' laws of the early 1950s, including the 1950 McCarran Act. However, following his appointment as Senate Minority Leader in 1953 – he became Majority Leader after the 1954 elections – Johnson did move quietly against McCarthy. He organised a committee to investigate the Wisconsin Republican, leading to McCarthy's Senate censure. Diplomat Charles Bohlen recalled his conduct during this period as that of a 'straight Democrat'.[33]

The McCarthy censure was an early indication of Johnson's undoubted skills as a legislative leader. Many commentators have made the point that Johnson's approach to Presidential leadership involved a rather inappropriate attempt to transfer to the White House the legislative skills of small group politicking and low-key consensus-building. Such skills are useful for Presidents; but so are decidedly non-Congressional skills of rhetorical national public leadership and high-profile policy redirection. On the specific issue of McCarthyism, Johnson retained the view that it reflected a mass hysteria, and that this had not been entirely extinguished by the mid-1950s.

The experience of internally directed anti-communism in the late 1940s and early 1950s reaffirmed Johnson's commitment to bipartisanship in foreign affairs. 'The more the two parties could agree', he told Doris Kearns, '. . . the less I worried about the public's tendency to go off on a jag'. He responded to criticisms about being insufficiently critical of Presidential foreign policy in the 1950s – 'petticoatin' around with Eisenhower' – by invoking the need to 'make absolutely sure that the Communists don't play one branch of government against the other, or one party against the other, as happened in the

Korean War'.[34] LBJ remained acutely conscious of the extent to which accusations of pro-communist sympathies in high places had damaged the Truman Administration. According to Harry McPherson, special counsel to President Johnson, it became an article of faith for LBJ 'that if Democrats wanted social progress, they should be seen to abhor communism'.[35]

As Senate Majority Leader, Johnson supported foreign policy bipartisanship, military preparedness, strong Presidential direction of foreign relations, foreign aid and internationalism generally. The launch of the Soviet Sputnik craft in October 1957 provoked a national panic over preparedness and about the advance of Soviet science. It impelled Johnson to schedule hearings on the US space programme. He urged the US to wake up, 'when the Russians get something in the air that we cannot get four feet off the ground'. His enthusiasm for his own call to 'roll up our sleeves', amid accelerating worries about the US–Soviet 'missile gap', led to LBJ becoming, in Robert Dallek's phrase, 'legislative father of NASA' – the National Aeronautical and Space Administration. As Vice President in May 1963, he announced that 'this generation of Americans' would not 'be willing to go to bed by the light of a Communist moon'.[36]

Johnson defended Eisenhower against conservative Republican accusations that Ike's invitations to Soviet Premier Nikita Khrushchev to visit America smacked of appeasement. The Texan actually met Khrushchev in September 1959, when the Soviet leader visited Capitol Hill. Khrushchev reportedly said that he hated LBJ's speeches, while Johnson said that Khrushchev would make an outstanding American Senator.[37]

Johnson's priority at this time was to achieve a higher foreign relations profile as the 1960 elections swung into view. In 1960, he joined a group of leading Congressional Democrats in urging Khrushchev not to withdraw from the May summit meeting in the wake of the shooting down of America's U-2 spy plane. Ike deemed this intervention 'a somewhat awkward attempt . . . to interfere in the day-to-day conduct of foreign affairs'.[38] Khrushchev's combative reply, and subsequent curtailing of the summit, provoked LBJ to suggest on the Senate floor that Moscow was running scared of Beijing. Johnson suggested that Khrushchev was acting 'under pressure' from his allies, 'at least one of which seems to be on the way to greater strength than that of the Soviet Union itself'.[39]

LBJ's experience as Vice President to John Kennedy was summarised, with more than a little insight by Anatoly Dobrynin: 'As vice president Lyndon Johnson had been excluded from the Kennedy inner circle and compelled to remain a passive spectator to great events, a galling situation for this dynamic man'.[40] As noted above, LBJ travelled widely on Kennedy's behalf, notably to South Vietnam and to West Berlin in 1961. Generally, however, and especially in connection with the 1962 Cuban missile crisis, Johnson's foreign policy role was peripheral. President Kennedy did call on his deputy's Senate expertise in regard to the sale of wheat to the USSR in 1963. Republicans and conservative Democrats were attacking the 1963 trade bill's provisions to finance the purchase of the wheat through the US Export-Import Bank. Passage of the trade bill became the symbolic first foreign policy legislative priority for LBJ when he assumed the Presidency on 22 November 1963.

Johnson's attitude towards the Soviet Union was sometimes more than slightly alarming. Like many other politicians of his generation, he used crass domestic anti-communism to further his ambition. He never entirely shook off the simplistic manner in which, as a rising Texan star in the late 1940s and 1950s, he had come to view Soviet communism. He told graduates at Howard University in 1961: 'The world today is a vast battleground between two systems of thought and two philosophies of society'.[41] As President, Johnson all too easily slipped, albeit usually in private, into the language of 'communist plots' and red conspiracies. Richard Helms, who became Director of Central Intelligence in 1966, recalled LBJ's requests for proof that the anti-Vietnam War movement was directed from Moscow or Beijing. Johnson told journalist Robert Spivack in 1965: 'So the kids are running up and down parading, and most of them are led by Communist groups'.[42] Following rioting in the Watts area of Los Angeles in 1965, LBJ wanted to know if the disturbances were part of a 'Communist conspiracy'.[43]

Yet Johnson was far too complex a political personality to be simply an ideologue, or simply an anti-communist extremist. Most of the time he was neither. Doris Kearns has suggested that his occasional fixation with 'plots' functioned as a form of emotional release.[44] After all, what Johnson had in abundance was pragmatism. One of his favourite stories concerned an aspiring school teacher being interviewed by a Southern school board. Did he believe the earth to be flat or round? The school board was reassured that the candidate was prepared to teach it either way.

Johnson's pragmatic intelligence was sometimes supplanted by prejudice and by lazy over-simplifications. Yet US Ambassador Foy Kohler was right to reassure Ambassador Dobrynin in 1965 that LBJ 'had never been a communist-baiter'.[45] (Leland Olds would not have agreed; but Johnson's McCarthyism does need to be set against the standards of the domestic politics of the early Cold War.) Dobrynin himself judged that Johnson 'never gave way to outright anti-Sovietism'.[46]

Johnson was not a foreign policy innovator. His dominant Presidential mood towards Moscow reflected a desire to avoid nuclear war by building on the progress in US–Soviet relations which had been made during 1963. The US had to meet aggression with force where necessary, and should always be prepared militarily. The Kremlin should not be appeased. Excessive domestic anti-communism was dangerous. A wise Democratic politician was one who used strong anti-communist rhetoric when it served his purposes, but who also knew the dangers of setting the anti-communist hare running. International communism had been weakened by the Sino-Soviet split, which it was in America's interest to see maintained. Communism could be beaten by a combination of resolve, ingenuity and international New Dealism. To destroy Soviet communism on his Presidential watch, however, would be a very tall order, especially given Johnson's own commitment to major domestic reform. For the foreseeable future, the main priority would be securing the conditions for a nuclear peace. Given that the Soviets seemed more rational and amenable than the Chinese, détente with Moscow seemed a realistic and worthwhile objective for his foreign policy.

Advisers

President Johnson inherited a 'collegial' style of decision-making procedure from President Kennedy. While he retained JFK's advisory personnel, he soon moved to modify the process. He developed what Patrick Haney has called a 'collegial-formalistic hybrid': more structured than the looser, JFK 'teamwork' approach, with greater reliance on a few key advisers and – unsurprisingly, given the Johnson personality traits discussed above – more geared to the imposition of Presidential control.[47] Like Kennedy, Johnson relied on his National Security Adviser (or 'special assistant') in the White House. McGeorge Bundy filled this post until February 1966, when he was eventually succeeded by Walt Rostow. The main formal role for Bundy and (later) Rostow was to channel and clear information to Johnson, although their substantive roles in policy formulation were far greater than such a job specification might imply. Johnson later described Bundy as 'sharp' and Rostow as 'philosophical', but both as 'ideal staff men'.[48] Somewhat less ideal was Robert Komer, who briefly replaced Bundy in 1966. Komer clashed with senior diplomats at the State Department and was switched to lead the pacification programme in Vietnam. Bundy and Rostow, at least by the standards of subsequent Administrations, succeeded in avoiding major public frictions with the State Department. One reason for this success was probably simply because of the relatively modest size of the NSC staff in this period: approximately twelve professional policy advisers under Bundy and eighteen under Rostow. Johnson's White House had only a 'very little' State Department of its own.[49]

At State itself, Dean Rusk rose to a position of influence with the President considerably greater than he had enjoyed under JFK. For Johnson, Rusk was 'loyal as a beagle'.[50] His view of the Department generally, however, was resentful and deeply affected by what Charles Bohlen understatedly called Johnson's 'rather strong desire for secrecy'.[51] LBJ told Federal Bureau of Investigation Director J. Edgar Hoover in 1965 that State was 'not worth a damn' and that it was staffed by 'a bunch of sissy fellows'.[52] (The President, of course, was not above pandering to Hoover's prejudice about the supposedly left-leaning Department.) Johnson was extremely concerned about State Department leaks and about the influence enjoyed there by Robert Kennedy, who by 1965 was LBJ's most hated political opponent.

Rusk built his influence around private meetings with Johnson, though the Secretary of State also chaired the interdepartmental Committee of Principals on arms control. Members of the State Department who tended to be especially involved in Soviet policy included senior figures like George Ball, John M. Leddy and Benjamin Read, as well as specialists from the Office of Soviet Union Affairs (European Affairs Bureau) like Robert Owen and Malcolm Toon. Llewellyn Thompson, Ambassador-at-Large until December 1966 and subsequently Ambassador to Moscow, was a key player in Soviet policy, generally in the 1963–66 period trying to explain Soviet attitudes to the policy-makers in Washington. Walt Rostow, before he took over from McGeorge Bundy at the White House, was chairman of the State Department Policy Planning Council, and was closely concerned with policy development towards the USSR.

Johnson's advisory system was bifurcated. On one side was the Presidential preference for formal processes and chains of command. This led Johnson to respect bureaucratic 'turf'. He was not an inveterate meddler in the internal affairs of the State Department.[53] Secretary of Defence Robert McNamara retained, until his departure from the Administration in 1967, his swathe of authority at the Pentagon. Johnson was not intimidated by the military, who sometimes attempted to approach him directly, rather than working through McNamara. Richard Helms remembered LBJ as probably not having 'the faintest idea' of how the CIA was organised internally. Johnson was inclined to respect the CIA's bureaucratic role as intelligence provider, rather than incorporating it as a regular part of the policy-making apparatus.[54]

Alongside his formalism, however, LBJ had a 'shadow', informal advice process, extending to figures such as Senator Richard Russell of Georgia, former President Eisenhower, and old friends like Abe Fortas and Arthur Krim. Clark Clifford was, before he succeeded McNamara at the Pentagon in 1967, LBJ's 'general utility man'.[55] Walt Rostow recalled Johnson talking 'personally more often than anyone knew to old colleagues in the Senate'.[56] Johnson wisely avoided reliance on just one adviser, whether in the formal or the informal process. He also regularly consulted the 'Wise Men', an assemblage of senior or retired foreign policy figures, usually led by Dean Acheson.

At the top of the bureaucratic tree, LBJ also tended to favour informality. The 'Tuesday lunch' group was generally preferred to the larger, more formal (and leaky) National Security Council. The Tuesday group usually included the Secretaries of State and Defence, the chairman of the Joint Chiefs of Staff, the National Security Adviser (Bundy or Rostow), CIA head, appropriate White House aides and – at various times – senior State and/or Pentagon personnel. Important decisions tended to be made, however, not at the rather unstructured Tuesday sessions, but in *ad hoc* meetings with LBJ and one or two senior people.[57]

Of LBJ's senior staff, Bundy and McNamara in particular, Walt Rostow to a lesser degree, were hampered in the President's eyes by their Kennedy connections. Years later, LBJ gave his opinion that he should have cleaned out JFK's advisory house in 1963 or 1964, rather than retaining his predecessor's men.[58] Suspicion of 'Harvards' and Kennedy connections apart, however, the key personnel – Bundy, Rusk, Rostow, McNamara – did share a general world outlook with the President. This outlook might be described as 'Munich analogy tempered by Cuban missile crisis'. All Johnson's senior advisers were in their twenties or thirties during the era of appeasement. Writing later of Rusk's attitudes, Robert McNamara declared that he could not 'overstate the impact of our generation's experiences' – Munich appeasement, World War Two, Soviet takeover in Eastern Europe, Soviet threats to Berlin, the Cuban missile crisis, communist expansionism in the developing world – 'had on him (and, more or less, on all of us)'.[59]

LBJ, Rusk, Bundy, McNamara and Rostow all agreed that communism – Soviet or Chinese – was an aggressive force which needed to be stoutly resisted: that was the lesson of the Cuban missile crisis, as well as of appeasement in the 1930s. Yet the 1962 Cuban crisis had also brought home as never before the precarious nature of the nuclear balance between the superpowers. As Dean Rusk later testified, the 'overriding problem' for the US became that of 'avoiding nuclear war'.[60] And avoidance of nuclear war was increasingly seen as involving some kind of comity between Moscow and Washington: some kind of pragmatic, mutual understanding, which could defuse crisis and promote stability. The world, by the mid-1960s, was certainly more complex than it had been ten years before. Various factors, from nationalism in the developing world to the Sino-Soviet split and the growth of integrative independence in Europe, had contributed to what Walt Rostow called the new 'diffusion of power'. But increased international uncertainty simply bolstered the case for cooperation (within limits) between the superpowers – certainly for an enhancement of mutual understanding. In such terms did Rostow describe McNamara's hopes for a US–Soviet dialogue on arms control:

> . . . protracted negotiation would educate each side in the fears and anxieties and modes of thought of the other. And out of that mutual education might flow implicit as well as explicit agreements and the habit of taking rationally into account the probable reactions of one side to the initiatives of the other.[61]

Johnson's top advisers shared fairly conventional understandings of the nature of Soviet communism. The most serious student of the USSR among the top advisory group was Walt Rostow, who had published books on both Soviet and Chinese communism. To Rostow in 1953, Soviet ideology since 1917 amounted to the 'systematic modification of the complex and contradictory Marxist tradition to make it serve as the rationale for the pursuit of power by a political dictatorship'.[62] A year later, he forecast the emergence of a serious

Sino-Soviet split. For Rostow, as for the entire group of advisers, the Cold War was an intertwined struggle of geopolitics and ideology.[63]

Finally, in this section, a word about Johnson's two Ambassadors to Moscow. LBJ inherited Foy Kohler, a career diplomat who stressed the importance of fostering cultural and economic links with the USSR. (Averell Harriman suggested that LBJ send Bobby Kennedy as Ambassador to Moscow, since 'Khrushchev wanted to get along'. Johnson did not comply.)[64] Kohler looked to members of the Soviet elite, 'who have contact with the West, who have absorbed ideas from the West', to increase the demand for change within the communist system. Kohler's fundamental outlook was realist. He foresaw consumer demand in the Soviet Union, stimulated by contact with the West, as putting pressure on the structurally weak Soviet economy.[65] Kohler's successor, Llewellyn Thompson, had served as Ambassador to Moscow under Eisenhower and Kennedy. His term under LBJ was not distinguished. Johnson himself referred to Thompson's 'nagging health problems and the exhaustion that sets in after many years of service in difficult and demanding appointments'.[66] A CIA report in December 1967 portrayed Ambassador Thompson as 'more the practical diplomat than the thoughtful student of Soviet affairs' whose communications to Washington were 'often cryptic and prosaic'.[67] Thompson did play an important role in the diplomacy of the Middle Eastern Six Day War (June 1967) and in efforts to start arms control talks. He seems, however, to have been depressed while in Moscow, and sceptical about making progress towards détente while the war was being fought in Vietnam.

Public opinion and Congressional relations

Johnson is frequently criticised for prioritising domestic consensus-building over clear national leadership. That is certainly not how he saw his own leadership style. In *The Vantage Point*, he described this style as one of 'first, deciding what needed to be done regardless of the political implications and, second, convincing a majority of the Congress and the American people of the necessity for doing those things'.[68] At a 1966 press conference, Johnson noted that 'the polls vary from week to week, and month to month. Those are things that we do not ignore, but they are not one of my burdens'. (He was not, of course, so relaxed about public opinion as expressed at elections.)[69]

LBJ inherited a public opinion consensus which, especially in the wake of the Cuban missile crisis, favoured a strong degree of Presidential direction of Cold War foreign policy. The consensus was, of course, to be severely shaken by Johnson's own leadership of policy towards Vietnam. Regarding Soviet policy, LBJ did not face major problems in managing mass public opinion. Republican Barry Goldwater was successfully portrayed by the Democrats in the 1964 Presidential election as an anti-Soviet extremist. The public welcomed the immediate post-missile crisis efforts to improve relations with Moscow. During LBJ's Presidency, the public consistently regarded China as a greater threat to world peace than Russia. (A 1964 Gallup poll found 56 per cent of respondents seeing China as the major threat; only 27 per cent plumped for Russia. In 1967, the figures were 71 and 20 per cent respectively.) A 1967 poll actually revealed 48 per cent as believing that, in the event of an American war against China, Russia would side with the US. A February 1968 Gallup poll found the following to be the last liked nations for Americans: (in descending order of affection) Russia, North Vietnam, Cuba and – bottom of the pile – Communist China.[70]

Johnson's public statements on Soviet policy naturally varied in tone according to the developing state of relations between Washington and Moscow. Some of his highest profile speeches, notably the 1964 State of the Union Address, contained sharp criticism of the Soviet role in the Vietnam conflict. However, LBJ's general inclination – in speeches delivered and approved, though not of course written, by him – was to talk up the prospects for superpower détente. His 1965 State of the Union Address looked forward to a new closeness between the US and the post-Khrushchev Soviet leadership: 'I am sure the American people would welcome a chance to listen to the Soviet leaders on our television – as I would like the Soviet people to hear our leaders on theirs'. In June 1965, he told Chicago Democrats that, between the US and the USSR, 'there has been friendship and there can be greater understanding'. Johnson's most famous public statement on Soviet relations was probably that made at the 1967 Glassboro, New Jersey, summit meeting with Aleksei Kosygin: 'I said on Friday that the world is very small and very dangerous. Tonight I believe it is fair to say that these days at Hollybush have made it a little smaller still, but also a little less dangerous'. A year later, LBJ offered a very upbeat account of US–Soviet relations at his Commencement Address at Glassboro State College. Moscow and Washington had 'begun . . . to bridge the gulf that has separated them for a quarter of a century'. In 1966, Johnson actually made a bid to influence *Soviet* public opinion. In an *America Illustrated* interview, destined for distribution in the USSR, he referred to 'the two most powerful nations on earth with every reason to want peace and no rational reason to want war'.[71]

As the first President in over one hundred years to have had top-level Congressional leadership experience, LBJ naturally tended to prioritise the legislative relations aspect of his Presidential duties. Johnson's closest Congressional relationship was with Senator Richard Russell, who tended to favour a guarded neo-isolationist stance for the US.[72] The pivotal foreign policy leadership relationships, however, were with Senate Foreign Relations Committee chairman J. William Fulbright, with Senate Majority leader Mike Mansfield, and with the Republican legislative leaders (especially Senate Minority Leader Everett Dirksen).

Johnson's break with Fulbright, firstly over the 1965 Dominican Republic invasion and subsequently over LBJ's conduct of the war in Vietnam, represented one of the most extraordinary political dogfights of modern political history. In the Johnson era, it was surpassed in ferocity only by the rivalry between LBJ and Bobby Kennedy. Fulbright's position on Soviet relations amounted to an advocacy of 'peaceful co-existence' based on the view that notions of a monolithic Soviet-inspired communist 'threat' were now outmoded. In March 1964, Fulbright declared on the Senate floor: 'Insofar as a nation is content to practise its doctrines within its own frontiers, that nation, however repugnant its ideology, is one with which we have no proper quarrel'.[73]

LBJ's relations with Mansfield were calmer than with Fulbright. LBJ once complained: 'Why do I have to have a saint for Majority leader?'[74] Mansfield's line on the Soviet Union was similar to Fulbright's: however, the Majority Leader was more circumspect in expressing publicly his criticisms of the conduct of the war. Dirksen was an old Senate buddy, whose friendship LBJ spent many hours cultivating from the Oval Office telephone. The Republican leadership in Congress tended to reserve its criticisms of LBJ's Soviet policy for instances where it seemed to be following the 'peaceful co-existence' line too enthusiastically. In 1964, Dirksen alleged that Johnson was betraying American interests by selling wheat to the Russians, and by allowing the Atlantic military alliance to deteriorate: 'It is high time our Government recognized that Communist aggression never stops and never will until we formulate policies to meet the realities presented by a cold, relentless and inhuman enemy'.[75]

In 1964, Bobby Kennedy was elected as Senator for New York. Increasingly preoccupied by what aides called 'the Bobby problem', Johnson came to see RFK's malign influence behind the activities of anti-war Senators like Fulbright, Frank Church and George McGovern. 'Why is it they never find anything that the Communists have done that's wrong?', complained Johnson.[76] In June 1965, he told Senator Birch Bayh: 'The Russian Ambassador, hell, he's talking to all of our Senators! After he has lunch with one of our Senators, it takes me *two weeks* to get the fellow to where he doesn't think I'm a warmonger again!'[77] LBJ told aides that Soviet agents were in 'constant touch with anti-war senators'. Bobby Kennedy's proposal for a Vietnam bombing halt in May 1965 was 'one of many jags which pretty much originated in the Communist world'.[78] By early 1967, RFK was advocating a bridge-building, integrative policy towards China, as well as Russia.

LBJ's main foreign policy battles with Congress, of course, were over the war, rather than Soviet policy *per se*. As with public opinion, Johnson gained from majority Congressional approval for the policy of consolidating JFK's post-Cuban missile crisis efforts to achieve superpower détente. Congressional opposition to Johnson's Soviet policy tended to emanate from the right, and to be concentrated in areas where the legislature enjoyed special procedural leverage: treaty ratification, trade issues and defence budgeting.

The US–Soviet Consular Treaty, presented by LBJ for Senate approval in 1964 but not actually ratified (by a 66–28 vote) until 1967, provided a focus for conservative opposition to the Administration's policy of building bridges to Moscow. The treaty opened the way for the opening of consulates in either country, also providing diplomatic immunity for consular employees and setting up procedures for processing the detention or arrest of a citizen of the other country. Opposition to the treaty saw the mobilisation of conservative interest groups, notably the Liberty League, as well as the intervention of J. Edgar Hoover. Barry Goldwater in 1964 complained about the making of agreement with 'enemies sworn to destroy us'. Dirksen, echoing Hoover's objection, complained that the Senate was being asked to 'ratify an agreement that would increase Soviet espionage and cloak it with immunity from pros-ecution to boot'.[79]

Johnson also faced major Congressional opposition over proposals to expand East–West trade. In 1966–67, a Congressional coalition of Republi-cans and Southern Democrats waged a campaign to kill efforts to extend Export-Import Bank credits to a joint Italian-Soviet plan for a Fiat car plant to be built in the USSR. In 1967, the Administration was forced to abandon efforts to obtain a routine extension of the life of the Bank. In 1968, Congress declined to act on further Administration proposals on extending East–West trade. On defence issues, the Administration faced strong Republican charges to the effect that it was relying too heavily on missiles, rather than manned bombers. Congressional pressure was also an important factor in precipitat-ing the 1967 decision to deploy the Sentinel Anti-Ballistic Missile system. Also of relevance to anti-Soviet defence postures were the various efforts, led by Senator Mike Mansfield, to withdraw substantial numbers of American troops from Europe.[80]

The Cold War: partnership or antagonism?

President Johnson in 1963 inherited a recently extended and refined version of the doctrine which underpinned America's entire Cold War foreign policy: the doctrine of anti-Soviet containment. President Kennedy had in many respects remained committed to the version of containment theory sketched out by Secretary of State Dean Acheson and State Department Policy Planning head, Paul Nitze, in 1950. (Nitze was to serve in Johnson's Department of Defence, becoming Deputy Defence Secretary in 1967.) The 1950 Acheson-Nitze view (codified in National Security Council document 68) was that the USSR was an expansionist, revolutionary power, whose influence must be resisted by an American policy of militarised, global containment. The strug-gle was between 'freedom' and 'slavery', the US was freedom's protector, and

American interests and responsibilities were co-extensive. The logic of anti-Soviet containment involved an assumption that the fire of Soviet communism – the 'new fanatic faith' described in NSC 68 – could be extinguished by preventing it from spreading. A combination of internal economic inefficiencies and popular dissatisfactions would dislodge the communist tyranny, but only if pressure were constantly applied on the borders of its influence. The danger, of course, was that communism, with its appeals to equity, modernisation and popular mobilisation *would* spread to what President Kennedy called the post-colonial 'lands of the rising people'. The threat seemed to intensify as Soviet leader Khrushchev pledged in January 1961 to support wars of national liberation in the developing world. The Kennedy Administration committed itself to 'centering the periphery': to a combination of flexible military and politico-economic responses to Soviet-sponsored insurgency in the developing world. JFK also accelerated the US arms build-up. In October 1961, Deputy Defence Secretary Roswell Gilpatric announced that the US now had the ability to withstand a Soviet nuclear attack and to destroy the Soviet Union in retaliation.[81]

Following the 1962 Cuban missile crisis, Kennedy reverted to a 'softer' version of anti-communist containment. The shift in policy reflected the way in which international politics generally had changed in the wake of the crisis, as well as Washington's growing awareness of the possibilities accruing from Moscow's deepening rift with Beijing.[82] JFK's post-1962 Soviet policies also drew upon earlier criticisms of the 'hard' NSC 68 approach. The NSC 68 version of containment had actually been conspicuously opposed by two Soviet experts, Charles Bohlen and George Kennan, who were highly regarded by President Kennedy. (Bohlen and Kennan had been influential State Department figures during the Truman years. The latter had developed the original, European-centred, containment doctrine in 1946–47. Bohlen, former Ambassador to Moscow, served LBJ as Ambassador to France.) Bohlen and Kennan, although both objected strongly to Khrushchev's 1961 speech on wars of national liberation, argued against an extreme militarisation of US foreign policy. They tended to see Soviet foreign policy as following relatively limited, 'national interest', rather than world revolutionary, goals. Sometimes these goals – which included seeking better relations with the West, but also maintaining Soviet leadership in the communist world, and expanding influence in the developing world – conflicted. However, the West should not overreact to the occasional bellicose outburst from Premier Khrushchev. Before the various crises of the period, 1959–62, there were indeed indications that the Soviet leadership favoured a new relationship with the US, and that the 'co-existence cocktails (vodka and Coca-Cola) consumed at the 1955 Geneva summit, should be kept at the ready.[83]

The Cuban missile crisis effected an eventual calming of the confrontational tone of 1959–62. JFK seemed once more to appreciate the wisdom of the

Bohlen-Kennan approach to containment. At the American University in Washington DC in June 1963, JFK declared that mankind 'can accept differences in ideology, politics, economics'. But the human race 'cannot survive, in the form in which we know it, in a nuclear war'.[84] The post-missile crisis period saw the establishment of the 'hot line' teletype link between the White House and the Kremlin and, in July 1963, the signing of the Limited Test Ban Treaty. (The treaty banned nuclear weapons tests in the atmosphere, in outer space and under water. It was ratified by the Senate and came into force in October 1963.) Shifts in Soviet strategic thinking, towards a view of the US as a responsible (if still hostile) power, began to be recognised in the West.[85]

It is certainly possible to argue that the 'nuclear learning' engendered by the Cuban missile crisis itself ushered in the era of détente, defined as a distinct, muted and modulated, form of Cold War competition between the superpowers of America and Russia. Obviously, we should not exaggerate the degree to which 1963 represented a qualitative change in Cold War attitudes. Kennedy returned to a more hawkish public voice in the period after his American University address. Moscow embarked on a major nuclear weapons acquisition programme. In April 1963, Robert Kennedy summarised a document delivered, indirectly, from Khrushchev to JFK: 'The United States is run by capitalists who are interested only in their profits'. President Kennedy's concern 'about the Rockefellers and these capitalists' prevented him from moving against the US armaments industry and taking 'the step for world peace'.[86] Also, and despite Moscow's rows with Beijing, some important elements of the Washington foreign policy bureaucracy clung on to notions of monolithic communism.[87]

There was clearly a way to go before structural superpower geopolitical and ideological rivalry would be transmuted into civilised competition. However, the view, that Moscow–Washington rivalry after 1962 developed the characteristics of a 'controlled contest' is quite widely held. John Lewis Gaddis saw 'an increasing commitment on the part of both great nations involved to a "game" played by the "rules"'. Once it matured, the Cold War became a 'long peace', comparable to the 'peace' of Metternich and Bismarck.[88] Others go further, arguing that the Kennedy Administration's recognition of the USSR as a great and legitimate power in 1963 marked a qualitative change in, possibly even the *end* of, the Cold War. Increasing US awareness of the Soviet estrangement from China and acceptance that, for the foreseeable future, Germany would remain divided, underpinned this recognition.[89] Allen Lynch maintains that the Cold War 'ended sometime' in the 1960s.[90] Post-1962 'nuclear learning' and the waning of Soviet revolutionary zeal created, in this line of argument, a situation of great power partnership. The US and the Soviet Union sought international stability and the guaranteeing of the 'nuclear peace'.[91]

From Moscow's perspective, America's Cold War policies of containment and coercive deterrence represented improper constraints on the Soviet Union's legitimate international geopolitical aspirations. Consolidation and assertion of 'great power' status were important features of Soviet foreign policy thinking throughout the Khrushchev and immediate post-Khrushchev eras. (Nikita Khrushchev fell from power in October 1964. He was replaced initially by a plural leadership, with Aleksei Kosygin as governmental and Leonid Brezhnev as party leader.) Moscow was especially concerned that rivalry with China might jeopardise Russian international status, including Moscow's right to be recognised as supreme leader of the communist world.[92]

Khrushchev himself attempted to reconcile pragmatism and ideological correctness. In his 1956 'secret speech' (at the 20th Congress of the Soviet Communist Party) he committed himself to a programme of de-Stalinising the USSR, within the limits imposed by a prudent fear of losing control of the momentum of reform. Part of this programme included the identification of 'peaceful co-existence' with the capitalist world as a goal for Soviet foreign policy. Khrushchev actually looked, by the late 1950s to 'burying' – to use his own rather unfortunate term – capitalism through the example set by communist success. He declared in a September 1959 speech in China: 'The socialist countries . . . fire the hearts of men by the force of their example in building socialism and thus lead them to follow in heir footsteps'.[93] The goal was to exceed US industrial and agricultural production by 1970. Khrushchev later explained that 'there can be no such thing as peaceful co-existence in the sphere of ideology and the class struggle, but there can and must be peaceful co-existence in the sphere of relations among states with differing political systems'. He explained to journalists, as recalled by Khrushchev in his 'last testament': 'We, the Soviet Union weren't going to bury anyone; the proletariat of the United States would bury its enemy, the bourgeoisie of the United States'.[94] 'Peaceful co-existence' was thus recruited to serve the doctrine of class struggle. During the Johnson years, the Soviet leaders remained committed to this Khrushchevian ideological line. Dobrynin later described Soviet Foreign Minister Andrei Gromyko as always favouring 'improving relations with Washington, while never allowing himself to overstep major ideological barriers'.[95] This union of 'peaceful co-existence' and class struggle was a way of finessing the Trotskyist tradition of prioritising world revolution: a way of updating what Zubok and Pleshakov have called the 'revolutionary imperial paradigm' – the old idea that 'promoting world revolution was not a goal in and of itself, but rather provided the rationale for building a strong Soviet Union'.[96]

Khrushchev developed a relationship with President Kennedy which involved personal rivalry with eventual, apparently mutual, respect. The US–Soviet clashes of the early 1960s, from Berlin – the Berlin Wall was erected in 1961 – to the Cuban missile crisis itself, were also personalised leadership confrontations. In his memoirs published in the West in 1970, Khrushchev recalled JFK's death as a 'great loss'. Kennedy would never, thought

Khrushchev, have allowed the US to become 'bogged down' in Vietnam. LBJ was implicitly blamed for presiding over a deterioration in US–Soviet relations, following the advances of 1963. Khrushchev was, however, prepared to praise Johnson for his personal assurance 'that he would keep Kennedy's promise not to invade Cuba'.[97] From the early 1960s onwards, the Soviet leadership became increasingly preoccupied with the split with China, and with rectifying nuclear weapons imbalances *vis-à-vis* the US. The rift with Beijing became manifest with Khrushchev's 1961 denunciation of Chinese-backed Albania for obstructing his de-Stalinisation programme. Following the Cuban missile crisis, Moscow strove, with quite swift success, to achieve a state of US–Soviet nuclear parity. Also operating to influence the USSR's international outlook, however, were anxieties about high defence costs, the desire of Soviet consumers for Western technology and grain, and continuing problems of managing the anti-Western alliance.

Turning more directly to the nature of the Cold War itself, it may be asserted with some confidence that it indeed did (as most Cold Warriors assumed) involve a mixture of ideological and geopolitical rivalry. Disputes about the relative importance of geopolitics and ideology are almost impossible to reconcile. Such disputes invariably hinge on prior theoretical assumptions about how international politics operate.[98] One way out of the ideology *versus* geopolitics dilemma, however, is provided by the notion of 'inter-systemic conflict'. In this view, two 'distinct social systems', in Fred Halliday's words, clashed in a way which could – given the 'competitive and universalising dynamic' of the rivalry – end only with one system prevailing over the other.[99] The US–Soviet rivalry was also undoubtedly vitiated by the 'security dilemma': the situation, very familiar to students of the Cold War, when the enhancement of one state's security leads to worry, insecurity, suspicion and rearming on the part of others.[100] Détente may be understood as an effort to resolve the 'security dilemma'. Rivalry was also unquestionably sustained by more generalised mistrust, and by misperception regarding opponents and their goals.[101]

Pre-1989 theoretical arguments about the nature of the Cold War had a tendency to mutate from arguments explaining US–Soviet antagonism, to arguments explaining stability.[102] Theorists during the era of the Cold War became as concerned with questions about the maintenance of the Cold War 'system', as about devising explanations for antagonism. Thus mistrust, misperception – indeed culture as well, and even aspects of ideology – can be held to have stabilised the competitive system even as they fuelled the underlying antagonism. Various formulations of international relations theory sought primarily to explain the persistence (in the absence of actual nuclear conflict) of the Cold War system. Important here were theories of bipolarity, involving the practice – especially in the era after the Cuban missile crisis – of mutual restraint by the superpowers, and their imposition of order on anarchic international relations. Theories of hegemonic stability sought to describe

America's guarantee of the liberal economic order, while other notions of cooperative regime functions were again focused on the stability that defined antagonism.[103] From these discussions of the Cold War stability and international systemic persistence it is not a long journey to the idea of actual partnership.

During the 1960s, third countries frequently complained about the consequences of superpower détente. At one extreme, the Chinese authorities referred to actual 'collusion' between Moscow and Washington to do down Chinese communism, and to repress challenge to the global duopoly. Small and developing countries resented what often appeared as a superpower conspiracy to exclude them. West German commentators sometimes accused America and Russia of making collusive deals such as the 1968 Nuclear Nonproliferation Treaty, at Bonn's expense.[104] In 1967, Prime Minister Sato Eisaku of Japan charged that US–Soviet détente was blinding Washington to the 'basic nature' of the Russians who were still in occupation of the Kurile Islands.[105]

'Internalist' analyses of the Cold War – wherein Soviet and American elites were seen as (objectively) conspiring to secure their power in the face of an external enemy – were also consonant with ideas of superpower partnership. In 1987, Soviet spokesman Georgi Arbatov famously warned Washington that Moscow was about to do 'a terrible thing to you – we are going to deprive you of an enemy'.[106] For many parts of the Western left, the structures of the Cold War operated to serve the needs of defence contractors and the permanent war economy in East and West. Cold War priorities were used as an excuse to subjugate potential rivals. US–Japanese relations were frequently analysed in this manner.[107] Even more centrally, one important dimension of the Cold War appeared (in Walter LaFeber's words) as 'the ongoing struggle between the world's commercial centres and the outlying countries' – the 'periphery' – 'that provide markets and raw materials'.[108] 'World systems' theory was developed to analyse the structural articulation of power between the exploiting 'core' and the exploited 'periphery'. (In many of its versions, world systems theory conceived the entire globe as constituting one, capitalist system.)[109] Ideas of partnership were not confined to the political left, but were apparent in many mainstream and conservative accounts of the 'long peace' and the Cold War 'controlled context'. They also surfaced in various post-Cold War evocations of the lost stability of the vanished system.

Varieties of détente

The key concept, 'détente', is, of course an extremely slippery one. The word, 'détente', derives from the French term for relaxation of tension following the firing of the crossbow. The word is most associated with the Presidency of Richard Nixon (1969–74), but Nixon's predecessors were certainly very familiar with the term. In 1974, Dean Rusk defined 'détente' as a 'process', rather than a 'condition'.[110] In the minds of President Johnson and his senior staff, however, détente is perhaps best understood as an aspiration: the hoped for achievement of a vocabulary and lexicon of mutual understanding between the superpowers, a way of resolving confrontation, avoiding nuclear war and allowing regional disputes (even wars) to proceed without drawing Moscow and Washington into direct confrontation. More dynamic and progressive than the Soviet concept of 'peaceful coexistence', the Johnson Administration's aspirations towards détente involved the notion of building permanent bridges to the East, even attempting to develop a policy for Europe as a whole.[111]

Aspirational détente, of course, is only one among any number of versions of our slippery term. Détente may be understood as a phase, or phases, within the history of the Cold War. It may be understood as a way of *waging* the Cold War, rather than a transcendence of it. For Coral Bell, détente was 'an American diplomatic strategy consciously deployed within a triangular power balance, vis-à-vis both China and the Soviet Union'.[112] Richard W. Stevenson defined it as 'the process of easing of tension between states whose interests are so radically divergent that reconciliation is inherently limited'.[113]

In this book, we are concerned with superpower détente – with bilateral relations between Moscow and Washington, as well as the collision and interweaving of superpower interests that occurred in various regions and policy areas. The relaxation of US–Soviet tension was not the only version of détente on offer in the 1960s. West Germany and France had their own détente agendas, the mere existence of which exemplified the increasing international complexity against which Washington struggled to construct its policy. Since West Germany's *Ostpolitik*, in particular, constituted so important a part of this complexity, it may be useful here briefly to set out for readers' inspection the bare bones of this strategy.

Bonn established diplomatic relations with Moscow in 1955. For West Germany, this was no more than a recognition of reality. Establishing relations with Moscow was not seen as abrogating the Hallstein Doctrine, whereby any state which recognised the German Democratic Republic (East Germany) was regarded as hostile. West German politics in the mid-1960s involved a clear tension between forces which opposed US domination of Europe, and 'Atlanticist' elements led by Chancellor Ludwig Erhard and Foreign Minister Gerhard Schroder. Especially following his 1963 resignation as Chancellor, Konrad Adenauer positioned himself near the head of the 'anti-Atlanticist' faction. In an effort to head off Adenauer's championing of a European 'third force', increasingly independent of Washington, Erhard and Schroder embarked on a policy of opening-out to the East, largely in the form of establishing trade missions in Eastern European states and in negotiating new patterns of access to Berlin. Following the coming to power of a Social Democrat-Christian Democrat coalition in 1966, a new urgency was lent to the *Ostpolitik* programme. Under Foreign Minister Willy Brandt, the Hallstein Doctrine was set aside and Bonn looked increasingly to the establishment of good relations with Eastern

Europe. Important changes in the North Atlantic Treaty Organisation, noted
in Chapter 3, also were associated with this policy. A State Department paper
of May 1968 noted the various changes which had occurred in West Germany
(the Federal Republic of Germany) since the early 1960s, and the coming to
power of Kurt Kiesinger and Willy Brandt in 1966:

> The Adenauer-Erhard years were years of German dependence upon the United
> States, with the FRG accepting US tutelage in return for our security guarantees and
> our support for German efforts to rebuild a prosperous and respected nation. The
> fall of Erhard late in 1966, and the creation of the Kiesinger-Brandt government,
> signalled the evolution of German policy toward greater emphasis on he pursuit of
> reunification of their divided nation. The relative absence of crisis in Europe and
> the public belief that Soviet aggression had become somewhat less likely; the growth
> of a détente psychology; the passage of years since 1945 and the erosion of the post-
> war fears and sense of guilt; de Gaulle's rekindling of nationalism first in France
> and then elsewhere in Europe; all contributed to a greater German sense of inde-
> pendence from tutelage, and more active efforts to lay the groundwork for eventual
> reunification.

Brandt's 'main single policy innovation' was 'the pursuit of a more flexible
Eastern policy aimed at opening a dialogue with the Soviet Union, improving
relations with the Eastern European states, and seeking to extend the FRG's
ties with East Germany (short of recognition)'.[114]

President Johnson's attitude towards Bonn's *Ostpolitik* combined a strong
commitment to containing German power with a desire to channel and control
the Federal Republic's Eastern outstretch. In December 1966, LBJ remarked
on the danger of the US–European alliance failing to 'tie the Germans in'.
There might be 'some 17-year-old right now in Germany who would be a
20-year-old Hitler in another three years'.[115]

Besides West German *Ostpolitik*, the US also had to contend with French
President Charles de Gaulle's vision of a European 'third force', with American power in Europe drastically reduced. The French and German attitudes
frequently exasperated Washington. Vice President Hubert Humphrey complained in 1967 that the Europeans 'resent US power. Détente is what they
want'.[116] LBJ's main commitment was to the preservation of the Atlantic
alliance, avoiding if possible 'a public fight' with France.[117] The health of
NATO was of paramount importance.

Gaullism and West German *Ostpolitik* provided the context for détente in
Europe. On a global scale, as already noted, wider forces were converging to
loosen the cohesion of the superpower alliance systems. The most obvious such
force was the split between the USSR and China. As we shall see, the Sino-
Soviet split, which combined ideological and geopolitical features, became the
main frame of reference for Western analysts seeking to understand and predict
Soviet behaviour. Also of considerable significance in the evolution of détente
was the growing restiveness of East European nations against Soviet domina-

tion. A Central Intelligence Agency report of July 1964 noted that, for most East Europeans, 'the basic fact of Communist rule' was not questioned. However, the relationship with Moscow was 'being subjected to examination and experiment'.[118] In February 1965, the CIA concluded: 'So long as the USSR's own policy includes an element of détente, it will be difficult for the Soviets to restrain East European movement toward the West'.[119] US business interests in the mid-1960s certainly saw major opportunities being created by new patterns of trade with Eastern Europe.[120]

Other changes, associated particularly with the rise of global economic interdependence, also pointed towards a more diffuse, less confrontational structure of international power. Regional conflicts and nationalist forces in the developing world, at one level at least, created a new potential for big power collision. They also, however, increased the case for a more regularised, cooperative and crisis-defusing dialogue between Moscow and Washington. Various regional wars and crises; the economic rise of Japan; Moscow's problems with East European nationalism; Beijing's challenge to Moscow for the title of leader of international communism; Washington's problems with its West European allies; proliferation of nuclear weapons; all these factors were tending to increase the diffuseness of the international order. H. W. Brands writes that it 'was Lyndon Johnson's peculiar bad luck to preside over American foreign policy at the moment when the scales of world power were tipping away from the United States'.[121] The international order was still structured around Soviet–American competition. Yet, to a clear degree, the scales of power were tipping away from both superpowers. It was against this background that the Johnson Administration sought to develop the aspirations towards lasting and progressive détente which had been expressed in President Kennedy's American University address of June 1963.

Notes

1 Rusk, Oral History (Lyndon B. Johnson Presidential Library), p. 8.
2 See H. Sidey, A Very Personal Presidency: Lyndon Johnson in the White House (New York, Atheneum, 1968); J. Valenti, A Very Human President (New York, Norton, 1975).
3 D. M. Barrett, book review, Journal of American History, 82:1 (1995) 362.
4 Quoted in C. Solberg, Hubert Humphrey: A Biography (New York, Norton, 1984), p. 266.
5 J. W. Hurst and J. C. Cain (ed. R. L. Hardesty and T. Gittinger), LBJ: To Know Him Better (Austin, LBJ Library, 1995), p. 63.
6 K. W. Thompson (ed.), The Johnson Presidency (Lanham, University Press of America, 1986), p. 31.
7 Ibid., p. 219.
8 L. C. Gardner, Pay Any Price: Lyndon Johnson and the War for Vietnam (Chicago, Dee, 1995), p. 29. See also W. Heinrichs, 'Lyndon B. Johnson: change and continuity', in W. I. Cohen and N. B. Tucker (eds.), Lyndon Johnson Confronts the World: American Foreign Policy, 1963–1968 (New York, Cambridge University Press, 1994), pp. 9–30, 26; R. Dallek, 'Lyndon Johnson as a world leader', in H. W. Brands (ed.), The Foreign Policies of Lyndon

Johnson: Beyond Vietnam (College Station, Texas A and M University Press, 1999), pp. 6–18; B. Ward, *The Rich Nations and the Poor Nations* (New York, Norton, 1959).

9 See R. Dallek, *Flawed Giant: Lyndon Johnson and His Times 1960–1973* (New York, Oxford University Press, 1998), pp. 281–4.

10 A. Dobrynin, *In Confidence: Moscow's Ambassador to Six Cold War Presidents* (New York, Times Books, 1995), p. 118.

11 M. R. Beschloss (ed.), *Reaching for Glory: Lyndon Johnson's Secret White House Tapes, 1964–1965* (New York, Simon and Schuster, 2001), p. 177.

12 Ibid., p. 159.

13 G. Reedy, *Lyndon B. Johnson: A Memoir* (New York, Andrews and McMeel, 1982), pp. 157–8.

14 Solberg, *Hubert Humphrey*, p. 266.

15 J. D. Beam, *Multiple Exposure: An American Ambassador's Unique Perspective on East–West Issues* (New York, Norton, 1978), p. 150.

16 Reedy, *Lyndon B. Johnson*, p. 157.

17 D. Rusk, *As I Saw It* (London, Tauris, 1991), p. 278.

18 Hurst and Cain, *LBJ: To Know Him Better*, p. 49 (Robert Hardesty).

19 Quoted in Rusk, *As I Saw It*, p. 277.

20 M. R. Beschloss (ed.), *Taking Charge: The Johnson White House Tapes, 1963–1964* (New York, Simon and Schuster, 1997) p. 200 (31 Jan. 1964).

21 Beschloss (ed.), *Reaching for Glory*, p. 353.

22 Lyndon Johnson Presidential Library, Oral Histories (Rusk, p. 4; Read, p. 6; E. Rostow, p. 39).

23 Sidey, *A Very Personal Presidency*, p. 23.

24 H. McPherson, *A Political Education: A Washington Memoir* (Boston, Houghton Mifflin, 1988), p. 109.

25 See R. Dallek, *Lone Star Rising: Lyndon Johnson and His Times 1908–1960* (New York, Oxford University Press, 1991), p. 109; R. Caro, *The Years of Lyndon Johnson: The Path to Power* (New York, Knopf, 1982), p. 272.

26 Beschloss (ed.), *Reaching for Glory*, p. 181.

27 W. Isaacson and E. Thomas, *The Wise Men: Six Friends and the World They Made* (New York, Simon and Schuster, 1986), p. 641. See also D. Kearns, *Lyndon Johnson and the American Dream* (New York, Harper and Row, 1976), pp. 99–101.

28 Dallek, *Lone Star Rising*, p. 272.

29 Gardner, *Pay Any Price*, p. 12.

30 Dallek, *Lone Star Rising*, p. 292.

31 R. Dugger, *The Politician: The Life and Times of Lyndon Johnson* (New York, Norton, 1982), pp. 310, 365, 368–71.

32 Dallek, *Lone Star Rising*, pp. 376–7. See also M. Miller *Lyndon: An Oral Biography* (New York, Putnam's Sons, 1980), p. 172.

33 Bohlen, Oral History, p. 15. See also R. A. Caro, *The Years of Lyndon Johnson: Volume 3: Master of the Senate* (London, Cape, 2002), pp. 525–7.

34 D. Kearns, *Lyndon Johnson and the American Dream* (New York, Harper and Row, 1976), p. 149.

35 McPherson, *A Political Education*, pp. 110–11.

36 Dallek, *Flawed Giant*, pp. 11, 418. See also T. M. Gaskin, 'Senator Lyndon Johnson, the Eisenhower Administration and US foreign policy, 1957–1960', *Presidential Studies Quarterly*, 24:2 (1994) 341–8.

37 Dallek, *Lone Star Rising*, p. 560; *FRUS, 1961–1963*: Volume V: *The Soviet Union* (Washington DC, US Government Printing Office, 1998), p. 834.

38 R. Evans and R. Novak, *Lyndon B. Johnson: The Exercise of Power* (New York, New American Library, 1966), p. 222.

39 *Congressional Record* 106, Part 9 (2 June 1960) 11635.

40 Dobrynin, *In Confidence*, p. 115.

41 Gardner, *Pay Any Price*, p. 55.

42 Beschloss (ed.), *Reaching for Glory*, p. 292 (29 April 1965).

43 Ibid., p. 420. See also J. Califano, *The Triumph and Tragedy of Lyndon Johnson* (New York, Simon & Schuster, 1992), pp. 59–63.

44 Kearns, *Lyndon Johnson and the American Dream*, pp. 316–17.

45 *FRUS, 1964–1968*: Volume XIV: *The Soviet Union* (Washington DC, US Government Printing Office, 2001), p. 344 (19 Nov. 1965).

46 Dobrynin, *In Confidence*, p. 189.

47 P. J. Haney, *Organizing for Foreign Policy Crises* (Ann Arbor, University of Michigan Press, 1997), p. 70.

48 H. W. Brands, *The Wages of Globalism* (New York, Oxford University press, 1995), p. 13.

49 W. W. Rostow, *The Diffusion of Power* (New York, Macmillan, 1972), pp. 167, 358–68; J. P. Burke, *The Institutional Presidency* (Baltimore, Johns Hopkins University Press, 1992), pp. 84–9; E. S. Redford and R. T. McCulley, *White House Operations: The Johnson Presidency* (Austin, University of Texas Press, 1986), pp. 99–111; A. Preston, 'The little State Department: McGeorge Bundy and the National Security Council staff, 1961–65', *Presidential Studies Quarterly*, 31:4 (2001) 635–59.

50 V. D. Bornet, *The Presidency of Lyndon B. Johnson* (Lawrence, University Press of Kansas, 1983), p. 28.

51 Bohlen, Oral History, p. 26.

52 Beschloss (ed.), *Reaching for Glory*, p. 333 (19 May 1965).

53 Read, Oral History, p. 7.

54 Helms, Oral History, pp. 5–6; R. Jeffreys-Jones, *The CIA and American Democracy* (New Haven, Yale University Press, 1989), ch. 8.

55 Brands, *The Wages of Globalism*, p. 15; D. M. Barrett, 'The mythology surrounding Lyndon Johnson, his advisers, and the 1965 decision to escalate the Vietnam War', *Political Science Quarterly*, 103:4 (1988–89) 637–63; D. M. Barrett, 'Secrecy and openness in Lyndon Johnson's White House', *Review of Politics*, 54:1 (1992) 72–111.

56 *The Diffusion of Power*, p. 362.

57 Brands, *The Wages of Globalism*, pp. 21–3; D. Humphrey, 'Tuesday lunch at the White House', *Diplomatic History*, 8:4 (1984) 81–101.

58 See Beschloss (ed.), *Reaching for Glory*, p. 364. But also see D. Fromkin, 'Lyndon Johnson and foreign policy', *Foreign Affairs*, 74:1 (1985) 161–70.

59 R. S. McNamara, *In Retrospect: The Tragedy and Lessons of Vietnam* (New York, Times Books, 1995), p. 195.

60 Rusk, Oral History, p. 44.

61 Rostow, *The Diffusion of Power*, p. 389.

62 W. W. Rostow, *The Dynamics of Soviet Society* (London, Secker and Warburg, 1953), p. 85.

63 W. W. Rostow, *The Prospects for Communist China* (London, Chapman and Hall, 1954), pp. 215–19; W. W. Rostow, *The United States in the World Arena* (New York, Harper and Row, 1960), p. 546.

64 Beschloss (ed.), *Taking Charge*, p. 429.

65 D. Mayers, *The Ambassadors and America's Soviet Policy* (New York, Oxford University Press, 1995), p. 218; N. V. Sivachev and N. Yakovlev, *Russia and the United States* (Chicago, University of Chicago Press, 1979), p. 216.

66 L. B. Johnson, *The Vantage Point* (London, Weidenfeld and Nicolson, 1971), p. 475.

67 *FRUS, 1964–1968*: Volume XIV: *The Soviet Union*, p. 605 (8 Dec. 1967).

68 *The Vantage Point*, p. 28.

69 D. C. Foyle, *Counting the Public In: Presidents, Public Opinion and Foreign Policy* (New York, Columbia University Press, 1999), p. 183.

70 See G. Gallup (ed), *The Gallup Poll: Public Opinion, 1935–1971, Vol. 3, 1959–1971* (New York, Random House, 1972), pp. 1881, 2053, 2104–5. See also B. I. Page and R. Y. Shapiro, *The Rational Public: Fifty Years of Trends in American's Policy Preferences* (Chicago, University of Chicago Press, 1992), p. 227.

71 *PPPUS: Lyndon B. Johnson: 1965*: Volume 1 (Washington DC, US Government Printing Office, 1966), p. 3; ibid., Volume 2, p. 632; *PPPUS: Lyndon B. Johnson: 1967*: Volume 1 (Washington DC, US Government Printing Office, 1968), p. 652; *PPPUS: Lyndon B. Johnson: 1968*: Volume 1 (Washington DC, US Government Printing Office, 1969), p. 681; *PPPUS: Lyndon B. Johnson: 1966*: Volume 2 (Washington DC, US Government Printing Office, 1967), p. 1070.

72 See G. C. Fite, *Richard B. Russell Jr: Senator from Georgia* (Chapel Hill, University of North Carolina Press, 1991), pp. 450–2.

73 R. B. Woods, *Fulbright: A Biography* (Cambridge, Cambridge University Press, 1995), p. 335.

74 Califano, *The Triumph and Tragedy of Lyndon Johnson*, p. 44.

75 T. Dietz, *Republicans and Vietnam, 1961–1968* (New York, Greenwood Press, 1986), p. 59. See also B. C. Hulsey, *Everett Dirksen and His Presidents: How a Senate Giant Shaped American Politics* (Lawrence, University Press of Kansas, 2000).

76 J. Shesol, *Mutual Contempt: Lyndon Johnson, Robert Kennedy and the Feud that Defined a Decade* (New York, Norton, 1997), p. 381.

77 Beschloss (ed.), *Reaching for Glory*, p. 356 (15 June 1965).

78 Shesol, *Mutual Contempt*, p. 381.

79 *Congressional Quarterly Almanac* 1964, p. 334. See also *Congressional Quarterly Almanac* 1967, pp. 188–95.

80 See ibid., pp. 216–17, 980.

81 Good summaries of the debates surrounding JFK's foreign policy are contained in B. I. Kaufman, 'John F. Kennedy as world leader', *Diplomatic History*, 17:3 (1993) 447–71; and J. W. See, 'An uneasy truce: John F. Kennedy and Soviet-American détente', *Cold War History*, 2:2 (2002) 161–94. NSC 68 is printed in R. Maidment and R. Dawson (eds.), *The United States in the Twentieth Century: Key Documents* (London, Hodder and Stoughton, 1999), pp. 327–46.

82 See, 'An uneasy truce', argues that the 'ill-informed Lyndon Johnson' (p. 195) squandered the 1963 openings towards détente made by President Kennedy.

83 T. G. Paterson, J. G. Clifford and K. J. Hagan, *American Foreign Relations: A History since 1895: Volume 2* (Boston, Houghton Mifflin, 2000), p. 283; W. J. Thompson, *Khrushchev: A Political Life* (London, Macmillan, 1995), pp. 212–13.

84 *PPPUS: John F. Kennedy: 1963* (Washington DC, US Government Printing Office, 1964), pp. 461–3.

85 See, e.g., T. W. Wolfe, 'Shifts in Soviet strategic thought', *Foreign Affairs*, 42:3 (1964) 475–86.

86 *FRUS, 1961–1963*: Volume VI: *Kennedy-Khrushchev Exchanges* (Washington DC, US Government Printing Office, 1996), p. 263 (3 April 1963).

87 See A. M. Schlesinger Jr., *A Thousand Days: John F. Kennedy in the White House* (Boston, Houghton Mifflin, 1965), p. 415.

88 J. L. Gaddis, 'The long peace', in S. M. Lynn-Jones and S. E. Miller (eds.), *The Cold War and After: Prospects for Peace* (London, MIT Press, 1993), pp. 38–51, 42; J. L. Gaddis, *The Long Peace: Inquiries into the History of the Cold War* (New York, Oxford University Press, 1982); A. L. George, P. J. Farley, A. Dallin (eds.), *US.-Soviet Security Cooperation: Achievements, Failures, Lessons* (New York, Oxford University Press, 1988).

89 See J. G. Hershberg, 'The crisis years, 1958–1963', in O. A. Westad (ed.), *Reviewing the Cold War: Approaches, Interpretations, Theory* (London, Cass, 2000), pp. 303–25.

90 A. Lynch, *The Cold War Is Over – Again* (Boulder, Westview Press, 1992), p. 24. See also M. Cox, 'Rethinking the end of the Cold War', *Review of International Studies*, 20:2 (1994) 187–200.

91 See R. Crockatt, 'Theories of stability and the end of the Cold War', in M. Bowker and R. Brown (eds.), *From Cold War to Collapse: Theory and World Politics in the 1980s* (Cambridge, Cambridge University Press, 1993), pp. 59–81.

92 On Soviet foreign and defence policy, see R. L. Garthoff, 'Soviet perception of Western thought and doctrine', in G. Flynn (ed.), *Soviet Military Doctrine and Western Policy* (London, Routledge, 1989), pp. 197–309; R. B. Day, *Cold War Capitalism: The View from Moscow, 1945–1975* (Armonk, Sharpe, 1995); A. A. Gromyko and B. Ponomarev (eds.), *Soviet Foreign Policy, 1917–1980, Volume 2* (Moscow, Progress Publishers, 1981); J. Lenczowski, *Soviet Perceptions of US Foreign Policy: A Study of Ideology, Power and Consensus* (Ithaca, Cornell University Press, 1984); A. Lynch, *The Soviet Study of International Relations* (Cambridge, Cambridge University Press, 1987); M. Tatu, *Power in the Kremlin: From Khrushchev to Kosygin* (New York, Viking, 1969); R. L. Garthoff, *Deterrence and the Revolution in Soviet Military Doctrine* (Washington DC, Brookings Institution, 1990) sees Soviet policies as primarily defensive; A. Rubinstein, *Soviet Foreign Policy since World War II: Imperial and Global* (New York, HarperCollins, 1992) sees the USSR as an aggressive, expansionist power.

93 Quoted in Rostow, *The Diffusion of Power*, p. 38.

94 S. Talbott (ed.), *Khrushchev Remembers: The Last Testament* (London, Deutsch, 1974), pp. 531–2.

95 Dobrynin, *In Confidence*, p. 131.

96 V. Zubok and C. Pleshakov, *Inside the Kremlin's Cold War: From Stalin to Khrushchev* (Cambridge, Massachusetts, Harvard University Press, 1996), p. 13.

97 S. Talbott (ed.), *Khrushchev Remembers* (Boston, Little, Brown, 1970), pp. 462–3; see also *Khrushchev Remembers: The Glasnost Tapes* (Boston, Little, Brown, 1990), pp. 281–3.

98 For a recent contribution to this debate, see M. Trachtenberg, 'New light on the Cold War?', *Diplomacy and Statecraft*, 12:4 (2001) 10–17.

99 F. Halliday, *Rethinking International Relations* (London, Macmillan, 1994), p. 175.

100 See B. Buzan, *People, States and Fear* (Hemel Hempstead, Harvester Wheatsheaf, 1991), ch. 4. Also, R. Jervis, 'Was the Cold War a security dilemma?' *Journal of Cold War Studies*, 3:1 (2001) 36–60.

101 See D. W. Larson, *Anatomy of Mistrust* (Ithaca, Cornell University Press, 1997); R. Jervis, *Perception and Misperception in International Politics* (Princeton, Princeton University Press, 1976).

102 See K. N. Waltz, *Theory of International Politics* (Reading, Massachusetts, Addison-Wesley 1979); K. N. Waltz, 'Response to my critics', in R. O, Keohane (ed.), *Neorealism and Its Critics* (New York, Columbia University Press, 1986), pp. 322–45; R. N. Lebow, 'The long peace, the end of the Cold War, and the failure of realism', in R. N. Lebow and T. Risse-Knappen (eds.), *International Relations Theory and the End of the Cold War* (New York, Columbia University Press, 1995, pp. 23–56.

103 See J. Dumbrell, *The Making of US Foreign Policy* (Manchester, Manchester University Press, 1997), p. 15; R. O. Keohane, *After Hegemony: Cooperation and Discord in the World Political Economy* (Princeton, Princeton University Press, 1984).

104 See *FRUS, 1964–1968*: Volume XI: *Arms Control and Disarmament* (Washington DC, US Government Printing Office, 1997), p. 523 (W. Rostow to LBJ, 7 Nov. 1967).

105 N. B. Tucker, 'Threats, opportunities and frustrations in East Asia', in W. I. Cohen and N. B. Tucker (eds.), *Lyndon Johnson Confronts the World* (Cambridge, Cambridge University Press, 1994), pp. 99–134, 125–6.

106 Cited in C. W. Kegley and E. R. Wittkopf, *World Politics: Trend and Transformation* (New York, St. Martin's, 1995), p. 98; Halliday, *Rethinking International Relations*, p. 173; M. Kaldor, *The Imaginary War* (Oxford, Blackwell, 1990); H. W. Brands, *The Devil We Knew: Americans and the Cold War* (New York, Oxford University Press, 1993).

107 See F. Halliday, *The Making of the Second Cold War* (London, Verso, 1983), p. 27; M. Kaldor, *The Baroque Arsenal* (London, Deutsch, 1982).

108 See W. LaFeber, 'An end to *which* Cold War?', in M. J. Hogan (ed.), *The End of the Cold War* (Cambridge, Cambridge University Press, 1992), pp. 13–20.

109 See I. Wallerstein, *The Modern World-System* (New York, Academic Press, 1974).

110 Quoted in R. W. Stevenson, *The Rise and Fall of Détente* (London, Macmillan, 1985), p. 9. See also M. B. Froman, *The Development of the Idea of Détente: Coming to Terms* (Basingstoke, Macmillan, 1991), pp. 29–35.

111 See T. A. Schwartz, 'Lyndon Johnson and Europe: alliance politics, political economy, and growing out of the Cold War', in H. W. Brands (ed.), *The Foreign Policies of Lyndon Johnson: Beyond Vietnam* (College Station, Texas A and M University Press, 1999), pp. 37–60.

112 C. Bell, *The Diplomacy of Détente: The Kissinger Era* (London, Martin Robertson, 1977), p. 3.

113 *The Rise and Fall of Détente*, p. 7.

114 *FRUS, 1964–1968*: Volume XV: *Germany and Berlin* (Washington DC, US Government Printing Office, 1999), pp. 662–3 (5 May 1968).

115 Quoted in F. Costogliola, 'LBJ, Germany and "the end of the Cold War"', in Cohen and Tucker (eds.), *Lyndon Johnson Confronts the World*, pp. 173–210, 198.

116 *FRUS, 1964–1968*: Volume XII: *West Europe Region* (Washington DC, US Government Printing Office, 1998), p. 572 (3 May 1967).

117 See Brands, *The Wages of Globalism*, ch. 4.

118 *FRUS, 1964–1968*: Volume XVII, *Eastern Europe* (Washington DC, US Government Printing Office, 1996), p. 21 (22 July 1964).

119 Ibid., p. 40 (18 Feb. 1965).

120 See T. J. McCormick, *America's Half-Century: United States Foreign Policy in the Cold War and After* (Baltimore, Johns Hopkins University Press, 1995), p. 168.

121 Brands, *The Wages of Globalism*, p. vii.

2

US–Soviet relations, 1963–69

1963–64: JFK to LBJ

John F. Kennedy's death was confirmed to Lyndon Johnson some three quarters of an hour following the Dallas, Texas, shooting on 22 November 1963. Unsurprisingly, the key concern in early communications with America's chief international adversary was to emphasise continuity. Johnson met Anastas Mikoyan (first Deputy Chairman of the Soviet Council of Ministers) on 26 November, when Mikoyan arrived to represent the USSR at JFKs funeral. Mikoyan was assured 'that there would be no change in the Kennedy policy'. Although there were verbal skirmishes with Mikoyan over Cuba, LBJ stressed that the 'United States would meet anyone more than half way'.[1]

At subsequent meetings, the Soviet Ambassador, Anatoly Dobrynin, was reassured that his private channels to Secretary Rusk, National Security Adviser McGeorge Bundy and Ambassador at Large Llewellyn Thompson would remain intact.[2] Thompson told Dobrynin that, although LBJ would continue JFKs policies, the new President's style was different. Johnson would probably 'devote a larger proportion of his time to domestic affairs'.[3]

Despite Nikita Khrushchev's swift condemnation of the 'villainous assassination',[4] Johnson's initial instincts were not so much to reject the idea of a conspiracy, possibly involving Moscow, as to head off panic which might propel the US into nuclear war. LBJ seems initially to have feared the possibility of a major Soviet attack following the assassination. He later recalled:

> What raced through my mind was that if they had shot our President . . . who would they shoot next? . . . when would the missiles be coming? I thought it was a conspiracy and I raised that question and nearly everybody that was with me raised it.[5]

The new President was still worrying, as he later told Doris Kearns, about his status as 'a pretender to the throne, an illegal usurper'[6]. He seems to have abandoned anxieties about a direct Soviet link to the assassination quite quickly, though he certainly retained a feeling that pro-Castro Cubans were involved.

Johnson, however, was alarmed by Federal Bureau of Investigation and CIA reports of arrested assassin Lee Harvey Oswald's Soviet links. He was horrified when Dallas prosecutors threatened to charge Oswald with killing JFK as part of 'a Communist conspiracy'.[7] The investigating bipartisan panel, headed by Chief Justice Earl Warren, was appointed on 29 November. Warren's brief included the injunction to apply oil to troubled waters. The Chief Justice was told that the substantiation of Soviet or Cuban involvement 'might even catapult us into a nuclear war'. LBJ persuaded Richard Russell to serve on the commission by invoking the threat to forty million American lives.[8] Attorney General Nicholas Katzenbach urged the commission idea on Johnson, arguing: 'Speculation about Oswald's motivation ought to be cut off, and we should have some basis for rebutting that this was a Communist conspiracy or (as the Iron Curtain press is saying) a right-wing conspiracy to blame it on the Communists'.[9] When House Minority Leader Charles Halleck objected to the choice of Warren to head the commission, LBJ responded that 'this is a question that could involve our losing thirty-nine million people. This is a judicial question'.[10]

Johnson seems genuinely to have considered the work of the Warren Commission as, in his words in *The Vantage Point*, 'dispassionate and just'.[11] He knew that the full implications of Oswald's Soviet ties had not been drawn out, not least because of the FBI's unwillingness to provide evidence of its own laxity in monitoring Oswald. Shortly before the commission issued its report, LBJ told Senate Majority Leader Mike Mansfield that Warren's panel 'don't quite find the motive yet that this fellow (Oswald) had for wanting to kill him (JFK). He (Oswald) was going back and forth to Russia'.[12] However, Johnson was appreciative that the Warren Commission had managed to ease the situation. The President was not unhappy if the true answers 'were lost, perhaps for all time'.[13] Clearly, Johnson's worries and fears about communism took second place to the demands of pragmatism.

Johnson was preoccupied in the immediate post-assassination period with providing evidence, to both domestic and foreign audiences, that he was in control of political Washington. The key early issue involved sales of surplus wheat to the USSR, which had been negotiated by the Kennedy Administration. It presented itself in the form of a foreign aid amendment (put down in the name of Republican Senator Karl Mundt of South Dakota), disbarring loan guarantees administered by the Export-Import Bank (these loans were designed to facilitate the Soviet wheat sales). Moscow's main concern with regard to the wheat sales was the US insistence that most of the wheat had to be delivered in American ships. The condition was primarily designed to assuage opinion in Congress and in the strongly anti-communist labour unions, whose members would have to load the wheat.[14] To conservatives like Mundt, the issue was one of 'trading with the enemy'. In the event, Johnson won the key votes. Private telephone conversations during this period showed LBJ's sensitivity to the 'soft on communism' charge. On 20 December, he told House Speaker John McCormack that he (LBJ) would 'take the rap' on the wheat sales: 'And then they can call me a Communist all over this country – Nixon can – and that will satisfy them'.[15] Johnson's preoccupation with the 1964 Presidential election, for which he viewed Richard Nixon as the likely Republican candidate, was evident in a meeting with Congressional leaders held on the same day. The trade bill, complained the President, 'just publicizes that I'm pro-Russian, right when Nixon is running against me',[16] But, whatever his misgivings, Johnson clearly saw the 'trade and aid' bill (which, of course, also provided funds for *anti*-communist activities by friendly governments) as a test of strength. He told Gould Lincoln of the *Washington Star* how he had called back legislators from holiday:

> . . . the whole Communist world was watching to see any sign of weakness or temporizing or compromising or running on the part of the President . . . If I'd let it go unchallenged, they'd have said, "Well, he's a weak sister. He hasn't got any steel in his spine, and hell, we don't need to pay attention to him. He's a pushover".[17]

Soviet specialists within the Administration were also concerned that the new President should pass his early tests. Foy Kohler, US Ambassador in Moscow, wrote on 10 December: 'Khrushchev, given his personal modus operandi and the imperatives of communist dynamics, must at some point test the will and determination of his new adversary'. Kohler favoured an early summit meeting as a way of postponing 'the test until the new administration has time to shake down a bit'. Khrushchev was unlikely to 'attempt an early showdown' with a meeting with LBJ imminent.[18] The balance of opinion, however, was that it would be preferable to delay a summit until following the November 1964 elections. A victorious Johnson, argued Llewellyn Thompson, could then face Khrushchev 'with a mandate from the people based upon his campaign platform'.[19]

At the beginning of 1964, with the immediate problems of the transition solved and the assassination hysteria diverted, LBJ set his sights on what he described to Robert McNamara on 2 January as a 'peace offensive' with the Soviets.[20] The initiative seems to have been driven by Johnson himself, in response to a communication issued by Khrushchev to the world's governmental heads on 31 December 1963. LBJ was piqued by the letter's propagandistic tone and its use of the term, 'imperialism'.[21] Yet Khrushchev did state his readiness to move to an international agreement peacefully to resolve territorial disputes. Johnson declared in private that the US should be more proactive: 'I am tired, by God, of having him [Khrushchev] be the man who wants peace and I am the guy who wants war'.[22] At a National Security Council meeting on December 5, LBJ referred to the 'sense of hope that was developing in President Kennedy's last months', attributing 'one-half of the explanation' for it to JFK's nuclear build-up. LBJ urged his Administration to show 'patience and understanding' of other political systems, but never to tolerate 'Communist subversion'.[23]

Johnson assigned Mac Bundy to the job of devising 'some initiative', to establish a momentum for *American* leadership for peace and for sustaining the hope of 1963. He told Bundy: 'Now you-all are supposed to be a brains group and have a lot of imagination and be soft on Russia'.[24] In December 1963, a CIA report on Soviet grain shortages pointed up the possibilities of using wheat sales in particular, and trade generally, as a tool of leverage and/or bridge-building with Moscow.[25]

The rest of this chapter considers (mainly) bilateral US–Soviet relations as they developed after January 1964. Areas, such as the Vietnam War and the 1968 Czechoslovakian invasion, which are covered in later chapters, will only be touched upon briefly.

1964: step-by-step and Khrushchev's fall

Throughout LBJ's first full year in office, the US and Soviet leadership were committed to 'step-by-step' moves, designed to ease international tension. These moves included bilateral agreements, increased trade and commercial links, defence spending restraint and control of the production of fissionable materials. In private meetings in the early part of 1964, LBJ revealed himself as keen to advance the 'step-by-step' agenda, but wary of its domestic repercussions. In April, 1964, for example, Johnson supported an expansion in trade with the USSR, but opposed 'large industrial sales . . . certainly in the next six months because of the difficulty of dealing domestically with such sales'. (The total value of US–Soviet trade in 1964 was a modest 167,000 dollars.) Johnson was also concerned that the 'step-by-step' agenda should not inhibit US resistance to communist advances in the developing world. His desire to prevent 'another Cuba' was evident in early April when he referred to the crisis in the island of Zanzibar: 'We couldn't just wait and let Africa go communist'.[26]

LBJ and Khrushchev swapped 'pen pal' letters during this period. Johnson wished to add the question of Soviet 'subversion' in Vietnam to the agenda between the superpowers. However, the President was prepared to take the initiative on nuclear cutbacks, announcing on 20 April that, following earlier cuts, the US would now be making an overall 20 per cent reduction in plutonium output and 40 per cent in uranium. Khrushchev made parallel announcements. The symbolism of all this was very important, despite problems of mutual verification. It was also certainly the case that the US had excess fissionable capacity. JFK had favoured cuts but wished to postpone them until after the 1964 elections. Referring to Franklin Roosevelt's Works Progress Administration, LBJ himself in April declared that the US 'must not operate a WPA nuclear project, just to provide employment when our needs have been met'.[27]

Nevertheless, real progress towards détente was being made. A CIA cable of 8 May reported, via Yugoslavia, that 'ranking Soviet officials in Moscow had expressed the view that in President Johnson the Soviet Union has the best chances since World War II to restore normal relations between the United States and the Soviet Union'.[28] Khrushchev even proffered, through Dobrynin, his vote for LBJ in the November Presidential election. Ambassador Kohler reported from Moscow on 6 March that Senator Barry Goldwater, LBJ's eventual opponent in the elections, was regarded there as 'the Devil Incarnate'.[29] In June, Khrushchev told LBJ that the plutonium and uranium cutbacks had been 'met with widespread approval throughout the world'. He proposed the next stage in the 'step-by-step' process as troop reductions in Europe: 'As long as John and Ivan, gripping sub-machine guns, are tensely eyeing one another across the boundary between the two German states, the situation will remain dangerous, regardless of what anyone says'.[30]

Moscow, one presumes, did not expect any moves on European troop reductions prior to the November elections. Actually, the comity between the superpower leaders was nowhere more evident than in Moscow's attitude towards the elections. A range of US actions – in Africa, Southeast Asia, Cyprus and elsewhere – was criticised by the Soviets. As Dobrynin informed LBJ at the beginning of September, Khrushchev 'frankly thinks' that 'Tonkin Gulf, Cyprus or the Congo do not necessarily, in his words, you know, decorate the US policy'. Yet, the Soviet leader appreciated that 'during the election campaigns some unfortunate things occur'.[31] (The August 1964 Gulf of Tonkin resolution significantly expanded the US commitment to South Vietnam. In September 1964, the US was supporting Moise Tshombe, its former enemy and leader of the Katanga rebellion, in the Congo. In November, the US intervened with Belgium to free hostages and oppose a leftist insurrection there. LBJ sought to prevent a war between Greece and Turkey over Cyprus, whose Greek Cypriot President Archbishop Makarios was making overtures to Moscow. In June 1964, Turkey was warned by Washington not to invade the island.) Dobrynin was briefed by McGeorge Bundy to the effect that 'in the polemics with Goldwater, Johnson might have to say some things that might displease Moscow'.[32] The Soviets should understand that such things should not be taken too seriously.

Khrushchev, of course, was unable to register his metaphorical vote for LBJ as America's leader. The 'real palace revolution'[33] that ousted Khrushchev in October excited in Washington an apprehension that soon gave way to cautious optimism. The CIA was briefing on the prospects for a post-Khrushchev USSR well before October. In March 1964, a CIA report suggested that the coming struggle would be between those who 'advocate a continuation of the Khrushchevian status quo' (including the dynamics of de-Stalinisation) 'and those who would perhaps disavow Khrushchev's reformism'.[34] A CIA analysis of 'Khrushchev, aged 70', noted that, though no longer a 'party ruffian' the Soviet leader had lost respect. His foreign policy had been driven by 'a strong desire to gain world recognition of the USSR as a great-power equal of the

US'. However, Khrushchev, although he had abandoned the anti-Western stances of 1957–58, had proved unreliable, with considerable 'vulnerability to self-deception' (particularly over the U-2 and Cuban missile crises).[35] Washington was keenly aware of Khrushchev's difficulties. Walter Stoessel of the US Embassy in Moscow reported that 'Soviet youth and labor are restless and food shortage has people disgruntled'.[36] LBJ himself referred to Kohler's view that 'compared to the problems that Khrushchev has, why, we ought to be joyful. He has them in every country with every Communist Party, and eight hundred million Chinese Communists'.[37]

Washington accepted that Khruschchev's fall (announced on 15 October 1964) was due to a variety of reasons: perceived failures in foreign policy, particularly in respect of Berlin and Cuba; what Thomas Hughes of State's Bureau of Intelligence and Research called Khrushchev's 'rambunctious, shotgun initiative style of leadership';[38] and failures in holding together the fabric of international communism. Such problems extended beyond the Sino-Soviet split, to Eastern and, indeed, Western Europe. On 20 October, Llewellyn Thompson cited the 'declaration of independence' – the 'Togliatti memorandum' – issued by the Italian communists, as a factor in Khrushchev's fall.[39] The almost exact coincidence of the Moscow palace revolution with the first successful test of China's nuclear bomb was widely noted. Thompson suggested that Khrushchev may have been about to force an even more open break with Beijing, and that this was resisted by more cautious elements in the Soviet hierarchy.[40] The CIA spied a 'hint of a new German policy' – a more accommodationist line on West Germany, with consequent opposition by East Germany and its supporters in Moscow.[41] The general CIA line, however, was that Khrushchev's fall was primarily due to domestic factors: party infighting, agricultural failures and what CIA Director John McCone described as 'the bitter controversy over allocation of economic resources, centering in a dispute over priority for consumer goods versus military programs'.[42]

Despite keen insights into Khrushchev's complex difficulties, American analysts were wrong-footed by the Soviet leader's sudden exit. Hughes offered the reassurance that Aleksei Kosygin (the new Chairman of the Soviet Council of Ministers and effective head of Soviet government) and Leonid Brezhnev (the new Communist Party First Secretary) were not hardliners.[43] (Mikoyan continued as titular President, a role he had assumed in July 1964.) For Thompson, however, 'the few clues we have would appear to indicate that the Stalinists are in the ascendancy'.[44] Ambassador Kohler saw Khrushchev's fall as signifying an 'institutionalized instability' in the Soviet system, linked to Khrushchev's own commitment to the legitimising role of the Communist Party Central Committee. Most US Soviet experts agreed that a plural leadership was unlikely to survive. Party insiders like Anastas Mikoyan and Nicolai Podgorny were likely to figure in the succession struggle, in which it was difficult to distinguish 'Stalinists' from 'liberals'. Mikhail Suslov, the party 'gray cardinal' who was later to be seen as perhaps the major figure in Khrushchev's ousting, did not attract much attention in these early American analyses. Despite the power of the Central Committee, the party base enjoyed by Brezhnev – a 'vain and ambitious man', according to Kohler[45] – gave him the real advantage. (Dobrynin later likened Brezhnev to LBJ. Both came from 'plain families', were 'masters of the domestic political game', but lacked foreign policy expertise. Dobrynin regarded Kosygin as more honest, intelligent and open-minded than Brezhnev. Kosygin's 'common sense' compensated for *his* weakness in foreign affairs and made him, behind Foreign Minister Andrei Gromyko, the country's best negotiator.)[46] US analysts agreed that there would be no sudden policy shifts and that, in Khrushchev's wake, the new leaders would pursue a style of regularised, bureaucratised managerialism. Llewellyn Thompson saw the first priority of Brezhnev and Kosygin as domestic policy, the second as the restoration of order in the forces of international communism, and only the third as foreign policy and US relations.[47]

Most US foreign policy analysts concentrated on the implications of Khrushchev's fall for Chinese policy. The CIA report of 22 October judged that, following the Chinese atomic test, 'any substantial rapprochement would be on Mao's terms'.[48] Kohler noted that, with Khrushchev's fall, 'Mao Tse-Tung remains the only old-line world-known Communist figure'. Restoring Soviet-oriented discipline on international communism would be very difficult,[49] David Klein from the White House staff saw the possibility of either a rather desperate attempt to restore relations with Beijing, or else a complete break with China.[50] Kohler's long term prediction was for 'the evolution of Soviet society in the direction of a national socialist state in loose association with Communist Parties which have won power or lost their revolutionary elan, while the ChiComs [Chinese Communists] develop a small but tight and expanding organization dedicated to perpetuating Marxist-Leninist revolutionary orthodoxy'.[51]

The Chinese nuclear test served, despite the uncertainties engendered by Khrushchev's ousting, to strengthen perceptions of a burgeoning community of interest between Moscow and Washington. This was evidenced in extreme form in the revival of 1963 proposals to take military action, possibly with Soviet complicity, against the Chinese nuclear capability. A June 1963 briefing paper, prepared for the July Moscow conference on the Limited Test Ban, had raised the possibility of 'Soviet, or possibly joint US-USSR, use of military force' against China.[52] Robert Johnson, of State's Policy Planning Council, considered the case for 'direct action against Chinese Communist nuclear facilities' in a paper written in April 1964 and considered in December 1964, by the Committee on Nuclear Proliferation (a high-level interagency committee, appointed by LBJ and chaired by Roswell Gilpatric). Summarising Johnson's paper, the Gilpatric Committee noted that 'Soviet cooperation or acquiescence would be improbable, the degree of improbability depending on the circumstances of the attack; i.e., whether or not ostensibly in response to aggressiveness in Southeast Asia, etc'.[53]

The step-by-step approach was reaffirmed by the post-Khrushchev leadership. Brezhnev, responding to positive American reactions to the leadership changes, indicated his willingness to make further troop reductions in Europe. The new leaders welcomed cooperation in the exploration of outer space and expressed their faith in 'certain obligations concerning non-attack on Cuba'.[54] At his December 9 meeting with Soviet Foreign Minister Gromyko, LBJ promised a two to three billion dollar defence spending reduction between 1964 and 1966, and welcomed a Soviet promise to cut 500 million roubles in the upcoming defence budget. Gromyko looked forward to movement in the Geneva disarmament talks. It was time to tackle the problem of weapons 'stockpiles as high as Mont Blanc'.[55]

1964 saw significant moves towards bilateral accords. Indeed, in June, the first ever bilateral, US–USSR, treaty (on arrangements for setting up consulates in either country) was signed in Moscow. Progress on a civil air agreement opened the prospect of direct New York-Moscow flights by 1965. Prospects for enhanced trade seemed good. In May, Kosygin testily reminded Dean Rusk that Russians 'now have more to sell, beyond vodka and caviar'.[56] The possibility of a formal non-aggression pact was raised. Cultural exchanges, seen in Washington as implanting in Soviet minds 'the benefits of genuine peaceful coexistence', increased.[57] LBJ was reluctant to undertake a summit meeting in Presidential election year. His indications to Moscow of his reluctance to travel, in the absence of a Vice President who could remain in the US, were not entirely convincing. However, a 1965 summit, following consolidation of power by the new Kremlin leaders, seemed likely.

1964, however, was not devoid of reminders of the darker side of the Cold War. In January, Yuri Nosenko, a KGB officer who had served on the Soviet disarmament delegation in Geneva, defected to the US. He was imprisoned for almost five years by the CIA, who mistakenly believed that the defection was a ruse to discredit information being provided by Anatoli Golitsyn, another (and less reliable) KGB figure who had crossed over in 1961.[58]

Also in January, in what Washington called an 'inexcusably brutal act',[59] Soviet fighter aircraft downed an American T-39 which had flown into East German airspace. In March, LBJ protested to Khrushchev about a shootdown, in similar circumstances, of a RB-66 aircraft.[60] The high-level Moscow–Washington correspondence of 1964 tended to treat 'darker side' incidents as dangerous holdovers from a more primitive, though recent, past. Even the friendliest correspondence and meetings, however, had an edge: a mixture of concern, regret and fear that Soviet–American relations might again spin out of control. In April, for example, Khrushchev complained to LBJ about US document-checking procedures in Berlin. Even apparently trivial incidents, insisted the Soviet leader, were sometimes links in a chain 'with which certain circles are striving to keep' the US and USSR 'from throwing off the shackles of the "Cold War"'.[61]

'Certain circles', of course, in Moscow as in Washington, were sceptical about the step-by-step strategy. However, the Cold War 'shackles' were kept in place equally firmly by (predictably unpredictable) incidents, deriving as much from constant middle-level diplomatic, military and intelligence competition, as from any conspiracy. In April, extensive bugging was discovered at the US Embassy in Moscow. In September, Soviet officials ransacked a hotel room used by US military attachés, whose recklessness Dean Rusk privately blamed for the intrusion.[62] Despite all this, there was a clear willingness in 1964 in both Moscow and Washington to 'play the game': to accept setbacks, to select an appropriate diplomatic tone according to circumstances and level of contact, and – at least at the highest levels – to keep in motion the dynamic of détente.

1965: breakdown

Towards the end of 1965, Ambassador Kohler reported Gromyko as indicating, rather obviously, that it 'was our policy in Vietnam above all which aggravated our relations'.[63] As detailed in Chapter 4, the war in Vietnam occasioned a major rupture in the step-by-step incrementalism of 1964 détente. US air attacks on North Vietnam in February, carried out while Aleksei Kosygin was in Hanoi, marked the close of the *petite détente* of 1963–64.

US estimates of Soviet intent before February 1965 tended to conclude that Moscow still placed the highest priority on improving relations with the West. A CIA evaluation concluded that long-term forces in the Soviet Union favoured 'relaxation of tensions with the West'. The hard edge of superpower conflict was in the developing world, but, even there, it was a 'double contest': the US *versus* the Soviet Union *versus* China.[64] Even in the Third World – for example, in the Congo – Moscow, according to the CIA in January 1964, was 'reacting rather than acting'.[65] Soviet policy was likely to be influenced by constraints imposed by the USSR's 'unfavorable power relationship with the US', by internal economic problems and by East European assertiveness.[66] The key to Soviet international attitudes was seen as lying in the competition with China. The Sino-Soviet split was, as Ambassador Kohler put it much later in the year, the 'mainspring' of Soviet behaviour.[67] Regarding the precise configuration of the Kremlin collective leadership, Washington seemed more than a little bemused. There was general agreement that Brezhnev's star was in the ascendant. In September, however, Thomas Hughes reported a 'current report' to the effect that 'Mikoyan and Kosygin are to resign, Brezhnev replacing Mikoyan as President', Suslov becoming party head and Shelepin replacing Kosygin as Premier. A Suslov-Shelepin regime, according to Hughes, would be likely to favour 'a harder line towards the West'.[68]

The February breakdown in US–Soviet relations produced several diplomatic and legislative casualties. LBJ's expressed intent, in his 1965 State of the Union Address, to pursue a meeting with Soviet leaders, had been followed through – indeed, virtually agreed by Moscow.[69] The prospects for a summit now collapsed. Hopes for progress on disarmament, for Senate ratification of the consular convention, and for East–West trade legislation were disappointed. A special committee chaired by J. Irwin Miller and operating under LBJ's personal sponsorship, recommended in April a significant expansion of US–Soviet trade as a way of reconciling deeper divisions. 'In this intimate engagement', concluded Miller, 'men and nations will in time be altered by the engagement itself'. Significant expansion of US–Soviet trade would have involved major modifications in the way various laws, designed to limit exports in the name of national security, were administered. Congress was also told that trade liberalisation was bound to enhance 'internal liberalization in individual Communist countries'.[70] (In this way, the trade agenda could be used to answer criticisms that the Administration, in its push for détente, was ignoring human rights violations inside the USSR. In September, Mac Bundy was advised that he should reply to a Jewish delegation, protesting about Moscow's treatment of Soviet Jewry, with 'appropriate noises' – 'there's little we can actually do'.)[71] On the trade issue, LBJ knew almost instinctively that, given the US–Soviet tensions over Vietnam, significant enthusiasm on Capitol Hill for any major initiative was unlikely.

Soviet Foreign Minister Gromyko evinced a sense of personal betrayal in protesting at US actions in Vietnam and in LBJ's ordering of the invasion of the Dominican Republic in April.[72] The 'pen pal' link never really recovered from Khrushchev's fall, and cultural exchanges were virtually suspended. Kohler reported that the Soviets would increasingly refrain from allowing 'themselves to be seen holding hands with US in public'.[73] Personal attacks on LBJ appeared in the Soviet media (Johnson had been acutely sensitive even to the fairly moderate personal criticism which had appeared in 1964).[74] Progress stalled on European issues, with Moscow continuing to interpret the US plan for a Multilateral Nuclear Force in Europe as a way of arming West Germany with nuclear weapons. The American publication of the 'Penkovsky Papers' was condemned by Dobrynin as 'premeditated action', designed by Washington to torpedo détente.[75] Supposedly the diary of a Soviet double agent, the Papers actually were the product of collusion between the CIA, a Soviet KGB defector and a *Chicago Daily News* journalist. Kosygin advanced the view that the Soviets could 'concoct a similar book' about the leadership of the Democratic party, but chose not to.[76]

The diplomatic record for 1965 reveals occasional deep pessimism about prospects for détente. Adlai Stevenson, then US Representative to the United Nations, reported gloom among liberal internationalist members of the Soviet delegation and secretariat. Such people were 'now in an extremely difficult position and were accused of being "apologists of American imperialism" '.[77] Superpower animosity spilled over into various regional crises, notably the Dominican Republic invasion. However, not all indicators and analyses were negative. The conflict, ignited in the disputed region of Kashmir, between India and Pakistan in August-September 1965 actually revealed the degree to which US and Soviet interests on the subcontinent were now running in tandem. Faced with the prospect of Chinese intervention, Washington and Moscow entered into an alliance of objective pragmatism. Rejecting the anti-Soviet thrust of prior US policy in the region, LBJ welcomed a Soviet offer of mediation following a UN-brokered ceasefire in September. At first, as Thomas Hughes reported in October, prospects looked 'dim'. The Soviets were 'taking their cues on this question from the Indians', while Pakistan's leader Mohammad Ayub Khan preferred 'discussions to take place in the [UN] Security Council rather than under Soviet auspices'.[78] Negotiations under Soviet direction, however, took place at the central Asian site of Tashkent. They followed intense American pressure on Pakistan – pressure which effectively terminated the alliance between Washington and Islamabad. A peace was achieved in January 1966. For George Ball, the episode demonstrated that it was time for the Soviets to 'break their lance' on the subcontinent.[79] The US felt itself stretched very thin in this period: in Vietnam, of course, but also in Indonesia, where the CIA was closely involved in the events which led to the violent anti-communist purges following the fall of President Sukarno.[80] Dean Rusk later recalled explicit American encouragement for Soviet mediation (one is almost inclined to write, burden-sharing) in the subcontinent: 'If the Russians failed at Tashkent, at least the Russians would have the experience of the frustrations that we have had for twenty years in trying to sort things out between India and Pakistan'.[81]

CIA evaluations of US–Soviet prospects, even in this year of crisis in Vietnam, were actually quite upbeat. In April, the Agency concluded that 'the experience of the past two months, coupled with the urgent requirements of domestic economic reform and growth, seems likely over the longer term to strengthen the Soviet leaders' incentive to move back toward détente and accommodation with the US as the main focus of their policy'.[82] Kohler advised that reasserting Soviet influence in the communist world was now the Kremlin's main priority. However, détente still had 'influential friends' in Moscow.[83] The State Department Bureau of Intelligence and Research reported on 23 November that the 'hardening of the Soviet demeanour toward the US continues to be limited and apparently intended more as a tactic than a fundamental reorientation of policy'.[84]

1966: learning to live with the war

'In US–Soviet context, Soviet propaganda speaks of American imperialism but Soviet policy is based on tacit assumptions and in some cases even overt cooperation with US'.[85] This comment by John Guthrie (Deputy Chief of Mission at the Moscow Embassy) encapsulated the superpower dynamic of 1966: a commitment to keeping the détente train on the rails, despite the Indochinese disruptions. Early in the year, LBJ launched a major programme of East–West 'bridge-building', designed to encourage greater economic contact between the competing power blocs. (As well as reaching out to the East, 'bridge-building' was designed to shore up differences in NATO.) Talks between Gromyko and Rusk in September, and between Gromyko and LBJ at Camp David in October, seemed to indicate a breakthrough over arms control and nuclear non-proliferation. (A US–Soviet agreed proposal on non-proliferation was delivered to NATO ministers in December.) A conversation with Gromyko, described by LBJ as 'very, very frank', convinced the President of a shift in the Soviet position, with Moscow now being more willing to inter-cede for peace in Vietnam.[86] Johnson told British officials on 14 October that US–Soviet relations were 'better at present' than at any time since he became President.[87] On 6 December, Kosygin publicly acknowledged the existence of a US–USSR 'community of interests', which could be enlarged if only a solution could be found in Vietnam.[88]

LBJ's public diplomacy during 1966 reflected the incremental détente agenda, and some progress was made upon it. Following the US bombing of Hanoi and Haiphong in June–July, Johnson told the press that it would not jeopardise arms control. The superpowers would find 'an acceptable compromise on language we can both live with'.[89] On 13 July, he invited Soviet cooperation in a new programme of oceanographic research.[90] Speaking to the American Legion in August, LBJ sounded almost like a post-Cold War President, keen to establish that global interdependence required the US to continue its internationalism: 'we know now that so interwoven is our destiny with the world's destiny, so intricate are the bonds between us and every continent, that our responsibilities would be just as real in the absence of a Communist threat'.[91] A major foreign policy address in October, to editorial writers in New York City, set out the case for incremental détente. The speech built on an intra-Administration initiative, launched in July, actively to 'develop areas of peaceful cooperation with the nations of Eastern Europe and the Soviet Union'.[92] In the October speech, LBJ declared that the US and USSR would 'not let our differences on Vietnam or elsewhere ever prevent us from exploring all opportunities' to relax tensions. He announced the imminent signing of the civil air agreement and proposed measures to regularise cross-border relations in Europe. LBJ also indicated the relaxation of export restrictions on hundreds of items relevant to trade with the USSR. The Export-Import Bank would further facilitate this trade, and guarantee credit to Poland, Hungary, Bulgaria and Czechoslovakia. The President promised to 'press' Congress for East–West trade legislation, giving him authority to extend Most Favoured Nation tariff treatment to the USSR – though not to North

Vietnam, North Korea, Cuba, East Germany or the People's Republic of China. The speech affirmed the need – despite, even in some sense because of, the situation in Vietnam – to encourage 'healthy economic and cultural relations' with the Soviet Union and (East Germany apart) Eastern Europe.[93]

As noted in Chapter 1, Congress (as LBJ no doubt realised) was not in cooperative mood. Wilbur Mills, Democratic chairman of the House Ways and Means Committee, refused even to introduce the East–West trade amendments. This lack of Congressional enthusiasm in election year was also seen in the efforts to kill the Export-Import Bank credits. The consular convention remained unratified. In April, Kohler explained to Ambassador Dobrynin: 'Congressional figures – including those well disposed towards the USSR – have to take into account the fact that even if there were enough positive votes, any debate on such questions at this time would provoke a big argument further affecting US–Soviet relations'.[94]

Leonid Brezhnev's reaction to LBJ's August address to the editorial writers was negative. The Soviet leader declared that progress in improving US–Soviet relations required a halt to American 'aggression' in Vietnam.[95] Washington, however, tended to discount such reactions. The Soviets, it was felt, wanted – perhaps needed – progress on détente. They simply felt, due to worries about their profile in the communist world, the need to keep alive their protests on Vietnam.

In other ways, however, 1966 did witness significant superpower tensions. The year began with Kohler reporting a 'vicious anti-American campaign' in Moscow.[96] Cultural exchanges, that reliable barometer of US–Soviet atmospherics, stuttered, though an agreement was reached in March. Dean Rusk commented that the Soviets did not want the agreement publicised and that they were particularly sensitive to Chinese charges of 'collaboration' with the US.[97] Perceived Soviet encouragement of the French decision, announced by General de Gaulle in February, to quit NATO's integrated command structure also raised tensions. (De Gaulle visited Moscow in June. He told Ambassador Bohlen that, in his view, 'the Soviet Union at the present time was interested in having a general détente with the West' in Europe.)[98] Characteristically optimistic, John Guthrie noted that 'in their efforts to establish a special relationship in Europe with France', the Soviets had virtually ignored the interests of the French Communist Party.[99]

American analysts in 1966 looked on détente as a desirable state for superpower relations, but one whose achievement had experienced recent setbacks. A State Department Policy Planning Council paper (23 March 1966) put the blame squarely at Moscow's door:

> The argument that the détente marked by the 1963 test ban was intended by the USSR to open a phase of continuing improvement in Soviet-American relations does not stand close analysis. The Soviets had more limited aims in view and soon returned to traditional priorities.

The paper, drafted by John Huizenga, argued that a détente settlement with Moscow, made on Moscow's terms, would not be worth having; it would amount to appeasement. However, a worthwhile détente could be achieved if the desires of the Soviet people – 'to become a modern society and to share the benefits of normal intercourse with other advanced societies' – were played upon.[100] Other 1966 overviews of the US–Soviet outlook were more straight-forwardly optimistic. Llewellyn Thompson was confident that 'Soviet youth . . . no longer accepted the outmoded dogma' peddled by the Kremlin. The leaders, however, were still in thrall to ideology. Communist belief 'often bars them from working out a regional solution to a given problem or at least places limits upon their freedom of action'.[101] A CIA analysis in February suggested that Soviet rigidity had been exacerbated by the resurgence in the power of 'party professionals' following Khrushchev's fall.[102] Yet a CIA National Intelligence Estimate, dated 28 April 1966, actually (and perceptively) judged that the Kremlin was moving out of the ideological rigidity identified by Llewellyn Thompson. The Brezhnev-Kosygin regime was committed to sureness and stability. The new leaders 'do not seize upon every crisis . . . as an opportunity to advance their cause suddenly and dramatically'. They exhibit 'a growing appreciation of the complexity of the world, the unpredictability of events, and the limits on Soviet ability to direct, or profit from, political change in foreign countries'.[103]

Most Washington analysts concluded in 1966 that the Vietnam War had not lessened the Soviet drive for détente in any fundamental way. The CIA pointed to Moscow's continued participation in the Geneva disarmament process and to the fact that 'Berlin, that sensitive touchstone of US–Soviet relations, has remained quiet'.[104] The USSR's internal economic problems, only slightly alleviated by the 'lucky harvest' of 1966, pointed towards defence spending reductions. Kohler reported Moscow's 'practically insoluble problem of resource distribution'.[105] Some analyses came close to identifying a nascent Soviet wish for some kind of partnership with the US. John Guthrie wrote in November that the apparent freeze in US–Soviet relations which began in February was more apparent than real – a 'controlled' freeze: 'Basic to this view is Kremlin's knowledge at bottom that it could not live with an actively hostile United States'. Ultimately, Moscow knew 'its security problems cannot be definitively resolved without us'.[106] Even Huizenga's more guarded paper of 23 March noted: 'The disorders and conflicts looming in the Third World suggest the possibility of parallel action by the US and USSR to contain the risks'.[107]

As ever, the US analysts put their strongest emphasis, in explaining Soviet behaviour, on reactions to China. The Sino-Soviet split was clearly seen to be working in America's interest. Llewellyn Thompson advised LBJ to take the opportunity, in his October meeting with Gromyko, to 'exacerbate the Sino-Soviet quarrel'.[108] The Great Proletarian Cultural Revolution was launched by Mao Zedong in May 1966. Designed to reenergize the Chinese revolution, Mao's initiative embodied outright condemnation of Soviet revisionism and imperialism. At one level, the Cultural Revolution itself served to draw the US and the USSR closer together. Gordon Chang later wrote of Moscow and Washington as, in 1966–67, 'still seemingly trying to arrange some sort of *Pax Superpowerica* over the world'.[109] To the considerable degree that the excesses of the Cultural Revolution served to isolate China from much of the communist world, the Soviets, by the end of 1966, appeared somewhat more relaxed about the threat to their international leadership. Llewellyn Thompson also noted that Kosygin and Brezhnev 'must be genuinely worried about the chaotic situation inside Communist China and would like better relations with us not only in the event of unforeseen contingencies but also to deter us from any inclination we might have to get together with Communist China in opposition to the Soviet Union'.[110] Guthrie argued that Moscow knew that it would eventually 'need US cooperation in handling awakening Chinese giant'.[111]

During 1966, senior figures in Washington were beginning to appreciate that the Chinese upheavals might result in some kind of major international realignment. A closer US–Soviet relationship, as suggested by Guthrie, was clearly one possibility. The craziness of the situation in China, where Mao appeared to be encouraging the disruptive questioning of all authority, was well captured in Llewellyn Thompson's record of a conversation with the Soviet Ambassador: 'I said I thought the Chinese had lost their minds. Dobrynin agreed'.[112] The CIA reported in December that, given the unpredictability of the situation, it should not be assumed that Chinese verbal attacks on Moscow would necessarily provoke 'a commensurate Soviet effort to improve relations with the West'.[113] Academic witnesses before Senator Fulbright's Foreign Relations Committee in March argued that the time had come to end the policy of trying to isolate China. On the advice of NSC staffer James Thomson, LBJ in December set up a China advisory panel, whose membership included the academic J. F. Fairbank, to investigate the possibility of greater flexibility toward China. Dean Rusk in this period seems to have been concerned that the US should pre-empt the possibility of a new Chinese leadership seeking closer ties to Moscow.[114]

1967: Glassboro

US–Soviet relations during 1967 were dominated by the Vietnam War, naturally, but also by conflict in the Middle East. When Johnson and Kosygin met in Glassboro, New Jersey, on 23–25 June, the Middle Eastern Six Day War had just ended in an Israeli victory, Egyptian humiliation, and with Soviet policy in disarray. The Arab–Israeli conflict, which had brought the US and USSR into something dangerously close to direct confrontation, dominated the summit, which also focused on Vietnam and nuclear weapons. These themes will be taken up in subsequent chapters.

The possibility of a summit had been raised in October 1966, in LBJ's conversations with Gromyko. Dobrynin later recalled the President's comment: 'The more we meet, the better it will be for us all'.[115] Kosygin took the initiative by attending a special session of the UN General Assembly in New York. The Soviet leader, of course, was technically visiting the UN rather than the US. The special session had been instigated by Moscow to deal with Israeli occupation of Arab territories in the wake of the Six Day War.

Kosygin initially indicated that he would be prepared to meet the American President in New York. The White House favoured Washington, Camp David or possibly a military base. McGeorge Bundy advised LBJ on 21 June: 'After a week of pulling and hauling, some may call it a tactical surrender' if the President ventured anywhere near New York.[116] Kosygin resisted any 'official' American site, especially a military one. He appeared sensitive to Arab and Chinese charges of being treated in the US as an honoured, official guest, even as quasi-ally. LBJ gave his view to Republican Senator George Aitken at this time that 'Kosygin had an obsession about China, he was scared to death'.[117]

Despite the inevitable dancing on diplomatic eggshells, Johnson's advisers felt that a meeting was desirable. Walt Rostow counselled LBJ to 'cover your flank to the left' (in terms of domestic criticism) by meeting Kosygin.[118] Johnson was advised that Kosygin was a sensible, unKhrushchevian leader, who would be impressed by 'your strength as well as your responsiveness'.[119] Referring to Khrushchev's behaviour at the UN, the CIA noted that Kosygin 'will certainly keep his shoes on his feet'.[120] Zbigniew Brzezinski, then working on State's Policy Planning Council, advised that LBJ should disabuse Kosygin of any idea that, following the Six Day War, 'the United States is out to humiliate the Soviet Union'. But Kosygin should not be encouraged – as Khrushchev was when he met JFK in Vienna – 'that a policy of bluff and bluster will get the Soviet Union anywhere'.[121] Nathaniel Davis told his boss, Walt Rostow, that LBJ should take seriously the rumours of Politburo personnel changes. Kosygin was 'a moderate in trouble' and should be offered the President's support – presumably in the form of undertakings on trade and arms control.[122]

The meeting finally took place at Hollybush, the Glassboro, New Jersey, home of the president of Glassboro State College, Thomas Robinson. The venue was arranged by state governor Richard Hughes, following Kosygin's rejection of the New Jersey air force base at Maguire. The meeting was cordial rather than productive, with significant progress being made only on the issue of nuclear non-proliferation. There were humorous incidents. It proved impossible to set up a proper taping system, so a White House secretary simply eavesdropped on the conversations between LBJ, Kosygin and two interpreters. Following the meeting, Kosygin was taken to visit Niagara Falls. One of his American handlers reported to LBJ that, before Kosygin boarded the aircraft, 'I took occasion to remove from the magazines beside the Chairman's (sic) chair, two which headlined pornography and violence in the United States and one which headlined "Russia Real Loser in Mid-East War"'. At Niagara, the local mayor patiently explained to the Soviet Premier that the US was a capitalist country.[123]

At Hollybush, according to the 23 June debriefing notes, Kosygin was 'contained but jolly'.[124] Johnson opened with a typically homely analogy: 'It had often happened that the oldest brother, himself, and the oldest sister had to take special powers in order to avoid disputes and differences between them so as to set a good example for the other children in the family'. In what might have served as an epigraph for the whole summit, Kosygin declared that the two sides seemed to agree 'on a global scale', but in 'this overall global concept only'. The first session saw LBJ rather surprisingly on the defensive, emphasising US non-aggression and the fact that, during his Presidential watch, 'we have not concluded any new military alliances with other countries'.[125] During the afternoon session of 23 June, Johnson emphasised that China represented 'the very greatest danger to both (our) countries at present'. Kosygin referred to 'forces in the world which were interested in causing a clash between the United States and the USSR'.[126] It was not entirely clear whether he was referring to Beijing only, to those 'rightists' who Khrushchev believed responsible for the death of JFK, or to Soviet–American defence interests. At lunch on 25 June, both leaders emphasised their desire to cut military budgets. The final, 25 June, meeting saw Kosygin again raising the spectre of dark forces threatening to destabilise US–Soviet relations, while LBJ offered the idea of annual summits as a way of smoothing difficulty and preventing misunderstanding.[127] In the evening, Johnson telephoned Eisenhower. Kosygin, said LBJ, had 'played about the same old broken record in private that he did in public'. The President complained about Kosygin's reluctance to set a timetable for talks on arms control. Kosygin had been polite and anxious to make 'clear they didn't want any confrontation', though there had been 'two or three little low blows below the belt every now and then'. Kosygin was very concerned about China, but his visit was primarily linked to USSR support for Egypt in the Six Day War:

> He came over here, in my judgement . . . to give Israel hell and try to get some of the polecat off him. He smelled bad in sending them all that arms, and just, by God, getting whipped in three days, and he wanted to divert the attention and get us on the defensive . . .[128]

Kosygin's comment about global superpower agreement and sub-global disagreement applied to various regional crises during 1967 – not only Vietnam, but also Cyprus and the Congo. (In July, the US aided the Mobutu regime in the Congo against forces loyal to Tshombe.) The East–West trade agenda was not advanced at Glassboro, and remained blocked by disputes in Congress about the extension of the Export-Import Bank's statutory authority. These attacks on the Bank emanated not only from opponents of trade with the East, but also from liberals who wished to restrain the financing of arms sales to developing countries. The total of imports and exports to the USSR in 1967 was worth just over one hundred million dollars. (This compared with a figure of five hundred million for UK–Soviet trade). Progress on bilateral relations, however, was made in 1967. The Senate ratified the consular convention in March, and the Outer Space Treaty (discussed in Chapter 3) in April.

The year 1967 saw a series of specific Soviet–American clashes. One, literal, clash involved (in White House staffer Nathaniel Davis' phrase) 'games of naval chicken' between US and Soviet ships in the Sea of Japan.[129] W. R. Macomber of the State Department informed Senator Fulbright of a Soviet effort 'to interfere with random US Navy exercises'.[130] In March, a Soviet trawler, fishing off the Alaskan coast, was temporarily seized by American vessels. Dobrynin was prepared to put this down to 'the game of American politics', wherein Soviet trawling had become a significant political issue for Alaska; by the end of 1967, a fishing agreement between the US and USSR had been reached. (Both this agreement and White House proposals to ease restrictions on Russian ships entering US ports provoked protests from US labour unions.)[131] On the espionage front, efforts were made to secure deals regarding personnel (notably regarding Imamv Ivanov and Buel W. Thom) held in either country on spying charges. A dispute, eventually resolved in 1968, also rumbled on over each country's desire to find a better site for its embassy.

The most vexing and unexpected irritation concerned the defection of Svetlana Alliluyeva, daughter of Jozef Stalin. Chester Bowles, now serving as Ambassador to India, was approached by Alliluyeva, who had arrived in India with the intention of settling outside the USSR, and having her (as it turned out, rather uncontroversial) book, *Twenty Letters to a Friend*, published. When the Indian government refused to accept her, Bowles arranged for Svetlana Stalin to travel to Rome, and subsequently to Switzerland. Within a few months she was in the USA, initially on a visitor's visa. Bowles explained to Walt Rostow: 'If we had refused to help her she would have gone to the press and the roof would have blown off at home'. The 'public outcry' at Washington's refusal to assist would have been 'overwhelming'.[132] The Soviet reaction was to attribute the US line to 'ill-will' and a desire to embarrass Moscow in the period leading up to the celebrations for the fiftieth anniversary of the Bolshevik Revolution. Soviet diplomat Yuri Tcherniakov alleged in May that Stalin's daughter suffered from 'mental disturbances'. He contrasted Washington's eagerness to discomfort Moscow over this issue with comparative Soviet silence about 'theories and arguments' concerning the murder of President Kennedy.[133] From Washington's viewpoint, the episode was more a nuisance than a propaganda triumph. It was, as Rusk told Dobrynin in July, 'a problem we had not asked for'.[134]

For American analysts in 1967, the future of US–Soviet relations seemed to a considerable degree to turn on the outcome of the revolutionary upheavals in China. John Roche of the White House staff surmised in January that Moscow had contingency plans to seize Chinese nuclear facilities if such facilities were overrun by revolutionary Chinese Red Guards. It seems likely that during this period, serious consideration was given again to possible US action – either unilaterally or even in collusion with the USSR – against Chinese nuclear sites. (Washington was also especially exercised over possible deployment of a Chinese nuclear-capable submarine.)[135] In January, Peter Jessup of the NSC staff disagreed with Roche over the likelihood of actual Soviet intervention:

> It is probable that Soviet planners are well aware of the potential unifying factor in the Chinese picture should there be foreign intervention. After a tradition of so many decades of 'foreign devils', the Russians would be most unlikely to intervene short of all-out war.[136]

Washington was consciously engaged in 1967 in analysing the possibility of, and limits to, 'parallel action' – the phrase was used by LBJ himself in May – between America and Russia.[137] In September, a major CIA National Intelligence Estimate on the USSR noted various ambivalences and paradoxes in Soviet foreign policy. There was a clear Soviet emphasis 'on the desirability of an all-out European détente and security system'. A desire to be seen as leader of international communism, however, pulled Moscow in other directions, especially in the developing world. The Politburo was riven by disagreements, especially over the Middle East and resource allocation. However, there was no simple split between militants and moderates, or between traditionalists and modernisers. The leading Soviet personnel – Brezhnev, Kosygin, Podgorny and Suslov – 'all seem to be near the middle of the Soviet political spectrum'. The leadership had 'not outgrown a dogmatic attitude that the world should conform to the Soviet image of it, but their foreign policies often reflect an understanding that there are definite limits to their ability to shape and exploit the course of international events'.[138] The leaders of the Soviet Union also clearly had problems with satisfying consumer aspirations at home. A CIA report of September 1967 described the average Soviet citizen as approaching the Bolshevik Revolution 'anniversary celebration with cynicism'.[139]

US analysts were preoccupied with the Soviet nuclear build-up, and with the degree to which the US should (openly or covertly) accept 'parity' with the old enemy in this area. A December study in the State Department concluded that, although the US had not become more vulnerable as a result of Soviet missile acquisitions, American 'vulnerability' would inevitably become a major domestic political issue. Enhanced Russian nuclear strength would also increase Moscow's confidence in the developing world.[140] Brzezinski, also in

December, directly addressed the possibility of a superpower partnership. There would, he wrote, be no 'US–Soviet condominium'. Washington must not accept parity. Superpower cooperation was only feasible and desirable in certain policy areas – in space, for example, and possibly in certain regions, notably Latin America. In others, particularly in other areas of the developing world, the US had to resist the 'sporadic adventurism' which was the likely future course for Moscow. Commenting on an 8 per cent (admitted) increase in the Soviet defence budget, Brzezinski commented that there was 'little connection between the external state of US–Soviet relations and the pace of Soviet military programs'. The latter 'seem to have a momentum of their own'.[141]

1968: yearning for a summit

Throughout the cataclysmic year of 1968 – the year that saw the communist Tet offensive in Vietnam (January–February); LBJ's post-New Hampshire primary, 31 March speech, announcing that he would not seek re-election in November; Martin Luther King's assassination (April); Robert Kennedy's assassination (June); the riotous Democratic Party convention at Chicago (July); and Richard Nixon's election as President in November – Johnson hoped for a successful summit meeting in Russia. His Presidency, however, was running out of time and steam. The 31 March announcement, in effect, inaugurated an extra long 'lame duck' period, as Moscow looked to LBJ's successor. The (20 August) Soviet invasion of Czechoslovakia, to be discussed in Chapter 7, fatally damaged Johnson's hopes for a meeting.

The year opened with the *Pueblo* incident. On 23 January, Washington was informed that the intelligence ship *Pueblo*, operating just outside territorial waters in the Sea of Japan, had been captured by North Korean ships. LBJ later described the affair as 'the first link in a chain of events – of crisis, tragedy, and disappointment that added up to one of the most agonizing years any President has ever spent in the White House'.[142]

The seizure was almost immediately linked in Washington to the Soviets. The CIA interpreted the incident as an instance of 'collusion between the North Koreans and the Soviets' and as 'another attempt to divert us from our efforts in Vietnam'. The launch of the Tet offensive only eight days after the seizure seemed to support the view, which Johnson continued to hold into his short retirement, that the *Pueblo* capture was part of a much wider international communist conspiracy. On 24 January, Walt Rostow supported a 'symmetrical suggestion' to seize a Soviet ship.[143] The almost reflex attachment of blame to Moscow indicated the shallowness of Washington's acceptance of the norms of US–Soviet détente. Nathaniel Davis complained to Soviet diplomat Igor Bubnov on 26 January that 'the *Pueblo* was no closer, in fact not so close, as the Soviet ships doing the same sort of work off our shores'.[144]

Mitchell Lerner argues that the vulnerability of Soviet ships was a strong reason for not suspecting Russian involvement. Within a few days of the *Pueblo* seizure, Moscow had in fact delivered a series of assurances that this was a purely North Korean initiative.[145] While still suspecting Soviet involvement, LBJ called Kosygin, outlining the American case and, in effect, requesting the Soviet leader's good offices in securing release of the crew. At this stage, LBJ told the *Pueblo* crisis group of advisers: 'Our primary objective is to gain time, to give all concerned an opportunity for reasoning together'. It was desirable to 'give the Soviets time to bring influence to bear on North Korea if they will'. Some 14,000 reservists were mobilised and serious consideration given to the possible bombing of North Korea. However, the President was worried: 'when we send our vast armada, won't the Soviets and the Chinese say they must be ready to protect their little brothers?'[146] Kosygin replied to LBJ on 27 January, indicating that he disputed America's interpretation of events but that he had relayed Johnson's message to the North Koreans. On 29 January, the US Embassy in Moscow reported that Soviet Foreign Minister Gromyko, although he maintained that the *Pueblo* had entered North Korean territorial waters, had indicated that Moscow might intercede: 'something would be done to reach settlement'.[147] Top-level meetings in Washington on 29 January resolved that Moscow would be advised in advance of any military action. The advisory group judged 'that communication with the USSR was in pretty good shape'.[148] Ambassador Thompson reported on 6 February that Kosygin condemned the 'many hotheads in the Pentagon who needed tranquillizers', but favoured a 'prompt settlement'.[149] Johnson was also worried about hotheads. He complained to George Ball about 'the Thurmonds and the Rivers' – Senator Strom Thurmond and Representative Mendel Rivers, chairman of the House Armed Services Committee – 'who want to blow up a city'.[150] Walt Rostow was concerned that failure to strike might 'damage our credibility with the Russians', though the counter-argument (also presented by Rostow), to the effect that an attack might provoke Moscow unnecessarily, won the day.[151]

Various meetings occurred between US and North Korean negotiators before the 82-man crew (and one deceased) were released on 22 December. Washington continually sought to orchestrate these meetings in order to maximise Soviet leverage on North Korean leader Kim-il-Sung. Nicholas Katzenbach of the State Department wrote on 22 February: 'Our hope is that the Russians will get to the North Koreans before the next meeting . . .'.[152] The extent of Soviet influence on Kim is very unclear. Moscow criticised Washington's reluctance to appreciate the sensibilities of small countries. Dobrynin in August called the *Pueblo* affair 'a big country – little country problem'.[153] Dean Rusk certainly thought that Soviet influence had been crucial in securing the crew's release. (In December, the US issued an expedient admission of guilt, complete with disclaimers, to obtain the release.) According to Rusk, it was 'one of those situations where a small belligerent country can act with a lack of responsibility simply because other countries don't want war'.[154]

It was, of course, 'a big country – little country problem' – the Soviet invasion of Czechoslovakia – which destroyed LBJ's hopes for capping his Presidency with some important token of foreign policy success. 1968 did see some progress in the agenda of détente. The direct New York – Moscow air service was instituted in June and the Nuclear Non-proliferation Treaty signed in July. Referring also to the fishing, space, new cultural exchange and consular convention agreements, Walt Rostow told LBJ on the very day of the Czech invasion that 'the year since Glassboro has been, certainly the most intense and successful post-war year in US–Soviet' relations.[155]

Johnson's campaign for a symbolically impressive summit, centred on questions of arms control, but encompassing other key areas of policy, began in earnest soon after the 31 March speech. Dobrynin was actually the first non-American to hear the news of LBJ's decision to stand down.[156] Johnson contacted Kosygin in early May with a view to commencing strategic arms limitation talks. Kosygin responded that direct talks might begin in Geneva in August. At a 29 July meeting in Washington, Johnson asserted his desire to facilitate talks – lead from the top – in the face of some advisorial caution. Focusing on the Czech situation, Defence Secretary Clark Clifford warned: 'there is so much cooking now'. LBJ, however, was keen to take the initiative, not always 'sitting with our hands in our pockets, just merrily, merrily going along'. He clearly felt that seizing the summit initiative would help dispel the impression that the events of 1968 were destroying the cohesion of America's political class: 'What I'm really concerned about is that they're more in command of our forces than I am'. The Soviets were 'beginning to think we're jelly'.[157]

By mid-August, arms control talks – according to Rusk, possibly the 'most important talks between our countries since World War II' – seemed imminent, while Dobrynin offered the prospect of a major summit in October, probably in Leningrad.[158] Against this background, the Czech invasion was, as Rusk put it to the Soviet Ambassador in September, 'like throwing a dead fish in the face of the President of the United States'.[159] Yet still Johnson persisted. His 'lame duck' status actually caused him to lose some of his familiar caution about domestic criticism. Walt Rostow informed LBJ on 4 October that the Soviets 'are suggesting a meeting which would be guaranteed before the event to be modestly fruitful with regard to strategic weapons talks' (though not, by implication, regarding Vietnam nor establishing a timetable for withdrawal from Czechoslovakia).[160]

As the months went by, the figure of Richard Nixon began to impinge increasingly on the subject of talks with the USSR. In August, Rusk 'declined to answer' Dobrynin's 'question as to whether or not there was a "new Nixon"'.[161] Given Nixon's strongly anti-communist past, Moscow certainly was casting its vote again for a Democrat. Dobrynin relates how he was actually instructed to offer financial aid to Democratic candidate Hubert Humphrey, who told the Ambassador that 'it was more than enough for him to have Moscow's good wishes'.[162] In November, following his election victory, Nixon refused a White House request to accompany Johnson to a summit. Though LBJ pursued the idea of a final summit right up to his last days in office, Nixon's November refusal really marked the end of any realistic hope. Johnson was exasperated: 'They are ready for talks. We are ready. There is support for this at Defense. When Nixon comes in, it could be a year before you get back to the point where we are now'.[163] For Walt Rostow in December, the missing of this opportunity was likely to be a matter 'we shall regret more than any other in the years ahead'. The human race 'may move down the wrong fork in the road for what will, with hindsight, look like relatively trivial reasons'. LBJ wrote the words, 'I agree', in the margin of Rostow's memo.[164]

Inevitably, the final months of Johnson's Presidential tenure had the appearance of a clock winding down. Nixon, with his own agenda, was hardly likely to commit himself to the fag-end of Johnson's. However, there were still crises to be managed. From February onwards, Washington was concerned that the *Pueblo* crisis might develop into a second Korean War. In late February, Cyrus Vance advised that Moscow be consulted on the possibility that North Korea might 'sponsor a major raid' on South Korea.[165] Soon after the Czech invasion, a Soviet aircraft crashed in the Norwegian sea while buzzing the USS *Essex*. In September, LBJ himself reminded the National Security Council that the assault in Czechoslovakia had been accompanied by a Soviet missile alert. He mentioned this 'for the benefit of those who are optimistic about the Russian willingness to improve relations and reach agreements'.[166]

Most analysts in 1968 were not optimistic. Llewellyn Thompson reported in January that he was just running a 'holding operation' in Moscow, although the regime would not for ever be able to resist 'pressure for liberalization'.[167] Dean Rusk, in a long assessment of the still volatile Chinese situation, outlined the possibility of a 'lessening of overt Sino-Soviet tensions'. He favoured a continuation of the new flexibility towards China.[168] In November, the US Embassy in Moscow conveyed Kosygin's view (in conversation with Robert McNamara) that philosophic and pragmatic US–Soviet differences 'will continue to exist: they are irreconcilable'.[169] The hopes of 1963–64 had not been vindicated. However, some senior advisers felt that time was on America's side – that human history might not take 'the wrong fork in the road'. Echoing Thompson's point about liberalisation, Dean Rusk argued in April that communist societies were now clearly 'facing the problem of the individual. This produces a pull of attraction to the West'.[170]

Notes

1 *FRUS, 1961–1963*: Volume V: *The Soviet Union* (Washington DC, US Government Printing Office, 1998), pp. 834–5 (26 Nov. 1963).
2 Ibid., pp. 845–8 (18 Dec. 1963).

3 Ibid., p. 832 (24 Nov. 1963).

4 *FRUS, 1961–1963*: Volume VI: *Kennedy – Khrushchev Exchanges* (Washington DC, US Government Printing Office, 1996), pp. 311–13. Khrushchev apparently became convinced that JFK had been killed as part of a rightist conspiracy to accelerate the Cold War. See C. Andrew and V. Mitrokhin, *The Mitrokhin Archive: The KGB in Europe and the West* (London, Allen Lane, 1999), p. 294.

5 M. R. Beschloss (ed.), *Taking Charge: The Johnson White House Tapes, 1963–1964* (New York, Simon and Schuster, 1997), p. 14.

6 D. Kearns, *Lyndon Johnson and the American Dream* (New York, Harper and Row, 1976), p. 170.

7 Beschloss (ed.), *Taking Charge*, p. 31.

8 R. Dallek, *Flawed Giant: Lyndon Johnson and His Times* (New York, Oxford University Press, 1998), pp. 48–53.

9 Beschloss (ed.), *Taking Charge*, p. 46 (25 Nov. 1963).

10 Ibid., p. 64 (29 Nov. 1963).

11 L. B. Johnson, *The Vantage Point* (London, Weidenfeld and Nicolson, 1971), p. 27.

12 Beschloss (ed.), *Taking Charge*, p. 561 (28 Sept. 1963).

13 *The Vantage Point*, p. 25.

14 See *FRUS, 1961–1963*: Volume V: *The Soviet Union*, p. 847 (McGeorge Bundy, 18 Dec. 1963).

15 Beschloss (ed.), *Taking Charge*, p. 112.

16 Ibid., p. 114.

17 Ibid., p. 135.

18 *FRUS, 1961–1963*: Volume V: *The Soviet Union*, pp. 840–2.

19 Ibid., p. 841 (10 Dec. 1963).

20 *FRUS, 1964–1968*: Volume XIV: *The Soviet Union* (Washington DC, US Government Printing Office, 2001), p. 1.

21 *The Vantage Point*, p. 465; *Department of State Bulletin*, 3 Feb. 1964, pp. 158–63.

22 Beschloss (ed.), *Taking Charge*, p. 145 (2 Jan. 1964).

23 NSF: NSC Meetings File, box 1, 'Summary record of NSC meeting, Dec. 5, 1963'.

24 Beschloss (ed.), *Taking Charge*, p. 144 (2 Jan. 1964).

25 NSF: CF: Europe and USSR: USSR, box 230, folder, 'Wheat sales', 'Popular discontent...' (8 Dec. 1963).

26 NSF: NSC Meetings File, box 1, 'Summary record of NSC meeting 526, April 3, 1964' (Zanzibar); ibid., 'Summary record of NSC meeting 527, April 16, 1964' (trade). On Zanzibar, see T. Lyons, 'Keeping Africa off the agenda', in W. I. Cohen and N. B. Tucker (eds.), *Lyndon Johnson Confronts the World* (Cambridge, Cambridge University Press, 1994), pp. 245–78, at p. 252. On 'step-by-step', see *FRUS, 1964–1968*: Volume XIV: *The Soviet Union*, pp. 86–7 (Khrushchev to LBJ, 5 June 1964), and p. 175 (telegram from Kohler, 11 Nov. 1964).

27 G. T. Seaborg, with B. S. Loeb, *Stemming the Tide: Arms Control in the Johnson Years* (Lexington, Heath, 1987), p. 51; Johnson, *The Vantage Point*, pp. 466–7, 602–3.

28 NSF: CF: Europe and USSR: Yugoslavia, box 232, folder, 'memos 1'.

29 *FRUS, 1964–1968*: Volume XIV: *The Soviet Union*, p. 41 (Kohler); p. 104 (Dobrynin, 4 Sept. 1964).

30 Ibid., p. 86 (5 June 1964).

31 Ibid., p. 104.

32 A. Dobrynin, *In Confidence* (New York, Times Books, 1995), p. 122.

33 Ibid., p. 128.

34 *FRUS, 1964–1968*: Volume XIV: *The Soviet Union*, pp. 43–4 (19 March 1964).

35 Ibid., pp. 59–64 (17 April 1964).

36 Ibid., p. 45 (25 March 1964).
37 Beschloss (ed.), *Taking Charge*, p. 310 (8 April 1964).
38 *FRUS, 1964–1968*: Volume XIV: *The Soviet Union*, p. 119 (15 Oct. 1964).
39 Ibid., p. 145.
40 Ibid., p. 147.
41 Ibid., p. 149 (22 Oct. 1964).
42 Ibid., p. 124 (16 Oct. 1964).
43 Ibid., pp. 119–20.
44 Ibid., p. 163 (31 Oct. 1964).
45 Ibid., p. 161.
46 Dobrynin, *In Confidence*, p. 173.
47 *FRUS, 1964–1968*: Volume XIV: *The Soviet Union*, p. 147 (20. Oct. 1964).
48 Ibid., p. 151.
49 Ibid., p. 161 (28 Oct. 1964).
50 Ibid., p. 131 (16 Oct. 1964).
51 Ibid., p. 163.
52 G. H. Chang, *Friends and Enemies: The United States, China and the Soviet Union, 1948–1972* (Stanford, Stanford University Press, 1990), p. 245.
53 Document reproduced in S. Maddock, 'LBJ, China, and the bomb: new archival evidence', Society for Historians of American Foreign Relations (SHAFR) *Newsletter*, 27: 1 (1996) 1–5, 3. See also R. L. Garthoff, 'A comment on the discussion of "LBJ, China, and the bomb"', SHAFR *Newsletter*, 28: 3 (1997) 27–31. (Garthoff, who worked for the Gilpatric Committee says that in its meetings, 'very little attention was given to the possibility of military action against China' (ibid., p. 29).)
54 *FRUS, 1964–1968*: Volume XIV: *The Soviet Union*, pp. 165–6; Dobrynin, *In Confidence*, p. 133.
55 *FRUS, 1964–1968*: Volume XIV: The Soviet Union, pp. 196–7.
56 Ibid., p. 77 (30 May 1964).
57 Ibid., p. 190 (4 Dec. 1964) (W. Tyler).
58 See Andrew and Mitrokhin, *The Mitrokhin Archive*, pp. 478–9.
59 *FRUS, 1964–1968*: Volume XIV: *The Soviet Union*, p. 17.
60 Ibid., p. 69 (17 April 1964).
61 Ibid., p. 49 (2 April 1964).
62 Ibid., p. 117 (10 Oct. 1964).
63 Ibid., p. 362 (23 Dec. 1965).
64 Ibid., p. 216 (27 Jan. 1965).
65 Ibid., p. 207 (7 Jan. 1965).
66 Ibid., p. 216.
67 Ibid., p. 361 (13 Dec. 1965).
68 NSF: CF: Europe and USSR: USSR, box 221, folder, 'memos (1) X', 'Purported changes in the Soviet leadership', 3 Sept. 1965. According to V. M. Zubok, a major split occurred in the Politburo in early 1965 over policy towards China. Kosygin, Suslov and Shelepin believed it was possible to achieve improved relations with Beijing. They managed to defeat an opposing faction, led by Gromyko and Yuri Andropov, who favoured accelerated détente with the US. 'The mood in the Politburo held that there was no need to hurry with détente: the deployment of Soviet ICBMs made the Soviet "position" of "strength" more credible every year . . .'. (V. M. Zubok, 'Unwrapping the enigma: what was behind the Soviet challenge in the 1960s?', in D. B. Kunz (ed.), *The Diplomacy of the Crucial Decade* (New York, Columbia University Press, 1994), pp. 146–82, at p. 163).
69 See R. L. Garthoff, 'The aborted US–USSR summit of 1965', SHAFR *Newsletter*, 32: 2 (2001) 1–3.

70 *National Diplomacy 1965–1970* (Washington DC, Congressional Quarterly, 1970), p. 64; Johnson, *The Vantage Point*, p. 472.

71 NSF: CF: Europe and USSR: USSR, box 221, folder, 'memos X', H. H. Saunders to Bundy, 18 Sept. 1965.

72 *FRUS, 1964–1968*: Volume XIV: *The Soviet Union*, p. 298 (25 June 1965).

73 Ibid., p. 318 (20 Aug. 1965).

74 See ibid., pp. 344–5 (18 Nov. 1965).

75 Ibid., p. 340 (15 Nov. 1965).

76 Ibid., p. 358 (24 Nov. 1965).

77 *FRUS, 1964–1968*: Volume XIV: *The Soviet Union*, p. 290 (28 May 1965).

78 NSF: CF: Europe and USSR: USSR, box 221, folder, 'memos X', 'Soviets accommodate Indians', 6 Oct. 1965.

79 R. J. McMahon, 'Disillusionment and disengagement in South Asia', in Cohen and Tucker (eds.), *Lyndon Johnson Confronts the World*, pp. 135–71, at p. 164. See also R. J. McMahon, 'Ambivalent partners: the Lyndon Johnson Administration and its Asian allies', in H. W. Brands (ed.), *The Foreign Policies of Lyndon Johnson: Beyond Vietnam* (College Station, Texas A and M University Press, 1999), pp. 168–86, at p. 172; H. W. Brands, *The Wages of Globalism* (New York, Oxford University Press, 1995), ch. 5. LBJ complained in December 1965 that 'when he needed Ayub he [Ayub Khan] was in Peking or Moscow' (*FRUS, 1964–1968*: Volume XXV: *South Asia* (Washington DC, US Government Printing Office, 2000), p. 504 (14 Dec. 1965)).

80 The CIA concluded in November 1965 that, although the Indonesian military was 'almost totally Soviet-supplied', it was 'likely that the Soviets themselves do not particularly wish to become entangled in the thickets of Indonesian politics' (*FRUS, 1964–1968*: Volume XXVI: *Indonesia, Malaysia and Singapore; Philippines* (Washington DC, US Government Printing Office, 2001), pp. 376–7 (22 Nov. 1965)).

81 Dean Rusk OH, p. 36. See also D. Kux, *The United States and Pakistan, 1947–2000: Disenchanted Allies* (Washington DC, Woodrow Wilson Center Press, 2001), pp. 153–77.

82 *FRUS, 1964–1968*: Volume XIV: *The Soviet Union*, p. 285 (9 April 1965).

83 Ibid., p. 271 (5 April 1965).

84 Ibid., p. 351.

85 Ibid., p. 439 (25 Nov. 1966).

86 Ibid., p. 424.

87 Ibid., p. 427.

88 Chang, *Friends and Enemies*, p. 275.

89 *PPPUS: Lyndon B. Johnson: 1966, vol. 2* (Washington DC, US Government Printing Office, 1967), p. 710 (5 July 1966).

90 Ibid., p. 724.

91 *National Diplomacy, 1965–1970*, p. 68.

92 *FRUS, 1964–1968*: Volume XVII: *Eastern Europe* (Washington DC, US Government Printing Office, 1996), p. 54.

93 *PPPUS: LBJ: 1966, vol. 2*, p. 1128 (7 Oct. 1966).

94 *FRUS, 1964–1968*: Volume XIV: *The Soviet Union*, p. 389 (26 April 1966).

95 Ibid., p. 421.

96 364 (10 Jan. 1966).

97 Ibid., p. 381 (14 March 1966).

98 *FRUS, 1964–1968*: Volume XII: *Western Europe* (Washington DC, US Government Printing Office, 2001), p. 122 (11 June 1966).

99 *FRUS, 1964–1968*: Volume XIV: *The Soviet Union*, p. 439 (25 Nov. 1966).

100 Ibid., pp. 384, 387.

101 Ibid., pp. 404–5 (15 July 1966).

102 NSF: CF: Europe and USSR: USSR, box 221, folder, 'memos X1', CIA Special Report, 25 Feb. 1966.
103 *FRUS, 1964–1968*: Volume XIV: *The Soviet Union*, p. 391.
104 Ibid., p. 409 (28 July 1966).
105 Ibid., p. 400 (Kohler, 12 July 1966); 'lucky harvest', ibid., p. 438.
106 Ibid., pp. 439–41.
107 Ibid., p. 384.
108 Ibid., p. 421.
109 *Friends and Enemies*, p. 275.
110 *FRUS, 1964–1968*: Volume XIV: *The Soviet Union*, p. 429 (14 Oct. 1966).
111 Ibid., p. 440.
112 *FRUS, 1964–1968*: Volume XXX: *China* (Washington DC, US Government Printing Office, 1998), pp. 394–5 (20 Sept. 1966).
113 Ibid., p. 485 (1 Dec. 1966).
114 Chang, *Friends and Enemies*, p. 274.
115 *In Confidence*, p. 145.
116 *FRUS, 1964–1968*: Volume XIV: *The Soviet Union*, p. 499.
117 Dallek, *Flawed Giant*, p. 432.
118 *FRUS, 1964–1968*: Volume XIV: *The Soviet Union*, p. 499 (21 June 1967).
119 Ibid., p. 507 (McGeorge Bundy, 22 June 1967).
120 NSF: CF: Europe and USSR: USSR, box 230, folder, 'Hollybush', CIA report, 15 June 1967.
121 *FRUS, 1964–1968*: Volume XIV: *The Soviet Union*, p. 495 (16 June 1967).
122 Davis to Rostow, 20 June 1967, NSF: CF: Europe and USSR: USSR, box 230, folder, 'Hollybush'. According to Dobrynin (*In Confidence*, p. 167), Kosygin lacked 'a mandate from the Politburo' and was not supported by Brezhnev.
123 Ibid., J. W. Symington to LBJ, 27 June 1967, folder, 'Hollybush 3'.
124 *FRUS, 1964–1968*: Volume XIV: *The Soviet Union*, p. 525.
125 Ibid., pp. 515, 519, 520.
126 Ibid., p. 535.
127 Ibid., pp. 539, 555.
128 Ibid., pp. 558, 560, 562.
129 Davis, 'The Sea of Japan incidents', 12 April 1967, NSF: CF: Europe and USSR: USSR, box 223, folder, 'Memos'.
130 19 July, 1967, Central Foreign Policy Files, POL 23-10: US-USSR (2668) (National Archives).
131 See ibid., letter from J. Curran, National Maritime Union of America, 1 Dec. 1967.
132 *FRUS, 1964–1968*: Volume XIV: *The Soviet Union*, p. 467 (18 March 1967).
133 Ibid., p. 476 (23 March 1967, Dobrynin); p. 438 (31 May 1967, Tcherniakov).
134 Rusk-Dobrynin, 26 July 1967, Central Foreign Policy Files, POL US-USSR 1/1/67 to 1/1/69.
135 See Garthoff, 'A comment on the discussion of "LBJ, China and the bomb"', p. 30.
136 *FRUS, 1964–1968*: Volume XXX: *China*, p. 512 (27 Jan. 1967).
137 *FRUS, 1964–1968*: Volume XIV: *The Soviet Union*, p. 486 (draft letter to Kosygin, 19 May 1967).
138 Ibid., pp. 582, 585, 587, 590.
139 NSF: CF: Europe and USSR: USSR, box 224, folder, 'Memos XVI', CIA Special Report, Sept. 1967.
140 *FRUS, 1964–1968*: Volume XIV: *The Soviet Union*, pp. 608–9 (18 Dec. 1967).
141 'The Soviet Union and the United States', 12 Dec. 1967, Central Foreign Policy Files, POL US-USSR 5/1/67 to POL 17.
142 *The Vantage Point*, p. 532.
143 Quotations from M. Lerner, 'A failure of perception: Lyndon Johnson, North Korean ideology, and the *Pueblo* incident', *Diplomatic History*, 25:4 (2001) 647–75, at pp. 647, 648.

144 'Memorandum', Davis-Bubnov lunch, 26 Jan. 1968, Central Foreign Policy Files, POL US-USSR 5/1/67 to POL 17.

145 'A failure of perception', p. 648.

146 *FRUS, 1964–1968*: Volume XXIX, Part 1: *Korea* (Washington DC, US Government Printing Office, 2000), p. 499 (25 Jan. 1968).

147 Ibid., p. 552.

148 NSF: Files of W. W. Rostow, box 10, folder, 'The President's file for Korea and Vietnam', Rostow 'Report on meeting of advisory group', 29 Jan. 1968.

149 *FRUS, 1964–1968*: Volume XXIX, Part 1: *Korea*, p. 611.

150 Ibid., p. 612 (7 Feb. 1968).

151 Ibid., p. 619 (8 Feb. 1968).

152 Ibid., p. 639.

153 Ibid., p. 695 (13 Aug. 1968).

154 Rusk OH, p. 29.

155 *FRUS, 1964–1968*: Volume XIV: *The Soviet Union*, p. 685 (20 Aug. 1968).

156 See *In Confidence*, p. 172.

157 *FRUS, 1964–1968*: Volume XIV: *The Soviet Union*, pp. 666, 668, 673.

158 Ibid., p. 676 (15 Aug. 1968).

159 Ibid., p. 719 (20 Sept. 1968).

160 Ibid., p. 735.

161 Ibid., p. 678 (15 Aug. 1968).

162 Dobrynin, *In Confidence*, p. 176.

163 *FRUS, 1964–1968*: Volume XIV: *The Soviet Union*, p. 767 (26 Nov. 1968).

164 Ibid., pp. 780–81 (11 Dec. 1968).

165 NSF: Files of W. W. Rostow, box 10, folder, 'Vance report – Korea', Vance, 20 Feb. 1968.

166 NSF: NSC Meetings File, box 2, 'Summary notes of 590th NSC meeting, Sept. 4, 1968'.

167 *FRUS, 1964–1968*: Volume XIV: *The Soviet Union*, pp. 624–5 (11 Jan. 1968).

168 *FRUS, 1964–1968*: Volume XXX: *China*, p. 648 (22 Feb. 1968).

169 *FRUS, 1964–1968*: Volume XIV: *The Soviet Union*, p. 747 (11 Nov. 1968).

170 NSF: NSC Meetings File, box 2, 'Memo for the record: 26 April 1968'.

3

Nuclear weapons

Johnson, McNamara and US nuclear strategy in the 1960s

Lyndon Johnson's attitude towards nuclear weapons combined a sensible horror of their destructive power with a faith, characteristic of his generation, in the superiority of American technology. The years following the Cuban missile crisis were, understandably, ones of intense public jitters about the nuclear bomb. LBJ's early efforts to establish with Moscow a momentum of nuclear de-escalation were, at least at one level, a response to this public mood. Johnson frequently sought to reassure the public that America's bomb was in safe hands. 'The control of nuclear weapons' declared LBJ in July 1964, 'is one of the most solemn responsibilities of the President of the United States – the man who is President can never forget it'.[1] These remarks were made in response to a suggestion from Republican Presidential contender Barry Goldwater that the military head of NATO might be given more leeway in ordering the use of nuclear weapons. LBJ's 'daisy girl' campaign TV broadcast of 7 September 1964 implicitly asserted that Goldwater might actually use the bomb. (LBJ himself, of course, is memorialised in American government textbooks as the President who said that the only power he had was nuclear, and he could not use that.) LBJ also regularly reminded Americans that the nuclear arsenal was 'under careful control'; 'complex codes and electronic devices' ensured that nuclear decisions could not be made without appropriate Presidential direction.[2]

Johnson's central and supreme concern during his Presidency was to avoid a nuclear war. He opened and concluded his first National Security Council meeting on nuclear issues with this statement:

> The greatest single requirement is that we find a way to ensure the survival of civilization in the nuclear age. A nuclear war would be the death of all our hopes and it is our task to see that it does not happen.[3]

Secretary Rusk later emphasised that LBJ and all his senior advisers had an overwhelming commitment to avoiding nuclear war. That was the legacy of the Cuban missile crisis.[4]

Johnson did not pretend to be an expert on nuclear strategy. He certainly retained from his days as head of the Senate Armed Service Preparedness Subcommittee a strong emotional commitment to US nuclear superiority. McGeorge Bundy later recalled a Presidential boast about American rocketry: 'We have more than anyone – twice as many'.[5] In fact, the 1960s saw huge increases in the Soviet nuclear stockpile. By 1968, LBJ was forced to confront the prospect of 'parity' with Russia. Strictly speaking, 'parity' was a strategic concept, involving recognition of the nuclear balance of terror rather than of any quantitative 'equality'. However, for LBJ, 'parity' shaded into 'equality'. He never accepted it as a policy goal, remaining emotionally committed to both superiority and to arms control.

In November 1964, Johnson and Defence Secretary McNamara decided to cap the surge in American nuclear weapons acquisition inherited from the Kennedy era. LBJ is often accused of wanting both guns and butter. He did appreciate, however, that some kind of trade-off between military and domestic spending was unavoidable. He also recognised the counterproductive dynamics of unrestrained superpower arms competition. The President told Walter Heller, Chairman of the Council of Economic Advisers, in December 1963: 'We're not going to make more atomic bombs than we need because that makes Russia make more'.[6] His ideal was an arms control package which would freeze into it a comforting, if strategically irrelevant, American numerical superiority, as well as allowing scope for US technological innovation.

Early in the Kennedy Presidency, it became evident that the 'missile gap' – the idea, fostered not least by LBJ's Preparedness Subcommittee, that the USSR had been allowed to draw ahead in the nuclear race – was a myth. JFK and McNamara stepped up the acquisitions programme regardless. The LBJ-McNamara decisions of November 1964 involved capping the land-based Intercontinental Ballistic Missile (ICBM, Minuteman) force at 1,000 and the Polaris/Poseidon missile submarine missile programme at 41. (President Eisenhower had requested 19 nuclear submarines, under the Polaris programme, and 400 ICBMs by fiscal year 1964). The US stockpile of ICBMs increased from 294 in 1962 to 1,054 in 1968. The November 1964 decision essentially represented a commitment to greater weapons efficiency and accuracy, as well as a judgment about the institutionalisation of American superiority. It also reflected the rise of the new technology of the MIRV – multiple, independently targeted re-entry vehicles (involving several warheads, aimed at a multiplicity of Soviet targets, on one ICBM or submarine-launched missile). The Pentagon in 1964 committed itself to developing both ICBM multiple warheads (Minuteman III) and submarine-launched MIRVs (Poseidon).

As Paul Nitze later noted, US and Soviet strategic policy diverged radically in the mid-1960s.[7] The US appeared rather blithely to accept its superiority. These questions of 'parity' *versus* 'superiority' had, by the late 1960s, actually become almost impossible to quantify. Nathaniel Davis informed his boss,

Walt Rostow, on 14 April 1967 that there were – according to Raymond Garthoff in the State Department – 'some two dozen ways to slice the data about the nuclear weapons balance – to prove we are ahead, to prove the Soviets are ahead, to prove they are catching up, or to prove we are widening our margin'. Figures for overall defence spending, for long-range bombers, for land-based ICBMs, for defensive missiles, for submarine-launched ballistic missiles, for numbers or payload – explosiveness – of warheads all told different stories. What was clear, however, was that, at least in terms of land-based ICBM installations, by 1968 – as Davis put it – 'we will be approaching numerical parity'.[8] The rise in Soviet destructive power should not be overstated. By 1967, the US was capable of delivering 1,054 warheads from its ICBM force against the USSR, and 656 from the Polaris submarines. In addition, the US had 500 long-range (B-52) bombers, capable of delivering nuclear bombs. This force was capable of roughly twice the destructive power predicted for it in 1963. By 1967, the Soviets had increased their land-based ICBM holdings from 200 in 1964 to over 700. Their submarine nuclear force had risen slightly. The new Soviet ICBM SS-9 could carry a massive 25-megaton warhead, a payload large enough – targeting problems notwithstanding – to obliterate the US ICBM silos in one strike. International Institute for Strategic Studies figures suggest that the Soviets achieved a numerical land-based ICBM superiority of nearly 500 by 1972, while the US retained a clear lead in submarine-launched ballistic missiles and in long-range bombers. The level of Soviet ICBM acquisitions was certainly not predicted accurately in the CIA estimates for the period 1964–67.[9]

In point of fact, numerical weapons calculations were being rendered slightly irrelevant – not only by the problem of how to 'slice the data', but also by Robert McNamara's developing doctrine of Mutual Assured Destruction (MAD). (McNamara himself referred to it as 'assured destruction capability'.) McNamara came to the view that this was the key to nuclear strategy only in 1967. Before then, he had concentrated, first on 'no cities' strategy – trying to structure nuclear conflict in terms of 'counterforce' strikes on military targets – and, subsequently, on various 'damage limitation' strategies. 'No cities' and 'damage limitation' were alternatives to the 'massive retaliation' strategy – conceptualising nuclear war as a huge, single assault on centres of Soviet population and industry – of the Eisenhower years. 'Assured destruction' went further, actually welcoming the Soviet ICBM build-up in terms of its putative achievement of a rational balance between the superpowers. The key to MAD was the recognition that 'enough' in nuclear deterrence terms meant the ability to inflict devastating damage on the opponent, following a surprise initial attack by that opponent. McNamara declared in 1967: 'The fact is that both the Soviet Union and the United States presently possess an actual and credible second-strike capability against one another – and it is precisely this mutual capability that provides us both with the strongest possible

motive to avoid a nuclear war'.[10] In 1968, following his departure from the
Pentagon, McNamara identified the essence of successful nuclear deterrence
as the ability 'to absorb the total weight of nuclear attack on our country –
on our retaliatory forces, on our command and control apparatus, on our
industrial capacity, on our cities, and on our population'. The US must 'still
be capable of damaging the aggressor to the point that his society would be
simply no longer viable in twentieth-century terms'.[11] 'Assured destruction'
was a working and evolving, rather than an 'official' doctrine in the Johnson
Administration. Its logic pointed away from the numerical superiority to
which LBJ remained generally, although by 1968 perhaps not irretrievably,
committed. MAD, of course, also became one of the defining concepts of the
entire Cold War. Explicators of the doctrine would use the metaphor of two
scorpions circling one another in a bottle – each one terrified to attack for fear
of sustaining annihilation in an immediate counterblow. The logic of MAD,
and of nuclear deterrence itself, was potentially undermined by the possibility of irrational behaviour by nuclear decision-makers, as well as by the
launching of a first strike by accident. (MADness assumed rationality on the
part of decision-makers.) Also threatening to nuclear deterrence balances was
the prospect of qualitative technological change. Was it possible to knock out
one superpower's ICBM retaliatory force in a single attack? Was it conceiv-
able that technology might even one day enable the enemy to destroy silos,
nuclear submarines and long-range bombers in one, sustained, surprise
assault? Would development of *defensive*, anti-ballistic missile (ABM) technology ever allow one superpower to launch a nuclear attack on its rival with
impunity?

The emergence in Washington of 'assured destruction' theory in the mid-
1960s explains to an important degree why the Soviet ICBM build-up was not
greeted with more alarm. Even allowing for the persuasiveness of McNamara's
arguments – and for the Secretary of Defense's personal prestige – it is still a
little surprising to find so apparently low a level of agitation. 'Assured destruction' represented a mid-point between 'war fighting' and 'finite deterrence'
approaches to nuclear strategy. 'War fighting' positions – the view that the US
needed the capability of defeating the USSR at every level of a future nuclear
conflict – were never abandoned by influential sections of American strategic
opinion. As we have seen, the President's own preference was for a nuclear
superiority which fitted 'war fighting' strategies. In such a view, only across-
the-board superiority would actually deter Moscow.[12] (By contrast, 'finite
deterrence' – the view that, given the horror of nuclear war evidenced in both
superpower capitals, deterrence could be achieved via relatively small levels of
nuclear firepower – commanded little support in top American governmental
circles, though some of McNamara's musings on nuclear doctrines indicated
that the Secretary of Defense had some leanings towards this view.) Many
conservative, 'war fighting' critics of MAD found it difficult to conceive of the

Soviet leaders as rational seekers of a nuclear balance, rather than as crazed despots who might actually use ICBMs. From the Administration's viewpoint, it was also certainly a consideration that perceived US insouciance in the face of Moscow's build-up would give dangerous ammunition to Republican opponents. To LBJ, the apostle of preparedness and the inveterate promoter of domestic consensus, the build-up was a source of deep unease. Before resuming the discussion of general nuclear strategy, the intention is now to delve more deeply into developing American reactions to, and understanding of, the Soviet ICBM spurt.

Nuclear strategy: US reactions to the Soviet build-up

Before 1967, LBJ was generally reassured about American nuclear superiority and about Soviet intentions. At his initial nuclear briefing, Johnson was informed by McNamara that during 'the decade of the 60s, our advantage over the USSR in the nuclear area will not fall below two times'. A nuclear war would produce 'no winner, even though after such an exchange, the US would retain a superior capability'. CIA Director John McCone told the NSC that the main Soviet ICBM system was the SS-7, with a reliability of 65 per cent: 'With our hardened intercontinental missile force coming rapidly into being, the US numerical superiority in strategic weapons must be evident to Khrushchev'. Secretary Rusk 'emphasized that despite the problems which the Soviet Union is having in the economic field, and despite our nuclear superiority, the Russians are making a tremendous effort'.[13] In February 1964, the CIA advised that the USSR had 'little choice but to find ways to contain the arms race and reduce its burden on the Soviet economy.[14] In April, McCone warned LBJ that 'the Soviet ICBM program is not a static program'.[15] Movement on Soviet ICBMs was explained largely at this time in terms of 'Khrushchev's . . . strong desire to gain world recognition of the USSR's status as the great-power equal of the US'.[16] By the later part of 1964, American officials were complaining that Moscow's pro-disarmament gesturing at the ENDC (the Eighteen Nations Disarmament Committee, meeting in Geneva) stood in stark contrast to the actual Soviet nuclear acquisitions programme.

Further worries began to surface in 1965 and 1966, with the Joint Chiefs of Staff calling into question the decision to cap US nuclear expansion. A State Department Policy Planning study of February 1965 argued that, if past experience was anything to go by, the West should not relax its guard: 'Historically, the function of détente for the Soviets has been to provide a period of pause in offensive action whenever the relation of forces turned unfavourable'.[17] In May 1966, the Arms Control and Disarmament Agency (ACDA) used the indications of Soviet ICBM programme movements to strengthen its case for arms negotiations: 'the United States believes its forces to have achieved the reasonably high survivability required for deterrence,

while the Soviets appear to be just beginning to improve the survivability of
their strategic land-based ballistic missile forces'. Without an arms limitation
agreement, 'the damage the United States might expect to sustain in a nuclear
war will likely increase during the next few years as Soviet forces are increased
and improved'.[18] In November 1966, the CIA noted that, 'with the large-scale
deployment of dispersed and hardened' ICBMs, the Soviets could now have
confidence in their assured destruction capability.[19]

The tone of Washington's reaction to the ICBM build-up changed during
1967. Nathaniel Davis drew Rostow's attention in April to a Republican
National Committee study which described Russia as 'drastically narrowing
the ICBM gap'. The study also argued that the 'Russians are years ahead of
us in ABMs'. Some Congressional Republicans were beginning to scent
another 'missile gap'. Davis commented: 'So far as timing is concerned, we are
in a situation where the Russians are proceeding with both an ICBM build-
up and an ABM deployment, while (in these oversimplified terms) we are doing
neither – pending the outcome of our talks with the Russians'.[20] Walt Rostow
concluded in August that the nuclear balance figures were 'not alarming; but
I suspect it will be exploited as a political issue in 1968'. The US was increasing its warhead capacity with the MIRV programme and a Soviet first strike
remained extremely unlikely. However: 'numbers will be moving unfavourably
over the coming year'.[21] In September, the CIA recognised that the USSR was
achieving 'a rough strategic parity' with the US, but argued that ICBM build-
ups were irrelevant to the major Soviet foreign policy objective of power projection in the Third World.[22] CIA Director Richard Helms reported in
November that 'the Soviets, with an economy less than half the size of ours,
are spending roughly as much for defense and space as we are, excluding the
costs of Vietnam'.[23] A State Department study in December acknowledged the
Soviet strategic advance: 'In a second strike, we estimate they could inflict two
to four times more damage on the US today than they could in early 1965
(80–100 million fatalities as compared to 25–35 million)'. The USSR would
probably surpass the US in 'total intercontinental megatonnage' by 1968 or
1969. Parity or Soviet superiority in numbers of Polaris-type submarines might
even be achieved by the mid-1970s. The study, however, concurred in the view
advanced by McNamara – now departed from the Pentagon – that 'our deterrent will remain more than adequate even against quite unlikely increases in
the threat'.[24] In January 1968, the CIA concluded that Moscow was now
clearly committed to seeking 'major improvements in the Soviet strategic
posture, even at the risk of jeopardizing economic growth'.[25] The CIA judged,
however, that prospects for an arms limitation deal were high due to Soviet
fears of American (especially MIRV) technology: 'while the USSR is currently
in the final stages of its third-generation ICBM deployment and has an effective deterrent, this capability will begin to erode in the early 1970s if Moscow
does not match announced US plans for upgrading its strategic defense and

attack capabilities with the Sentinel [ABM], Poseidon and Minuteman III programs'. The USSR was making an effort in MIRV research, but was still lagging behind the US.[26]

McNamara's main aim was to convince Moscow that 'we possess strategic nuclear forces so powerful as to be capable of absorbing a Soviet first strike and surviving with sufficient strength to impose unacceptable damage on them'.[27] In December 1966, McNamara concurred with the Joint Chiefs of Staff (JCS) recommendation to replace Polaris with Poseidon submarines. MIRV technology, applied to the submarine fleet and to the land-based missiles, would sustain US superiority, or at least so it was hoped. By 1976, it was projected that, compared to 1966, the US second strike capability would have increased fourfold.[28] General Earle Wheeler, JCS chairman appointed in July 1964, argued in December 1966 that the US must 'maintain the kind of favourable power environment which helped us during the Cuban missile crisis'. Air Force Chief of Staff J. P. McConnell argued that the US was faced with nuclear threats from China and Russia: 'We are dealing with the descendants of Genghis Khan. They only understand force'.[29]

Despite such bellicose advice, the Kennedy era dash for absolute and incontrovertible ICBM superiority was not resumed. Johnson's own unease about the changing nuclear balance after 1966 was resolved in his increasing commitment to arms control: to the achievement of a deal which would not only be historic and strong enough to withstand Republican charges of appeasement, but also capable of standing as a lasting achievement of his increasingly troubled Presidency. By 1966–67, Dean Rusk was also a firm advocate of arms control, an advocacy which certainly influenced Johnson's own views. Some key advisers at the White House – notably Spurgeon Keeny, who had even opposed the Kennedy era nuclear acquisitions – were also set against a renewal of the arms race. There was no desire, beyond the ranks of military special pleaders, to inflate further a defence budget already swollen by the Vietnam War spending. The Soviet leadership was regarded by LBJ, McNamara and Rusk as rational, and as capable of appreciating the logic of deterrence. This certainly was the message coming to the top decision-makers from civilian Soviet experts. LBJ was repeatedly advised, for example, that, although they were certainly capable of aggression if in a tight spot, the Soviet leadership had essentially a 'defensive mentality'.[30]

One or two further points about American nuclear strategy in the 1960s will help clarify the ensuing discussion of nuclear non-proliferation, the antiballistic missile deployment and strategic arms limitation. NATO strategy in this era was built around the threat of a conventional Warsaw Pact invasion of Western Europe. McNamara's central concept here was 'flexible response', adopted as official NATO doctrine in 1967, but never really fully operationalised.[31] 'Flexible response' involved a new commitment to conventional responses to an attack on Western Europe. It was 'simply not credible that

NATO, or anyone else', declared McNamara in 1962, 'would respond to a small step – the first slice of salami – with immediate use of nuclear weapons'. For Western European allies, 'flexible response' conjured up visions of American abandonment of Europe. There was also, as McNamara acknowledged, a 'school of thought which believes that the United States and the Soviet Union might seek to use Europe as a nuclear battleground and thus avoid attacks on one another's homelands'.[32] For McNamara, 'flexible response' necessitated firm American central control of NATO decisions. The NATO Nuclear Planning Group was set up in 1966 as a way of meeting demands for alliance consultation in the face of this centralisation. America's difficulties of alliance management in Europe, of course, were exacerbated by the departure of France from the NATO integrated command structure in 1967.[33]

'Flexible response' brought with it a host of strategic implications. The notion of 'intra-war deterrence' – the sending of messages to Moscow about the consequences of crossing various combat thresholds – was developed in the early 1960s. 'Flexible response' was also not simply a European doctrine. As bequeathed by JFK to LBJ, it was a global policy. Moscow responded by augmenting the reach of its conventional forces. A late 1967 State Department report noted: 'they have developed forces which, while probably originally intended for the general war mission, now provide them with capabilities for distant, limited operations'.[34] There was also a major problem in gauging the reception in Moscow of the whole argumentation and logic of 'assured destruction' and 'flexible response'. MAD assumed sanity in the opposition and, as noted above, the Johnson Administration generally did view Soviet decision-makers as rational and mindful of the safety of their homeland. However, McNamara had little way of knowing how profoundly the logic of his position had penetrated Soviet minds. (He had little enough certainty of its acceptance in Washington!) Was Moscow receiving America's messages and interpreting them correctly? As promulgated by the Politburo and the Soviet military, Russian nuclear doctrine appeared unsophisticated to Western observers. On the surface at least, Soviet nuclear doctrine appeared to amount to little more than a determination that Russia could win a nuclear conflict – perhaps not excluding the possibility of getting in a retaliation first. Ultimately, American attachment to the doctrines of deterrence and 'assured destruction' was almost as much a matter of faith as of reason.

Recently declassified documents have ignited major debate about a particular aspect of Johnson-McNamara nuclear strategy: the putative 'nuclear taboo' – American leaders' resolve never to contemplate first use of nuclear weapons. A 1964 plan drawn up by the Warsaw Pact, and released from Czech archives, certainly indicated a willingness on the Soviet side to countenance such first use.[35] On the American side, it was generally assumed that first use would only seriously be considered in the event of certain knowledge about an imminent Soviet nuclear strike. In 1964, Deputy Under Secretary of State for Political Affairs, U. Alexis Johnson, referred to 'the understandable reluctance of responsible officials to agree to a general release of nuclear weapons'.[36] By 1964, it was widely assumed that the prospect of a major Soviet conventional assault on Western Europe was lessening. Llewellyn Thompson in July 1964 thought it 'so remote that it is scarcely worth considering'. However, some commentators have seen significance in Thompson's view that, in the unlikely event of a conventional Soviet 'grab for Europe', the US would have to consider the immediate, first use of nuclear weapons.[37] Certainly, Thompson does seem to have been echoing American military opinion that there could not be a blanket prohibition on nuclear first use.

The still frenzied and dangerous nuclear competition of the Johnson era raised major problems of a mutual misreading of intentions between the superpowers. As McNamara and LBJ appreciated, risks of such misreading and misunderstanding could be alleviated by actually talking to Moscow about nuclear issues. As we saw in Chapter 2, LBJ's efforts to establish a trust-building dialogue began in the 'pen pal' correspondence with Khrushchev over cuts in the production of fissionable material. Despite the difficulties posed by the Vietnam War, these efforts continued in the form of superpower co-operation over nuclear non-proliferation.

Nuclear non-proliferation and the US–Soviet 'community of interest'

The Treaty on the Non-proliferation of Nuclear Weapons (NPT), signed in July 1968, was a major achievement for LBJ and for arms control bureaucrats in his Administration, notably for Adrian Fisher, deputy director of the Arms Control and Disarmament Agency. Johnson's own commitment to the NPT was recognised in the internal National Security Council history of the negotiations, drawn up in December 1968: 'President Johnson's firm continuing desire to move ahead with the treaty provided the impetus that led to achieving compromise language without which further progress on the treaty would have been impossible'. The NSC history noted 'reservations about the NPT within the US Government', but acknowledged the important role of public and Congressional support. (The Pastore Resolution, endorsing the NPT, gained unanimous Senate approval in May 1966.)[38]

Signed by the original 'nuclear club' (the US, the USSR and Britain), as well as by over 50 other countries, the NPT prohibited nuclear states from transferring nuclear weapons, and non-nuclear states from receiving them. Several 'threshold' non-nuclear states – notably India, Israel, West Germany and Brazil – refused to sign. The process was also effectively conducted without the People's Republic of China, which condemned the NPT as an example of collusive behaviour between Moscow and Washington. France abstained from the negotiating process, though promised to observe the NPT without actually signing it. In line with the Pastore Resolution, the Senate moved to immediate consideration of the treaty in July 1968, with the Foreign Relations Committee recommending ratification by a 13-3 vote.

The principal objection to the treaty that was voiced during the Senate Foreign Relations committee hearings concerned possible new commitments to non-nuclear states. Senators worried that the NPT carried with it the obligation to defend any non-nuclear state threatened with nuclear attack. (Leading members of the Administration had, in fact, been careful to avoid giving blanket 'assurances' to non-nuclear countries in order to secure their support for the NPT. In June 1967, for example, Dean Rusk informed Soviet Foreign Minister Gromyko about the limits of any assurances to India. He raised 'the contingency of a conflict between India and China in which the USSR might support China'. Rusk 'would not care to have a nuclear war with the USSR just to have the Indians sign a non-proliferation treaty'.)[39] Most Senators dismissed worries about US commitments and 'assurances' to countries like India. Consideration of the NPT was, however, dropped by the Senate in the wake of the Soviet invasion of Czechoslovakia. Ratification occurred in 1969, with the treaty coming into force in 1970. Around a quarter of a century later, Jozef Goldblatt, disarmament campaigner and winner of the Nobel Peace Prize, described the NPT as a measure of 'paramount importance', constituting 'an obstacle to nuclear anarchy'.[40]

As already noted, to several non-nuclear states, the NPT appeared to epitomise a joint superpower imperialism. In February 1967, Dean Rusk told Willy Brandt, Chancellor of the Federal Republic of Germany, that this was the attitude of France, despite France's own nuclear status. Rusk tried, without success, to persuade Brandt that the NPT was in Bonn's interest.[41] During the 1968 UN General Assembly debate on the treaty, Japanese and Pakistani delegates argued that the NPT failed to provide an 'acceptable balance of mutual responsibilities'.[42] The US worked quietly to cajole small states into backing the NPT at the United Nations. Moscow, perhaps less adept at the diplomacy of joint superpower imperialism, preferred – in the words of Arms Control and Disarmament Agency (ACDA) Director William Foster – to ' "railroad" the measure through'.[43]

To some of the American principals, the NPT indeed was a harbinger of a new world order, policed by a Russo-American partnership. In May 1966, for example, Adrian Fisher, then serving as ACDA Acting Director, informed LBJ:

> if we and the USSR were to agree to a non-proliferation treaty, probably all of the non-nuclear powers that are in danger of going nuclear would find it difficult not to adhere to such a treaty. Thus the issue would not be whether a treaty would stand in the way of the supreme national interest of such countries. The issue would rather be whether a US–Soviet sponsored international consensus, finalized in a treaty, would be a factor to be taken into account in determining what the supreme national interest of these countries was. Clearly it would be.[44]

For supporters of the NPT within the Administration, what Walt Rostow called 'an argument on behalf of humanity' – the fewer 'independent fingers on the nuclear triggers' the better – coincided with narrower superpower interests. The problem of 'assurances' to non-nuclear states has already been mentioned. As Rostow explained it in *The Diffusion of Power*, commitments to *nuclear* allies were even more dangerous: 'if any state to which the United States was committed produced nuclear weapons and asserted an independent right to fire them, the United States would confront a grave dilemma' – a dilemma which had become apparent at the time of Anglo-French action over Suez in 1956. To avoid being trapped by allies into nuclear war, the US might have to abandon its commitments in crucial areas of the world. Moreover, if the NPT were to work at all, near-nuclear nations had to be convinced of the reliability of the US commitment. The US had a clear interest in holding the nuclear line against proliferation. For Rostow, the NPT actually did seem to presage a global order based on superpower, self-interested partnership. The treaty afforded a glimpse of 'what the world might be like if Moscow decided that its maximum attainable objective was a reasonably orderly and safe environment for the Soviet Union, achieved by close collaboration with the United States'.[45] During the negotiations, Rostow argued that, if a treaty were to be achieved, it would be on the basis of rationally conceived mutual superpower interest. There was no need for the US to make concessions. He told LBJ in August 1966: 'Either the Russians share an interest with us in non-proliferation or they don't. No bonus from the Free World should be required'.[46]

Backtracking to the beginning of the NPT process under President Johnson, it should be emphasised that the American commitment to the treaty was cemented as a result of the Chinese atomic test. Committees under Llewellyn Thompson and Roswell Gilpatric considered and presented the case for comprehensive non-proliferation in 1964–65. At this stage, some leading players, certainly Dean Rusk, favoured nuclear acquisition by Japan and India, as a curb on China.[47] Johnson's own commitment seems, rather characteristically, to have been ignited as a result of the rivalry with Bobby Kennedy, whose maiden Senate speech (in June 1964) criticised the President for neglecting the Gilpatric Committee recommendations.

Johnson immediately accused Gilpatric of briefing RFK: 'He's got Gilpatric working for him'. The President's initial reaction was to downplay the non-proliferation issue in public. He told McGeorge Bundy in July: 'I do not want to get into proliferation in any way so it looks like I'm copying Bobby'.[48] Yet LBJ was, as Atomic Energy Commission chairman Glenn Seaborg put it, 'stung into action' by Bobby Kennedy's speech.[49] LBJ quickly issued NSAM 335, directing ACDA to draft proposals to reinvigorate the ENDC Geneva disarmament talks. The US lobbied successfully at the UN to increase pressure on the USSR to support the Geneva process.

Between 1964 and the end of 1966, Moscow was keen to declare its public support for non-proliferation. Mac Bundy reported on a November 1965 conversation with Ambassador Dobrynin: 'On non-proliferation . . . the Soviet Government had exposed itself to severe criticism from quarters he need not name (I inferred China); that should prove its sincerity'.[50] During the 1950s and 1960s, Moscow in fact made a series of public proposals either to prohibit nuclear weapons entirely or to ban their use. In 1965, Kosygin proposed a 'non-use' provision in the NPT itself. Washington routinely dismissed such proposals either as absurd gestures or as moves in Sino-Soviet diplomacy.[51] The Soviet Union itself, of course, had been involved in nuclear proliferation, most obviously in Cuba and in China, whose path to nuclear status had been assisted by Soviet aid delivered under the terms of the 1957 Sino-Soviet defence agreement. Moscow's main concern in relation to nuclear proliferation was the possibility of NATO emerging as a quasi-independent nuclear entity. The original Soviet aid to China, and transfer to Cuba, were, at least at one level, responses to the perceived nuclearisation of Western Europe. Following the Cuban missile crisis and the Chinese nuclear test, Moscow sought a diplomatic, rather than a confrontational, response to the problem of NATO.[52] In order to explain the complex superpower diplomacy surrounding the emergence of the NPT, a short digression on the nuclear politics of NATO is necessary.

At least in the post-Khrushchev era, Moscow looked to the NPT to restrict any progress towards greater nuclear independence in Western Europe: especially to deny any prospect of West Germany gaining access to the nuclear trigger. A CIA report on the NPT negotiations in January 1968 concluded that, for Moscow, non-proliferation was primarily 'a means of promoting the political and military containment of West Germany'.[53] Ideally, the NPT would undermine existing nuclear arrangements in NATO; the exclusion of Bonn from nuclear access was, for the post-1964 Warsaw Pact, the *sine qua non*.

The precise sticking point in respect of a US–Soviet deal between 1964 and late 1966 was American support for the Multilateral Nuclear Force (MLF) in Europe. American abandonment of the MLF made possible the 1968 treaty. JFK had publicly launched the MLF, a proposal for an integrated European nuclear force, ultimately under American control, in 1961. The case for the MLF emanated from McNamara's calculations of strategic rationality, including the US aversion to independent nuclear deterrents in Europe, as well (ironically) as the perceived need to contain German nuclear ambitions. Washington agreed with Moscow that Bonn should not be allowed to assume anything approaching independent nuclear authority. In Washington's view, the MLF was a way of simultaneously recognising and containing West German ambitions.

The history of the MLF was tortuous. In his final year in power, Nikita Khrushchev actually appeared willing to make concessions. His main goal centred on using a non-proliferation agreement as a lever against Chinese nuclear development. In 1963–64, Wladyslaw Gomulka, the Polish communist leader, pressured Khrushchev to back away from any deal which would allow West German access to nuclear weapons.[54] Khrushchev's successors presented a clear-cut opposition to the MLF, accepting Gomulka's argument that the proposed new nuclear arrangements for Western Europe were incompatible with non-proliferation.

The MLF caused strains within the Western alliance as well as within the Warsaw Pact. President Johnson certainly did not drop support for the MLF simply to promote a non-proliferation deal with Moscow. Soon after Kennedy's death, the Johnson Administration developed a plan for a Polaris-armed surface fleet, manned by mixed-nationality crews. British opposition to the plan was intense. Prime Minister Harold Wilson defended the integrity of Britain's deterrent by explaining to LBJ that Moscow would never accept the MLF as a realistic way of channelling and restraining Germany nuclear ambitions.[55] Wilson proposed an Atlantic Nuclear Force, effectively a partnership between US and British nuclear submarines loosely attached to NATO. By late 1964, the idea of a mixed-nationality fleet had lost credibility, and Wilson's ANF proposal effectively killed the idea. Franz-Josef Strauss of West Germany's Christian Democratic Union brilliantly described the ANF as 'the only fleet that had not been created that torpedoed another fleet that hadn't yet sailed'.[56] Roswell Gilpatric recalled that the MLF 'languished primarily for lack of presidential support'.[57] British Defence Secretary Denis Healey recollected that the whole MLF/ANF idea was finally killed by 1966 'because nobody wanted it'.[58]

To Moscow, the MLF was not a farce, more a serious attempt by the US to export nuclear weapons, regardless of the dangers of rearming West Germany. US–Soviet exchanges continually and repetitiously circled this issue, with American leaders emphasising that they wished to retain the veto over nuclear use. The initial American tactic was to force the USSR into a position where Moscow had either to accept US-defined restrictions on proliferation or – in William Foster's words – see 'the MLF come into being with no commitment of this kind to limit its evolution'.[59] This line of approach foundered not only with the weakening of the MLF, but also with the rise of American suspicions that Moscow's real target was NATO itself. Dean Rusk told Andrei Gromyko in December 1964 that 'if Soviet concern about the MlF was with respect to non-dissemination, we could meet it because we ourselves are against proliferation'. However, 'if the Soviet Union was against NATO, we were afraid we could not do much about it'.[60] By November 1965, Mac Bundy was reporting Soviet opposition to NATO reform in general, especially in relation to what Moscow called the 'McNamara special committee' (the Nuclear Planning Group). Bundy assured Ambassador Dobrynin that Bonn would not be allowed direct access to nuclear weapons, and that Washington would not 'support the Germans in any effort to use any German nuclear role as an instrument of power against the Soviet Union'.[61]

The collapse of the MLF did not take the issue of German nuclear access out of the NPT negotiations. In UN exchanges, at Geneva and in bilateral meetings, US and Soviet representatives continued to contest the issue, in a complex debate over treaty language. In September 1966, Gromyko insisted that the NPT 'must contain a prohibition against non-nuclear countries producing or receiving nuclear weapons directly or indirectly', including 'through an alliance'.[62] The possibility of an integrated military entity in Europe one day gaining an independent right to fire nuclear weapons was discussed in Washington, and repeatedly raised by Moscow. Walt Rostow told LBJ in August 1966: 'as soon as a united Europe claimed a right to fire independently of the US we would pull back'.[63]

In October 1966, Andrei Gromyko, meeting Dean Rusk in New York, effectively agreed to compromise on treaty language as a way of reviving the treaty, and as a *quid pro quo* for the abandonment of the MLF. The final treaty language involved a ban on the 'transfer' either of weapons themselves or of the 'control' of weapons. White House staffer Francis Bator advised LBJ that he should tell Gromyko that 'the critical issue is the legal right and physical ability to fire', and that 'on that, the Soviet and US interests completely coincide'.[64] Moscow dropped demands to prohibit 'consultation over nuclear decisions or even direct reference to access'. Existing arrangements in NATO were, in effect, protected, and the force of Rusk's argument – that the US 'cannot agree to any wording which would amount to informing our allies that their nuclear defence is none of their business' – accepted.[65]

The final treaty language did leave the prospect of a future integrated European entity enjoying nuclear status in direct succession from Britain and France. Dean Rusk later recalled that, since such an integrated Europe would take a 'long, long time' to emerge, neither Moscow nor Washington were especially exercised by this eventuality.[66] Concessions to the non-nuclear states included the right to quit the NPT on three months notice by invoking a state's 'supreme interests'. Non-nuclear countries were required to conclude agreements with the International Atomic Energy Agency regarding inspection procedures. A related dispute over the status of EURATOM, the European Atomic Energy Community, and its jurisdiction over inspections, continued into the 1970s. When LBJ and Kosygin met at Glassboro in June 1967, many of these complex issues were still unresolved. Johnson successfully urged the Soviet leader to have a revised treaty tabled at Geneva as soon as possible, 'before the other countries concerned become disgusted with the endless delays'.[67]

The Glassboro meeting led directly to NPT signing. The treaty rested on what Rusk had called in 1964 a superpower 'community of interest' in managing global nuclear security.[68] Attempts were made to extend this mutual superpower dynamic beyond the NPT. Throughout the Johnson years, for example, ACDA continued to present the case for a Comprehensive Test Ban Treaty. The 1963 partial test ban stimulated a succession of US–Soviet disputes. In February 1965, McGeorge Bundy advised LBJ that it was probably best not to 'take a prosecutor's attitude' over Soviet tests which appeared to violate the 1963 agreement. The US was finding its Plowshare programme – nuclear explosions conducted for peaceful, excavative purposes – compromised by the earlier treaty. America also was likely to want to undertake tests of warlike devices which might fall foul of the Kennedy-Khrushchev treaty.[69] Soviet attitudes towards on-site inspection also seemed to rule out any strengthening of current prohibitions. Dobrynin argued in 1965 that the 'only reason for on-site inspections was political'.[70] Robert McNamara, at least early on in the Administration, favoured a move towards a comprehensive treaty. He believed that the 1963 treaty 'was working to the advantage of the Soviets because underground tests were enabling them to close the gap in weapons'.[71] LBJ, however, was not prepared to lead the charge for a comprehensive measure. Indeed, in a conversation with Glenn Seaborg in 1966, he expressed doubts as to the wisdom of any ban on testing at all. LBJ ordered a huge test in Nevada to go ahead in April 1968 despite its occurring on the opening day of the UN debate on the NPT. (In a bizarre episode, he took time to respond to criticisms of testing – and a bribe offer – from the deranged billionaire Howard Hughes.)[72] American proposals for a comprehensive test ban treaty remained stranded at the level of rhetorical good intentions. A similar fate befell hopes for a 'threshold' ban – the establishment of a regime of regulated underground tests, limited by explosive yield – in the face of opposition from the Joint Chiefs of Staff.[73] (The Threshold Test Ban Treaty was eventually signed in 1974.)

Superpower 'community of interest' was evident in Soviet willingness to countenance, against the wishes of Cuba, Latin American denuclearisation;[74] and in the progress on banning nuclear weapons in space. In April 1966, Rusk presented to LBJ a proposal for the prohibition of 'military fortifications, military manoeuvres, weapons test, and stationary nuclear weapons on a celestial body'.[75] Ambassador Kohler reported in July 1966 that the Soviets 'clearly cannot afford to engage in an arms race in space'.[76] The 'celestial body' proposals were expanded into the 1967 Outer Space Treaty, which forbade the deployment into space of any object 'carrying nuclear weapons or any other kinds of weapons of mass destruction'. Agreements were also made concerning the safe return of astronauts or equipment to home countries in the event of unplanned landings. Arthur Goldberg, US Ambassador to the UN, promoted the agreements, telling LBJ that they represented 'peace building'. President Johnson was actually offering a toast to the Outer Space Treaty in January 1967 when he was brought news of the death of three astronauts in a fire on the Apollo launching pad.[77]

Anti-ballistic missile (ABM) deployment

In a major public pronouncement on nuclear strategy, delivered in San Francisco on 18 September 1967, Defense Secretary McNamara announced the Johnson Administration's intention to proceed with deployment of 'a light and reliable Chinese-oriented' anti-ballistic missile system. By this time, the Pentagon had spent over two billion dollars in developing ABM technology, under the Nike-X programme. Long and short-range American missiles would intercept incoming ICBMs. The Army was committed to a full-scale, anti-Soviet deployment. In San Francisco, however, McNamara rejected this 'heavy' or 'hardpoint' system, designed to protect America's Minuteman long-range missiles against a Soviet attack. Such 'heavy' deployment could not achieve reliable protection, would be extremely expensive, and would become 'a strong inducement for the Soviets to vastly increase their own offensive forces'. A 'thin', cheaper system, argued McNamara, was feasible. It would be enough to achieve protection against a less intense and less sophisticated attack from China.[78]

McNamara, in fact, was opposed to ABM deployment *per se*. He argued in December 1966 that ABM deployment would encourage Soviet offensive force development.[79] He informed LBJ in January 1967 that such deployment would not succeed in any of its three possible objectives: protection of American cities against a Soviet assault, protection of American cities against a Chinese attack, or protection of the Minuteman force. Deployment 'by the US of an ABM defense which would degrade the destruction capability of the Soviet's offensive force to an unacceptable level would lead to an expansion of that force. This would leave us no better off than we were before'. As for China: 'the lead time required for China to develop a significant ICBM force is greater than that required for deployment of our defense – therefore the Chinese threat in itself would not dictate the production of an ABM system at this time'.[80] McNamara tended to the view that no ABM system could ever be completely reliable. In any case, reliability could never be *assumed* as part of any rational nuclear strategy. Of course, if one side were to assume that it had a reliable ABM defence, that side would be emboldened to attempt a first nuclear strike. The superpowers, in McNamara's mature view, should embrace Mutual Assured Destruction, not the destabilising will-o'-the wisp of nuclear defence.

McNamara's analysis was backed by CIA Director Richard Helms. He argued in December 1966 that the scale or type of American ABM deployment would not greatly matter. Moscow would assume that the US would go all the way to 'heavy' deployment. 'In the end after enormous cost to them and us, the condition of mutual deterrence would be likely to obtain as before'.[81] These views were widely held across the Administration. Nicholas Katzenbach, then deputising for Rusk at State, told Walt Rostow that an

American ABM would 'expedite full-scale Soviet deployment' of the limited (Galosh) ABM system it currently had in place around Moscow.[82] Cyrus Vance and Llewellyn Thompson also supported the McNamara line.

The debate over ABM deployment came to a head in December 1966, at a set-piece debate held at LBJ's Texas ranch. On his way to Texas by plane, McNamara angrily grabbed some charts, outlining the case for the ABM from Harold K. Johnson, Chief of Staff for the Army. For the pro-ABM side, America's 'heavy' anti-ballistic system was a legitimate response not only to the Soviet Galosh defences, but also to a Russian anti-bomber system ('Tallin'), which US military intelligence believed could be easily upgraded to shoot down American missiles. At the 1966 Texas debate, General Earle Wheeler, chair of the Joint Chiefs, argued that a US failure to deploy would convince Moscow that Washington 'was not willing to pay to maintain its present nuclear superiority'. The US government 'would be denying to many of our own people a chance to survive a nuclear exchange'.[83]

Presidential adjudication of the Wheeler-McNamara battle involved a classic Johnsonian compromise. Congress would be asked to fund the 'thin' anti-Chinese, Sentinel system, which would probably become operational in the early 1970s. It was also hoped that the 'thin' system would protect the US against an accidental Soviet attack, as well as providing at least some cover for the Minuteman force. As for the 'heavy' deployment, McNamara and Vance essentially secured a deal whereby funds for the system's development would be sought, but not expended if progress were made on bringing Moscow to disarmament talks.[84]

The compromise exemplified LBJ's skilled, but limited, leadership. McNamara later related how he had deliberately pushed Johnson into a position where a decision had to be made: 'It was one of the few times I left the president in a position where he had to choose in the starkest terms between one of the recommendations of the chiefs and my own . . .'.[85] Johnson wished to keep McNamara in his Administration, despite the Defense Secretary's increasing unease with policy in Vietnam. He also understood very well the dangers of provoking the Joint Chiefs of Staff into a mobilisation of their support on Capitol Hill. Congress had already voted huge appropriations for an ABM system, which some key figures on the Hill saw as a saviour of American lives. Senator Richard Russell frequently declared that, if only two people were to survive a nuclear war, then he wanted those two to be Americans. In his view, ABM deployment would enhance survivability.[86] LBJ probably agreed with McNamara's analysis. He certainly saw the problems of ABM deployment simply pumping up the arms race, telling Attorney General Ramsey Clark in January 1967 that the two superpowers might end up spending thirty to forty billion dollars on the ABM: 'we don't want to get into that arms race'.[87] Yet Johnson was not prepared to defy the Joint Chiefs – nor indeed the body of Congressional opinion represented by his old chum Richard Russell.

Johnson's solution was to give hostages to fortune by tying the ABM deployment into a new strategic arms limitation agenda.

The intra-Administration debate over the ABM focused on the rationality of Soviet decisions and likely responses, and on the prospects of a strategic arms deal with Moscow. The eventual decision to move to an anti-Chinese ABM system reflected an assumption that Beijing was less rational than Moscow. However, several Johnson advisers had already warned their boss against assuming too much rationality even in the Kremlin. Such warnings, of course, had serious implications not only for LBJ's hopes of finessing the 'thin' ABM deployment into a general strategic arms deal; but also for the theory of 'mutual assured destruction' itself. Katzenbach argued that the Soviets 'don't approach the problem as rationally as we do'. He evidenced the strong Soviet preference for linking offensive and defensive weapons negotiations, despite the fact 'that a purely defensive freeze would be to their advantage'.[88] Llewellyn Thompson considered that Soviet reactions were so linked to sensitivities about great-power status and defence of the homeland that they were 'not what we would consider rational'.[89] In August 1967, Spurgeon Keeny held that ABM deployment would 'pose serious risk to our arms control objectives'. It would be difficult to convince Moscow that the 'emerging Chinese ICBM threat', rather than Soviet missiles, was 'a primary basis for our decisions'.[90] In the same month, Walt Rostow told LBJ that 'the ChiComs have shown themselves systematically extremely cautious in military operations and extremely respectful of US military power, including our nuclear power'. An ABM system might be deployed against China, but there was 'no reason for panic'.[91]

US–Soviet exchanges over the ABM were far from propitious. In January 1967, Walt Rostow treated Ambassador Dobrynin to a disquisition on American democratic politics. Rostow 'explained in some detail why it might be possible for the Soviet Union to move slowly in small increments on the ABMs, but that in a democratic society with two Senators from each state, it would be extremely difficult to have an ABM system limited to one city or one region'.[92] By the time of the June summit in Glassboro, it was accepted in Washington that offensive and defensive missiles would be taken together in the strategic arms agenda. LBJ explained to Kosygin that he was under great pressure to develop ABMs, but emphasised that he did not wish to enter a new arms race.[93] Kosygin's stated views mirrored those of the American Joint Chiefs. Defensive missiles were there to save lives, not to make it possible for one side to cheat mutual assured destruction, by rendering its cities impervious to retaliatory attack. In exchanges with McNamara, Kosygin proclaimed his outrage at the Defense Secretary's reported view that the US should concentrate on cheap ICBMs, not expensive ABMs. The Soviet leader told LBJ at the 23 June afternoon meeting at Glassboro that he was 'shocked' by McNamara's views about 'offensive weapons being cheaper than defensive ones'. Johnson attempted to apply pressure. Referring to the January 1967 budget requests to Congress, LBJ said that 'the clock was ticking' and he 'did not know how long he could postpone' his recommendation to Congress on the ABM question.[94]

Kosygin's stated position on the ABMs – that they 'are not the cause of the arms race, but constitute a factor preventing the death of people'[95] – was disingenuous. As Dobrynin later wrote, various positions on the ABM had already been rehearsed in Moscow. Kosygin certainly was more committed than Brezhnev to ABM development. In any case, Kosygin lacked any mandate to make deals, or promises of deals on ABM systems. According to Dobrynin: 'Moscow at that time sought first of all to achieve nuclear parity in strategic offensive weapons'.[96]

The Soviet leader's attitude at Glassboro caused LBJ to recommit himself to the ABM deployment. He was prevailed upon by Walt Rostow to accept McNamara's reluctant, compromise espousal of the 'thin', anti-Chinese Sentinel deployment in August 1967, shortly before the Defense Secretary's San Francisco speech. McNamara continued, without any success, to press Dobrynin on the possibility of a specific deal on defensive weaponry.[97]

By late 1967, it seemed that only a comprehensive US–Soviet arms deal could prevent the US moving to full-scale, 'heavy' Nike-X ABM deployment.[98] There were some hopeful signs. For example, in September 1967, the CIA advised that Moscow was willing seriously to consider a comprehensive – offensive and defensive – nuclear arms agreement. The Soviets 'now recognize that the impressive buildup of . . . strategic strength will not necessarily bring gains in foreign policy'.[99] Without a major negotiating breakthrough, however, an ABM arms race was virtually certain. A State Department survey of December 1967 indicated that the Soviets were committed to ambitious, full-scale ABM deployments by the early 1970s. If the US simply abided by the 'thin' deployment, 'only for protection against China, this will remain a political issue in this country'.[100] Attention was now firmly on the prospects for strategic arms limits.

Strategic arms limitation

Early Johnson initiatives on arms control were made in connection with the 'step-by-step' strategy, which expired in the 1965 superpower antagonism over Vietnam. In February 1964, Robert McNamara argued that since the Soviets now had 'the essence of a deterrent', Moscow might accept a freeze on ICBMs, ABMs, medium-range missiles and bombers, and heavy bombers.[101] In the same month, the Soviets made a proposal to destroy all long-range bombers. According to Ambassador Kohler, Gromyko regarded this proposal as 'sufficiently limited to avoid impairing the present balance of forces' but also 'radical enough to impress' the world.[102] Early in 1964, ACDA developed a proposal for a freeze on development of strategic nuclear delivery vehicles. Moscow also offered, at the Geneva ENDC talks, a programme of 'general and complete disarmament', to be initiated by massive force cuts.

These early exchanges advanced no further than wishful posturing. Most commentators on the history of arms control dismiss them as largely symbolic efforts to sustain the détente of 1963. In December 1964, LBJ told Gromyko that, in their quest for guarantees for peace, Moscow and Washington were 'like children hunting for Easter eggs'.[103] 'General and complete disarmament' was regarded in Washington in the same light as Soviet espousal of nuclear non-use policy: as empty gesturing, designed to impress developing and non-aligned nations, and largely to be explained in terms of Sino-Soviet competition. The various freeze and weapons-cutting schemes never encompassed reliable verification. The Joint Chiefs of Staff noted in February 1964 that an adequate compliance and verification regime 'would be intrusive to a greater extent than the USSR has been willing to consider in the past'.[104] ACDA head William Foster explained that the Soviets were advancing a cuts agenda at Geneva 'but we are resisting this since there is no way of verifying such reductions'.[105] The American 'freeze' proposal evinced 'no enthusiasm' from the Soviet side.[106] America's allies also objected to agreements being made without adequate consultation (Britain was especially concerned about the status of its Polaris nuclear submarine programme).[107] Yet elements of the Washington bureaucracy kept the proposals afloat. The Gilpatric Committee report of January 1965, for example, contained an injunction to push for a verified freeze on strategic delivery vehicles, along with significant reductions in strategic force levels.[108]

Between 1965 and mid-1967, ACDA continued to develop the strategic arms limitation (SALT) agenda,[109] despite the disruptions in superpower relations associated with events in Vietnam. Though the main thrust of arms control now related to non-proliferation, it should be remembered that the NPT process itself involved some commitment to general arms limitation by the US and USSR. Largely in order to increase their credibility in the eyes of non- or near-nuclear states, the superpowers agreed in the final Nonproliferation Treaty to pursue arms limitation in good faith.

However, far more than the NPT, it was the US debate over ABM deployment which revived Presidential interest in strategic arms limits. As described above, the December 1966 discussions at LBJ's Texas ranch culminated in a commitment to begin a strategic arms dialogue with Moscow. Llewellyn Thompson's official approach to Gromyko and Kosygin (made on 27 January 1967) contained some important American concessions. Thompson declared that the US was happy for the talks to cover offensive and defensive weaponry. He also dropped the traditional American insistence – long a *sine qua non* for the Joint Chiefs of Staff – on on-site inspections. US overtures at this juncture were backed up by public statements by McNamara about the potency of

America's new MIRV technology, as well as by direct hints to Moscow that Washington was on the verge of ABM deployment. Moscow's attitude was ambivalent. Various exchanges between Thompson, Gromyko, LBJ and Kosygin raised the issues of nuclear superiority, parity and the point in the arms race at which new acquisitions would be frozen. Kosygin's attitude was noticeably prickly. Llewellyn Thompson reported his own response: 'I observed that if I had talked of who was ahead I would have had to say that it was the USSR because we had not yet installed any ABMs'.[110] The US Embassy in Moscow reported that Gromyko was unwilling 'to freeze present strategic balance which we have publicly boasted is in our favor'.[111] Kosygin informed LBJ that prospects for arms talks would greatly improve if 'such hotbeds of tension as that in Vietnam were liquidated'.[112]

Between January and June 1967, the arms control process failed to gather momentum. LBJ admitted to journalists in early March that no summit was imminent, and that inclusion of offensive missiles in the SALT agenda had been a deliberate concession to Moscow. The Glassboro summit saw little further progress. A position paper, prepared for LBJ's meeting with Kosygin in New Jersey, indicated the widespread American view that Soviet delay in commencing talks was traceable to 'divided views within the Soviet leadership on how to proceed'.[113] At the 25 June Glassboro session, Kosygin made it clear that Moscow wanted progress on Vietnam and the Middle East before the commencement of SALT talks. Johnson complained to Eisenhower that, despite some good signs, Kosygin never 'would set a time and never would set a place' for arms talks to begin.[114]

As noted in Chapter 2, Johnson cherished the hope – an increasingly desperate hope – of initiating a direct SALT dialogue during his Presidential watch. The continuing strength of this hope, despite the various setbacks, effectively relegated the immediate prospect of any 'thick', anti-Soviet ABM deployment. LBJ's personal commitment to the talks actually increased following his 31 March 1968 speech of withdrawal from the Presidential race. Ironically, of course, the speech also secured him an early status as a 'lame duck' President, arguably making Moscow even less likely to make an early move towards talks. Interwoven in the Presidential thinking was, firstly, the wish to cap his troubled times in office with a major diplomatic success – or at least with the clear initiation of a new era of arms control; secondly, the possibility of locking an American advantage into an arms deal; and, thirdly, the desire to leave a legacy of enhanced nuclear peace. Johnson felt that the US had made the running on arms control, and he was prepared to continue the effort. He remarked in July 1968 that he had been keen on an arms deal ever since assuming office. With the Vietnam crisis in early 1965, 'things kind of tapered off'; however, 'we have kept shoving'.[115] (This view, of course, contrasted sharply with Kosygin's perception, expressed at Glassboro, that the US was constantly racing ahead in the nuclear arms contest, with Moscow 'merely

following its lead'.)[116] If Johnson's commitment to arms control was charac-
terised by at least a degree of high-mindedness, this was more than matched
by Dean Rusk's increasing enthusiasm for the cause. During a Cabinet room
debate about how to keep the SALT craft afloat after the Soviet invasion of
Czechoslovakia, the Secretary of State argued that arms talks must be launched
at the highest level: 'I think if the President initiated the discussions, this would
be a sign to what General Eisenhower called the military industrial complex
that, Goddamn it, setting an agreement to limit offensive and defensive missiles is the national policy of the United States'.[117]

Johnson and Rusk had had to wait until late June 1968 for anything
approaching a positive response from Moscow. On 27 June, Kosygin agreed
to talks covering the limitation and reduction of offensive and defensive missiles. Plans for an October summit in the USSR, of course, were destroyed by
the Russian invasion of Czechoslovakia. Immediately prior to the invasion,
various attempts were being made in Washington to probe and understand
Moscow's arms control position. A CIA Office of National Estimates memorandum, presented to LBJ by Richard Helms in mid-July 1968, argued that
the Soviets were indeed ready to talk. They had now reached some kind of
nuclear parity with the US, at least on ICBMs, and would interpret a public
dialogue as a recognition of this. However, there was little indication that
Moscow actually wanted a deal. Although the Soviets were 'deeply conscious
of the economic burdens of continuing' the arms race, they understood that
prolonged negotiation was itself a form of arms control'.[118] A CIA Intelligence
Memorandum of 26 July argued that some Politburo figures saw talks as a
way 'at the least, of exploring the US position and seeking to delay US programs at little cost to the USSR'.[119] Following the Czech invasion, Johnson
was encouraged by CIA estimates to the effect that Moscow had not intended
deliberately to sabotage SALT negotiations. Indeed, during the latter part of
1968, the CIA interpreted Moscow's willingness to hold out the prospect of
arms talks as 'probably calculated to help offset the approbrium the USSR suffered from the Czech invasion'.[120] According to the CIA, Moscow did want
to limit strategic forces, although arms control could not match the maintenance of Soviet suzerainty over Eastern Europe as a policy priority. The
Russian leaders, however, certainly wished to use lengthy negotiations as a
way of postponing American Minuteman III (MIRV) deployments.[121] In
October, the CIA reported that Moscow was concerned about the new US
developments – especially Poseidon and Minuteman III – 'that threaten to
erode their relative position'. With 'rough numerical parity' in ICBMs having
been attained, 'the Soviets will probably give increased attention to other
options designed to enhance the survivability and effectiveness of their strategic attack forces'.[122]

Johnson and Rusk were unimpressed by CIA assessments that Moscow was
not keen to close a deal. Rusk tended to answer all criticisms by appealing to

the generalised benefits which an arms treaty would bestow. For example, he dismissed worries about the lack of on-site verification: 'We estimate that the potential risks to our deterrent due to possible Soviet evasion of the terms of the agreement are less serious than the risks we would face in the absence of an agreement'.[123]

Perhaps the most thoughtful American analysis of the Russian position came in Thomas Hughes' July 1968 analysis of why Kosygin had agreed to talks. The Director of Intelligence and Research at the State Department located his analysis within generalised interpretation of Soviet foreign policy-making:

> When the Soviet Politburo meets on a knotty question, it must balance the myriad interests of a large country, weighing such factors as effects on the economy, internal political implications, implications for Soviet military strength and reactions of both friends and adversaries abroad . . . Faced with the need for decisions and the difficulties of making them, Soviet leaders look for easy ways to meet these conflicting pressures . . . Soviet foreign policy thus tends to be made piecemeal.

Despite 'Marxist rhetoric which emphasizes the idea of scientific understanding of the whole historical process', it was actually a mistake to look for much consistency. Soviet policy was 'a series of fixes'. Policy objectives were 'mixed or contrapuntal'. (The Czechoslovakian invasion, apparently undertaken with little attention to the détente agenda, would soon appear to prove Hughes' point.) In June 1968, the Politburo had apparently made a discrete decision to begin talks, but not to commit itself to anything more. The decision did involve a defeat for the Soviet military, and appeared to have been made with one eye on the US Presidential election campaign: 'We suspect that the Soviets see the election campaign as a formative period for American attitudes on strategic spending in coming years, and hence a moment for attempting to exert their influence'. Hughes considered the proposition that Moscow, far from being reluctant to deal with the 'lame duck' Johnson, actually saw the advantage of making an agreement with an American leader 'working under a deadline and therefore more prone to make concessions'. There was little evidence, however, that Moscow really was looking to a deal in the foreseeable future. Rather, the 'Soviets presumably hope to strengthen those political forces in the US opposed to arms spending'. Such strengthening would be advantageous to Moscow even in the event of a Republican victory in November.[124]

When the Republican victory came, LBJ's priority became (as indicated in Chapter 2) the recruiting of President-elect Nixon to the arms control cause. On 20 November, Walt Rostow suggested that Nixon be given the 'option of coming along' to an arms summit 'like Attlee and Churchill to Potsdam'.[125] Five days later, Johnson told the National Security Council: 'The Czech invasion blew up earlier plans for the arms talks. We should get started even if we handle the talks so as not bind [sic] a successor'.[126] These eleventh hour efforts were, despite some lukewarm encouragement from Moscow, unrealistic. Nixon, whatever was agreed about the non-binding nature of talks, was not about to be roped into his predecessor's initiative. The Joint Chiefs and their allies in Congress feared lest LBJ's desire for a deal should indeed lead him to concede too much. The non-ratified status of the Nonproliferation Treaty made it difficult to make progress on SALT. Clark Clifford also raised the 'real concern' that the Senate might refuse to ratify any deal (especially one without on-site inspections) made by the departing President.[127]

SALT: the American negotiating position

During much of 1967 and 1968, large sections of the Washington defence and foreign affairs bureaucracy were concerned to produce a viable American negotiating position on SALT. Since talks did not commence until the era of President Nixon, Johnson's negotiating position was never tested. It was inevitably rather inchoate and obviously represented a stance that would have been modified in the course of actual negotiations with the Soviets. There is no question – indeed it would be extraordinary if this were not the case – that LBJ wished to freeze an American advantage into any arms control bargain. Writing to LBJ in late November 1968, Clark Clifford urged the President not to abandon hopes for a deal: 'If the Soviets were to accept an agreement along the lines of the one unanimously recommended to you, we would maintain a substantial part of our present strategic advantage; a year from now it will be more difficult to devise a proposal which takes account of existing strategic forces and is in our interest'.[128] Johnson told Bob Murphy, Nixon's foreign policy representative during the transition: 'We have substantial nuclear superiority over the Soviets. If a freeze goes into effect, we would be ahead'. (Murphy was unconvinced, saying that he found the idea of another Glassboro 'unappealing'.)[129] The crucial issue, of course, surrounding the locking-in of an American advantage involved the exclusion of MIRV deployments from the calculations. A brief survey of the development of the American SALT negotiating position will elucidate these points.

During 1967, the key trade-off between the US military and ACDA involved on-site inspections and the status of MIRV deployments. As noted above, the initial ACDA proposals did not include on-site inspections. This issue was further complicated by the exigencies of inspecting the new generation of mobile missiles. Thomas Hughes noted in April 1967 that Moscow had expressed 'concern over the impossibility of monitoring the *extent* of mobile missile deployment without an elaborate inspection system of the kind which the USSR would not accept'.[130] Even more than on-site inspections, however, the Joint Chiefs at this stage urged no surrender of the US strategic advantage, no concession on Soviet ABMs and no inclusion in any deal of MIRV capabilities. Between the decision to deploy the 'thin' ABM (announced in McNamara's San Francisco speech of September 1967) and Kosygin's accep- tance of the SALT talks offer (June 1968), the US military battled with arms control bureaucrats over these issues. Paul Warnke, now assistant to Clark Clifford at the Pentagon, voiced his frustration in April 1968. He argued that General Earle Wheeler's insistence on freezing-in American superiority was tantamount to destroying any commitment to arms control: 'We must face the fact that no agreement with the Soviet Union can be expected to maintain U.S. superiority'.[131] Dean Rusk on 26 April urged LBJ that there were 'convincing reasons to give the Soviets at this point a somewhat more concrete idea of just what we are prepared to talk about'.[132] At this time the key bureaucratic com- promise available to Johnson was a draft plan which accepted the Soviet case for purely national inspections, supplemented of course by informal satellite observation. The plan provided for numerical superpower equality on ABM launchers and on land-based intercontinental nuclear missiles. (Submarines were deemed inappropriate for the anticipated inspection regime.) Johnson, presumably bowing to General Wheeler's objections, declined to follow Rusk's advice and present the detailed plan to Moscow. Following the Soviet agree- ment to begin talks, and before the invasion of Czechoslovakia, Paul Warnke and Morton Halperin at the Pentagon worked on a proposal which might be acceptable to the Joint Chiefs. The version which received Presidential approval at the end of August 1968 provided for a freeze on ICBMs and on submarine-launched nuclear missiles. This latter provision involved a sub- stantial American advantage, only slightly offset by the freezing of fixed land- based launchers for IRBMs (intermediate range ballistic missiles), where the Soviets had the advantage. The Joint Chiefs conceded the issue of on-site veri- fication, though Clifford continued to argue that 'we should depend on uni- lateral verification' only 'as a fall-back'.[133] Mobile launchers for offensive and defensive missiles were (in a provision that would not be susceptible to veri- fication) to be outlawed. Glen Seaborg concluded: 'Essentially . . . what was being proposed was a quantitative, but not a qualitative freeze on strategic missile launchers, and an agreement to limit ABMs on both sides to an equal, but as yet unspecified, number'. The proposed treaty was 'a way to prevent eruption of the arms race into the ruinous escalation that both McNamara and Rusk predicted might follow extensive ABM deployment by either side'.[134] Actual strategic force reductions were not countenanced. While the inbuilt advantages to the US might have been modified in actual negotiation, the major omission from the proposal (as from Nixon's SALT I agreement of 1972) was MIRV technology. As Seaborg noted, the failure to restrict MIRVs was an 'ominous limitation': 'while the number of missile launchers might be held steady, the number of warheads could increase significantly'.[135] Accord- ing to Robert Divine, the 1968 SALT negotiating plan would, allowing for anticipated American MIRV advantages, have led to a five to one US advantage in deliverable nuclear warheads by the mid-1970s.[136] (When the plan was accepted in August 1968, the US was about to embark on final testing for both land and submarine-based MIRVed missiles).[137]

It is appropriate to end this chapter with some general comments about LBJ's nuclear policies. Firstly – despite the unrealism of his ambitions and the compromised nature of his motivation – Johnson does perhaps deserve some credit for pressing ahead with arms control in 1968. His motives were not entirely base. The major problem, at least in beginning the negotiations, was the Soviet invasion of Czechoslovakia, rather than issues on the American side. Certainly, the unwillingness to include MIRVs made it unlikely that any LBJ arms initiative would do all that much to halt the arms race. In this connection it is nevertheless worth noting the view of some Johnson advisers that the President would, in the last resort, have been willing to defy the Joint Chiefs and negotiate on MIRVs. Dean Rusk argued in 1986 that, had SALT talks commenced in September 1968, 'the state of the art in MIRVs was such that we might have been able to get them under control'. According to Walt Rostow, President Johnson knew 'the clock was ticking' on MIRVs and would have been prepared to negotiate with Moscow on the new technology.[138] It can only be observed that LBJ's attitude towards the Joint Chiefs, as evidenced in his stance over SALT negotiating positions in 1967–68, does not tend to bear out the judgment of Rusk and Rostow.

Secondly, in regard to both the ABM deployment and the SALT negotiating position decisions, we discern LBJ's familiar pursuit of the middle way. As is evident in so many other aspects of his Presidency, the tendency to interpret effective leadership as the negotiation of a middle-way compromise between competing positions was as likely to lead to enervation and drift, as to the creative and purposeful resolution of political conflict.

Lastly, some general remarks about Johnson's nuclear stance towards the Soviet Union. The Johnson era saw the development, albeit a stuttering and uncertain development, of the détente of 1963. It was, nevertheless, still an era of considerable nuclear danger. As seen in the first section of this chapter, the strategic outlook of the Johnson Administration was not entirely consistent. Mutual Assured Destruction had its own internal inconsistencies, and in any case, never commanded universal assent in Washington. In addition, nuclear 'first use' was not entirely ruled out in this period, even by the civilian Soviet expert Llewellyn Thompson. It was certainly not ruled out by Moscow. Robert McNamara's leadership at the Pentagon was brilliant, but mercurial. The fevered atmosphere of the post-McNamara period allowed little opportunity for the Administration fully to explore the strategic implications of (on the one hand) conceding nuclear parity to the USSR, and (on the other) developing a negotiating position which did not take account of MIRVs.

Johnson was fortunate in not having to face, with the partial exception of the 1967 Middle Eastern Six Day War confrontation, a direct US–Soviet crisis with nuclear implications. It is difficult to imagine Lyndon Johnson, who regarded nuclear war as the horror of horrors, and who saw avoidance of nuclear conflict as his first Presidential priority, acting irresponsibly in his nuclear decisions. Yet his grasp of nuclear doctrine was never entirely confident and secure. His consensual, 'middle way' leadership style was also singularly unsuited to the clarity of vision and purpose which a major superpower nuclear crisis would have required.

Notes

1 *The Johnson Presidential Press Conferences: Volume I* (London, Heyden, 1978), p. 172 (24 July 1964).

2 V. D. Bornet, *The Presidency of Lyndon B Johnson* (Lawrence, Kansas University Press, 1983), pp. 197–8.

3 'Summary record of NSC meeting, 5 Dec. 1963', NSF: NSC Meetings File, box 1.

4 Dean Rusk, Oral History, p. 44.

5 McG. Bundy, *Danger and Survival: Choices about the Bomb in the First Fifty Years* (New York, Vintage, 1988), p. 555. See also D. Shapley, *Promise and Power: The Life and Times of Robert McNamara* (Boston, Little, Brown, 1993), p. 390.

6 M. R. Beschloss (ed.), *Taking Charge: The Johnson White House Tapes, 1963–64* (New York, Simon and Schuster, 1997), pp. 119–20.

7 P. H. Nitze, *From Hiroshima to Glasnost* (London, Weidenfeld and Nicolson, 1989), p. 285. See also A. C. Enthoven and K. Wayne, *How Much is Enough? Shaping the Defense Program, 1961–1969* (New York, Harper and Row, 1971); D. Ball, *Politics and Force Levels* (Berkeley, University of California Press, 1980), pp. 157, 181; M. M. Boll, *National Security Planning: Roosevelt through Reagan* (Lexington, Kentucky University Press, 1988), pp. 110–15; F. Kaplan, *Wizards of Armageddon* (New York, Simon and Schuster, 1983), pp. 265–70; R. A. Divine, 'Lyndon Johnson and strategic arms limitation', in Divine (ed.), *The Johnson Years: Volume 3: LBJ at Home and Abroad* (Lawrence, Kansas University Press, 1994), pp. 239–78.

8 Davis to Rostow, 14 April 1967, 'ABMs and Politics', NSF: Files of Nathaniel Davis, box 1.

9 P. Towle, *Arms Control and East-West Relations* (London, Croom Helm, 1983), pp. 185–6; Divine, 'Lyndon Johnson', pp. 240–1.

10 G. F. Treverton, 'From no cities to stable vulnerability', in P. Bobbitt, L. Freedman and G. F. Treverton (eds.), *US Nuclear Strategy: A Reader* (London, Macmillan, 1989), pp. 190–204, at p. 196.

11 R. S. McNamara, *The Essence of Security* (New York, Harper and Row, 1968), pp. 52–3.

12 See R. N. Lebow and J. G. Stein, *We All Lost the Cold War* (Princeton, Princeton University Press, 1994), ch. 14. See also E. Beukel, *American Perceptions of the Soviet Union as a Nuclear Adversary* (London, Pinter, 1989), pp. 48–62; R. A. Levine, 'The evolution of US policy toward arms control', in G. W. Breslauer and P. E. Tetlock (eds.), *Learning in US and Soviet Foreign Policy* (Boulder, Westview, 1991), pp. 130–51.

13 'Summary record of NSC meeting, December 5, 1963', NSF: NSC Meetings File, box 1.

14 *FRUS, 1964–1968*: Volume XIV: *The Soviet Union* (Washington DC, US Government Printing Office, 2001), p. 21 (19 Feb. 1964).

15 Ibid., p. 48 (2 April 1964).

16 Ibid., p. 62 (17 April 1964) (CIA Special Report).

17 Ibid., p. 248 (15 Feb. 1965).

18 'Draft proposal', ACDA, NSF: Files of W. W. Rostow, box 10 (folder, 'Kosygin I').

19 National Intelligence Estimate, 17 Nov. 1966, NSF: CF: Europe and USSR; USSR, box 223 (folder, 'Memos 2').

20 As note 8.

21 *FRUS, 1964–1968*: Volume XIV: *The Soviet Union*, p. 569 (9 Aug. 1967).

22 Ibid., p. 589 (28 Sept. 1967).

23 NSF: NSC Meetings File, box 2, folder, 'NSC meetings vol 4 Tab 61', Helms briefing notes.

24 *FRUS, 1964–1968*: Volume XIV: *The Soviet Union*, p. 608 (18 Dec. 1967).

25 Ibid., p. 618 (9 Jan. 1968).

26 *FRUS, 1964–1968*: Volume XI: *Arms Control and Disarmament* (Washington DC, US Government Printing Office, 1997), p. 654 (26 July 1968); L. Freedman, *US Intelligence and the Soviet Strategic Threat* (London, Macmillan, 1977), p. 117.

27 Quoted in Divine, 'Lyndon Johnson', p. 244.

28 See ibid.

29 Ibid., p. 246.

30 See, e.g., L. Thompson (Moscow Embassy) to Rusk, 18 Feb. 1967, in *FRUS: 1964–1968*: Volume XIV: *The Soviet Union*, p. 444.

31 See F. J. Gavin, 'The myth of flexible response: United States strategy in Europe during the 1960s', *The International History Review*, 23:4 (2001) 847–69.

32 'Speech to NATO Council, Athens, 5 May 1962' in Bobbitt, Freedman and Treverton (eds.), *US Nuclear Strategy*, pp. 205–20, 211, 215.

33 See L. Kaplan, 'The US and NATO in the Johnson years', in Divine (ed.), *The Johnson Years: Volume 3*, pp. 119–49.

34 *FRUS, 1964–1968*: Volume XIV: *The Soviet Union*, p. 608 (18 Dec. 1967).

35 See 'US planning for war in Europe, 1963–64', National Security Archive electronic briefing book 31 (ed. W. Burr, 2000) (available on National Security Archive website).

36 Ibid. (US Air Forces Europe document, 26 May 1964).

37 Ibid. (Thompson to Seymour Weiss, 'Implications of a major Soviet conventional attack in Central Europe', 29 Dec. 1964).

38 NSF: NSC histories, Non-proliferation treaty, box 55, 24 Dec. 1968. See also R. L. Garthoff, *A Journey Through the Cold War: A Memoir of Containment and Coexistence* (Washington DC, Brookings Institution, 2001), p. 196.

39 NSF: CF: Europe and USSR: USSR, box 228, folder, 'Gromyko conversations 1', 27 June 1967.

40 J. Goldblatt, *Arms Control: A Guide to Negotiations and Agreements* (Oslo, PRIO, 1994), p. 83.

41 *FRUS, 1964–1968*: Volume XI: *Arms Control and Disarmament*, p. 437 (8 Feb. 1967); but see also p. 600 (17 May 1968).

42 G. T. Seaborg, with B. S. Loeb, *Stemming the Tide: Arms Control in the Johnson Years* (Lexington, Heath, 1987), p. 376.

43 Ibid., p. 374.

44 *FRUS, 1964–1968*: Volume XI: *Arms Control and Disarmament*, p. 319 (12 May 1966).

45 W. W. Rostow, *The Diffusion of Power* (New York, Macmillan, 1972), pp. 378, 383. Raymond Garthoff (*A Journey Through the Cold War*, p. 231) saw the NPT as 'an important example of the practical combination of unilateral and consultative actions feasible in the real world of East–West diplomacy'.

46 Rostow to LBJ, 12 Aug. 1966, NSF: Files of Walt Rostow, box 11, folder, 'Non-proliferation'.

47 See Seaborg, *Stemming the Tide*, p. 135.

48 M. R. Beschloss (ed.), *Reaching for Glory* (New York, Simon and Schuster, 2001), pp. 369 (24 June 1964), 380 (1 July 1964).

49 *Stemming the Tide*, p. 147.

50 *FRUS, 1964–1968*: Volume XI: *Arms Control and Disarmament*, p. 266 (24 Nov. 1965).
51 For Thomas Hughes (State Department Intelligence and Research) these proposals represented a 'benchmark in Sino-Soviet relations' (NSF: Files of Spurgeon Keeny, box 7, folder, 'Gromyko', 'Moscow's latest proposal . . .', 28 Sept. 1967).
52 See J. S. Nye, 'US–Soviet cooperation in a non-proliferation regime', in A. L. George, P. J. Farley and A. Dallin (eds.), *US–Soviet Security Cooperation: Achievements, Failures, Lessons* (New York, Oxford University Press, 1988), pp. 336–52, at p. 340.
53 NSF: CF: Europe and USSR; USSR, box 25, folder, 'Memos B', 9 Jan. 1968.
54 See 'The Warsaw pact and Nuclear Non-proliferation, 1963–1965', Cold War International History Project Working Paper 32 (D. Selvage) (available on Woodrow Wilson Center CWIP website).
55 H. Wilson, *The Labour Government, 1964–70* (London, Weidenfeld and Nicolson, 1971), p. 49.
56 Quoted in P. Ziegler, *Wilson: The Authorised Life* (London, Weidenfeld and Nicolson, 1993), p. 209.
57 R. Gilpatric, Oral History, p. 16.
58 D. Healey, *The Time of My Life* (London, Joseph, 1989), p. 305. See also P. Y. Hammond, *LBJ and the Presidential Management of Foreign Policy* (Austin, University of Texas Press, 1992), ch. 4.
59 *FRUS, 1964–1968*: Volume XI: *Arms Control and Disarmament*, p. 103 (14 Aug. 1964).
60 Ibid., p. 133 (5 Dec. 1964).
61 Ibid., pp. 265–6 (24 Nov. 1965).
62 Ibid., p. 371 (22 Sept. 1966).
63 Rostow to LBJ, 12 Aug. 1966, NSF: Files of Walt Rostow, box 11, folder, 'Non-proliferation'.
64 NSF: CF: Europe and USSR: USSR, box 222, folder, 'Memos 12', 9 Oct. 1966.
65 *FRUS, 1964–1968*: Volume XI: *Arms Control and Disarmament*, pp. 389–90 (10 Oct. 1966).
66 Rusk, Oral History, p. 16.
67 *FRUS, 1964–1968*: Volume XIV: *The Soviet Union*, p. 521 (23 June 1967).
68 *FRUS, 1964–1968*: Volume XI: *Arms Control and Disarmament*, p. 80 (16 June 1964).
69 Ibid., p. 190 (11 Feb. 1965).
70 Ibid., p. 198 (30 March 1965).
71 Seaborg, *Stemming the Tide*, p. 183.
72 Ibid., p. 239.
73 See *FRUS, 1964–1968*: Volume XI: *Arms Control and Disarmament*, p. 282.
74 See Goldblatt, *Arms Control*, pp. 149–52 (1967 Treaty of Tlatelolco).
75 *FRUS, 1964–1968*: Volume XI: *Arms Control and Disarmament*, p. 312 (2 April 1966).
76 *FRUS, 1964–1968*: Volume XIV: *The Soviet Union*, p. 400 (13 July 1966).
77 See Bornet, *The Presidency of Lyndon B. Johnson*, pp. 215–16; W. A. McDougall, *The Heavens and the Earth: A Political History of the Space Age* (New York, Basic Books, 1985), pp. 360–5.
78 M. H. Halperin, 'The decision to deploy the ABM: bureaucratic and domestic politics in the Johnson Administration', *World Politics*, 25:1 (1972–73) 62–95, at pp. 62, 64.
79 *FRUS, 1964–1968*: Volume X: *National Security Policy* (Washington DC, US Government Printing Office, 2002), p. 485 (22 Dec. 1966).
80 *FRUS, 1964–1968*: Volume XI: *Arms Control and Disarmament*, pp. 421, 423 (no precise date).
81 Ibid., p. 411 (10 Dec. 1966).
82 Ibid., p. 408 (10 Dec. 1966).
83 Divine, 'Lyndon Johnson and strategic arms limitation', p. 246.
84 See Shapley, *Promise and Power*, pp. 390–4.

85 Ibid., p. 391.

86 See Halperin, 'The decision to deploy the ABM', p. 74.

87 *FRUS, 1964–1968*: Volume XIV: *The Soviet Union*, p. 449 (20 Jan. 1967).

88 *FRUS, 1964–1968*: Volume XI: *Arms Control and Disarmament*, p. 408 (10 Dec. 1966).

89 Ibid., p. 409 (10 Dec. 1966).

90 Keeny to Rusk and McNamara, NSF: Files of Spurgeon Keeny, box 1, folder, 'ABM 2', 28 Aug. 1967.

91 *FRUS, 1964–1968*: Volume X: *National Security Policy*, p. 565 (2 Aug. 1967).

92 *FRUS, 1964–1968*: Volume XIV: *The Soviet Union*, p. 454 (27 Jan. 1967).

93 Ibid., p. 522 (23 June 1967).

94 Ibid., pp. 529–30, 534–5, 556, 565.

95 R. G. Garthoff, 'BMD and East-West relations', in A. B. Carter and D. N. Schwartz (eds.), *Ballistic Missile Defence* (Washington DC, Brookings Institute, 1984), pp. 275–301, at p. 295.

96 A. Dobrynin, *In Confidence* (New York, Times Books, 1995), pp. 150, 166. See also Bundy, *Danger and Survival*, p. 549.

97 Shapley, *Promise and Power*, pp. 393–4.

98 See Divine, 'Lyndon Johnson and strategic arms limitation', pp. 252–6.

99 *FRUS, 1964–1968*: Volume XIV: *The Soviet Union*, p. 589 (28 Sept. 1967).

100 Ibid., pp. 602, 612 (18 Dec. 1967).

101 *FRUS, 1964–1969*: Volume XI: *Arms Control and Disarmament*, pp. 16–17 (13 Feb. 1964).

102 Ibid., p. 36 (28 Feb. 1964).

103 Ibid., p. 136 (9 Dec. 1964). See J. Newhouse, *Cold Dawn: The Story of SALT* (New York, Holt, Rinehart and Winston, 1973), pp. 66–72; J. Prados, 'Prague Spring and SALT: arms limitation setbacks in 1968', in H. W. Brands (ed.), *The Foreign Policies of Lyndon Johnson: Beyond Vietnam* (College Station, Texas A and M University Press, 1999), pp. 19–36, at p. 20.

104 *FRUS, 1964–1968*: Volume XIV: *The Soviet Union*, p. 24 (22 Feb. 1964).

105 Ibid., p. 29 (29 Feb. 1964).

106 Ibid., p. 76 (A. Fisher, 16 June 1964).

107 See ibid., p. 17.

108 Ibid., p. 180.

109 The SALT acronym was adopted by the CIA in 1968 when material on strategic arms limitation talks (not 'treaty'; at this stage) required filing. See S. Talbott, *Endgame* (New York, Harper and Row, 1979), p. 28.

110 *FRUS, 1964–1968*: Volume XI: *Arms Control and Disarmament*, p. 444 (18 Feb. 1967).

111 Ibid., p. 453 (28 Feb. 1967).

112 Ibid., p. 450 (27 Feb. 1967).

113 NSF: CF: Europe and USSR: USSR, box 229, folder, 'Hollybush 1'.

114 *FRUS, 1964–1968*: Volume XIV: *The Soviet Union*, p. 558 (25 June 1967).

115 Ibid., p. 672 (29 July 1968).

116 Ibid., p. 521 (23 June 1967).

117 Ibid., p. 669 (29 July 1968).

118 Ibid., p. 664 (15 July 1968).

119 *FRUS, 1964–1968*: Volume XI: *Arms Control and Disarmament*, p. 655.

120 Ibid., p. 734 (7 Nov. 1968).

121 Ibid., pp. 735–7.

122 *FRUS, 1964–1968*: Volume X: *National Security Policy*, p. 749 (3 Oct. 1968).

123 *FRUS, 1964–1968*: Volume XI: *Arms Control and Disarmament*, p. 679.

124 'Moscow's decision to hold strategic arms talks', 12 July 1968, NSF: Files of W. W. Rostow, box 11, folder, 'Strategic missile talks'.

125 Rostow to LBJ, 20 Nov. 1968, ibid.
126 *FRUS, 1964–1968*: Volume XI: *Arms Control and Disarmament*, p. 739.
127 Ibid., p. 742 (25 Nov. 1968).
128 Ibid., See also C. Clifford, *Counsel to the President: A Memoir* (New York, Random House, 1991), pp. 559–60.
129 *FRUS, 1964–1968*: Volume XIV: *The Soviet Union*, p. 767 (26 Nov. 1968).
130 Hughes memo, 12 April 1967, NSF: Files of Nathaniel Davis, box 1.
131 See Divine, 'Lyndon Johnson and strategic arms limitation', p. 263.
132 Rusk to LBJ, 26 April 1968, NSF: Files of W. W. Rostow, box 11, folder, 'Strategic missile talks'.
133 *FRUS, 1964–1968*: Volume XI: *Arms Control and Disarmament*, p. 634 (8 July 1968).
134 Seaborg, *Stemming the Tide*, p. 436.
135 Ibid., p. 437.
136 Divine, 'Lyndon Johnson and strategic arms limitation', p. 266.
137 Prados, 'Prague Spring and SALT', p. 28.
138 Seaborg, *Stemming the Tide*, p. 442.

4

The Vietnam War, 1963–66

Vietnam, the USSR and the United States: 1963–65

During 1964 and 1965, the Johnson Administration made a series of decisions which transformed, escalated and Americanised the conflict in Vietnam. The country of Vietnam had been divided at the 17th parallel at the Geneva conference (of which Britain and the Soviet Union were co-chairmen) in 1954. Partition was to be a temporary measure, pending countrywide elections to install a government to succeed the recently defeated French colonial administration. Moscow had provided some aid to the (nationalist and communist-led) Viet Minh in its war against the French, and continued to support the communist Democratic Republic of Vietnam (DRV, or North Vietnam) after 1954. The main external sponsor of both the Viet Minh and the DRV, in this era at least, was China. The consolidation of communist authority in the North, and of US-backed anti-communist regimes in the South, provided the background to the re-emergence of serious conflict after 1960. During John Kennedy's Presidency, the Southern government in Saigon was engaged in a war with nationalist (Viet Cong) guerrillas, seeking to overthrow the pro-American regime and to reunify the country. The free, nationwide elections promised in 1954 were never to occur. For its part, the DRV (or, more correctly, the leadership of the Vietnam Workers' Party or Lao Dong, in the Northern capital of Hanoi) in 1960 created the National Liberation Front (NLF) of South Vietnam, to direct the Southern insurrection. Lyndon Johnson inherited an already militarised US commitment to Saigon's security, albeit as yet without American combat forces.

In January 1964, Soviet leader Nikita Khrushchev wrote an open letter to world governmental heads, calling for the reunification of Germany, Korea and Vietnam. Skating over the nature of Moscow's commitment to East Germany, Khrushchev wrote: 'the question of unification must be resolved by the people of those countries themselves and by their governments, without foreign military interference or occupation, as, for instance, occurs in South Korea and in South Vietnam'.[1] Johnson himself was soon faced by clear evidence not only of North Vietnamese sponsorship of the Viet Cong, but of direct DRV military incursions into the South. In May 1964, he remarked to his old Senatorial friend Richard Russell that the US might be prepared to quit South Vietnam if only Hanoi would refrain from making mischief: 'We tell them, every week, we tell Khrushchev, send China, Hanoi, and all of them word that we would get out of there if they just quit raiding their neighbors, and they just say, screw you'. Russell's view was that a full-scale war in Vietnam would prove to be 'the damnedest mess on earth'.[2]

The US escalation decisions of 1964–65 fell into four main phases: those decisions which culminated in the Congressional passage of the Gulf of Tonkin Resolution (granting LBJ authority to 'respond instantly with the use of appropriate force to repel any unprovoked attack against the armed forces of the United States')[3] on 7 August 1964; the December 1964 decision to embark on an escalation strategy – bombing of the North and possibly the commitment of ground troops; the February 1965 decisions to begin what would soon become the ROLLING THUNDER bombing of North Vietnam, and the sustained bombing of areas of South Vietnam under communist control; and the June–July 1965 decision, announced by LBJ on 28 July, to increase the US troop commitment to 125,000, with additional men to be sent as necessary. Historians disagree as to the importance of various stages in this decisional process, and the debate also remains stubbornly entangled in differing views as to JFK's intentions in Vietnam.[4] For present purposes, the first phase in LBJ's relationship with Moscow, in respect of the Vietnam War, may be deemed as extending from November 1963 to the passage of the Gulf of Tonkin Resolution. The recognition of the Gulf of Tonkin decisions, rather than the fall of Khrushchev, as a key turning point in this story has more than expositional significance. It emphasises that Moscow's stance towards Vietnam, at least in this early phase, was primarily reactive. There was no sudden switch in policy with the ousting of Khrushchev, although Hanoi certainly took the opportunity to press its case forcefully with the new Soviet leaders.[5]

Prior to August 1964, the USSR was concerned about the challenge mounted by Chinese activity in the region to Moscow's role as international leader of communism. However, Moscow did not see Vietnam as a site of vital interest. At this time, the Soviet leaders were arguably more preoccupied with the situation in neighbouring Laos, a country riven by a three-way conflict between neutralist, communist and US-backed rightists. In the early months of 1964, Moscow attempted to restrain Hanoi and to send warnings to the US about the dangers of escalation. At the end of July, Moscow threatened to resign as co-chairman of the Geneva conference on Laos unless the US stepped away from military involvement in Indochina. Official Moscow also criticised 'the Chinese splinters and those who support them'. Though Khrushchev himself in 1961 had championed the cause of 'wars of national liberation', Lao Dong was seen as extremist in the degree of its ideological commitment to the leading revolutionary role to be played by Third World nationalism.[6] In February 1964, the

CIA reported on Moscow's 'reluctance to undertake major new commitments in unproven territory'.[7] During these early months of Johnson's Presidency, it was generally assumed in Washington that Moscow's desire to build détente with the US would inhibit Russian involvement in Vietnam.

The 1964 Gulf of Tonkin Resolution was designed to bolster the regime of General Nguyen Khanh in Saigon, to help LBJ's re-election campaign, and to open the way for sustained airstrikes on the North, possibly even to the introduction of combat troops. The resolution also formed part of the Administration's 'crisis management' approach to the Vietnam crisis: the strategy, adopted from the handling of the Cuban missile crisis, of resolving crisis by sending clear messages of intent. By increasing the temperature surrounding the Vietnam issue, Washington was signalling to Moscow that the time had come to bring the errant Politburo in Hanoi to heel. Secretary Rusk told Republican Senator Bourke Hickenlooper on 6 August that what 'the Russians learned in Cuba could have an influence on the entire world'. The US, in the case of Vietnam, was seeking to make Moscow aware of its intentions: 'For months and months we have been trying to get to them a signal'.[8] (Beijing, of course, was also receiving a signal of US intent. However, the Chinese leaders were seen by Rusk and his fellow American decision-makers as less rational than the Russians, and as not having necessarily learned the lessons of the missile crisis.) The passage of the Gulf of Tonkin resolution followed supposed North Vietnamese attacks on two US ships, and retaliatory bombing of North Vietnam by the US. LBJ's handling of this sequence of events involved a high degree of deceit and disingenuousness.[9]

The official Soviet reaction to America's Gulf of Tonkin retaliation was actually quite moderate. Reporting on a speech made in the UN Security Council by Soviet Representative Morozov, a US State Department official noted: 'One almost had the impression that he was not defending a fellow Communist regime, or at least not *his* kind of Communist regime'.[10] Khrushchev contacted LBJ, urging 'composure and restraint' – albeit in the context of a condemnation of the US aim of 'strengthening somehow the position of the corrupt and rotten South Vietnamese regime'.[11] Johnson replied that the US reserved the right to respond to aggression. In the meantime: 'Anything you can do to restrain either the North Vietnamese or Peiping from further reckless action in this area will be most helpful to peace'.[12] On 8 August, Soviet Foreign Minister Gromyko was reported as having expressed to the Canadian Ambassador to Moscow 'the USSR's irritation at the uncomfortable situation in which it had been placed by the Tonkin Gulf crisis'.[13] Though strong warnings to the US were issued in the Soviet press, there was no significant Soviet military response to the crisis. The general view in Washington was that Moscow was primarily interested in the propaganda war with China, and certainly did not wish to allow events in Southeast Asia to undermine the inter-superpower 'bridge-building' in other areas.

In retrospect, it seems that the Tonkin Gulf crisis was actually more significant to the development of Soviet attitudes towards Vietnam than was apparent at the time. With the US seemingly spoiling for a fight, the Soviet leadership reviewed its policy. The appointment, in late August, of Ilia Scherbakov as Ambassador to Hanoi was indeed a sign of a policy shift. In November, Scherbakov reported that 'the socialist countries, particularly China, will render thorough assistance to the DRV. And the USSR will not be able to remain aside . . .'. Moscow, so Scherbakov advised, should try to mobilise 'world opinion for the soonest political settlement of the South Vietnamese problem on the basis of the Geneva Accords'.[14] The new policy – more aid to Hanoi, combined with efforts to facilitate a settlement – reflected a variety of Soviet aims and motives. There was a feeling of duty to a socialist ally. Soviet leaders may also have begun to calculate the possible geopolitical benefits of a more forceful resistance to US and Chinese influence in the whole South Asian region. Moscow certainly did not wish to be seen as irrelevant to the region's future. A greater military stake in Vietnam might also increase Moscow's leverage – both in terms of issuing warnings to the US, and in respect of organising an international conference to settle Vietnam's affairs.[15]

Moscow was certainly alive to the attractions of undercutting China's claims of credit in the event of a favourable settlement. In 1964 and early 1965, the Soviet and Chinese commitments to the DRV were, superficially at least, very different. The ideological affinity between Hanoi and Beijing manifestly superseded that between the Soviets and the DRV. Beijing encouraged the view that the battle against imperialism in Vietnam would be a long one, but that the purity and historical rectitude of Hanoi's aims would ensure ultimate victory. At one level, the Chinese commitment to the DRV threw down a gauntlet to those in Moscow who wished to 'collude' with Washington. Zhou en Lai, Chinese Foreign Minister and head of Beijing's delegation to the 1954 Geneva conference, declared China to be the 'great rear' of the 'Revolution in South-East Asia'.[16] In June 1964, Mao Zedong promised North Vietnam: 'Your business is my business and my business is your business'.[17] Mao seems consciously to have sought to use the commitment to revolution in Southeast Asia as a force for sustaining revolutionary fervour at home. A Beijing-Hanoi agreement of December 1964 provided for 300,000 Chinese troops to be sent to the DRV.

To President Johnson, the logic of the situation in Vietnam seemed to point, at least in Spring 1964 – LBJ did not have consistent views on this issue – in the direction of cooperation between Washington and Moscow. He made this explicit in a March 1964 conversation with Robert McNamara: 'Looks to me that the Russians would be more interested in saving Vietnam than we are'. To LBJ at this time, any commitment of Soviet aid to Hanoi appeared either to contradict Moscow's interests; or (more likely) to rest on the assumption that America would keep China at bay in Asia, whatever policy was being followed by the Kremlin. He even compared Moscow's position towards China with France's attitude towards Soviet power in Europe.[18]

LBJ's view, as sketched above, tended to ignore the degree to which Hanoi might succeed in orchestrating the competition between the big communist powers, so that Soviet and Chinese aid increased in parallel. This point was cogently made in July 1965 by John McCloy (one of LBJ's 'Wise Men' group of advisers). McCloy argued that the Soviets might be brought increasingly to what he called an ' "annealing" of the Sino-Soviet relationship, i.e., the Soviets competing with the Chinese and acting on parallel lines, although with no necessary resolution of the basic policy differences between them'.[19] In other respects, the contrast between the tepid Soviet attitude and the perceived boiling hot enthusiasm of Beijing for the DRV (and Viet Cong) cause was more apparent than real. For one thing, even in this relatively early phase of the war against the US, Hanoi was not unmindful that Vietnamese nationalism had traditionally been asserted *against* China. When Hanoi decided at the Ninth Plenum of the Lao Dong, in December 1963, to escalate the war in the South, it did not intend to cast itself adrift from Moscow. In fact, in 1963, Hanoi reportedly rejected a large offer of Chinese aid because it came only on condition that the DRV should refuse all Soviet aid.[20] In August 1964, UN Secretary General U Thant not only told Johnson that Ho Chi Minh, the leader of the DRV, was more nationalist than communist. He was also 'probably pro-Moscow rather than pro-Peking now'.[21] In addition, though Beijing was committed to the NLF and to the doctrine of 'people's war', the China did not necessarily share Hanoi's absolute priority of reunification under socialism. R. K. Brigham, in his study of the diplomacy of the NLF, argues that Beijing 'preferred a pro-China southern regime to a Moscow-leaning unified Viet Nam'.[22] The 'people's war' doctrine did not encompass any automatic commitment to direct intervention in such conflicts. Beijing frequently declared that the anti-imperialist war in Vietnam would and could be won without the China's People's Liberation Army (PLA) actually participating in the fighting.[23] In July 1965, Llewellyn Thompson pointed out to Secretary Rusk that China's apparently universalistic revolutionary zeal should perhaps not be taken too seriously: 'The Chinese did not invent nor have they been in the past the principal supporters of the doctrine of national liberation. The Soviets are equally committed to the concept of wars of national liberation'.[24] Both China and Russia were in the 'great rear', rather than on the exposed cutting edge, of the Vietnam conflict.

The visit of a DRV delegation to Moscow in November 1964 was the occasion of an agreement, at least in principle, to provide substantial Soviet aid. A heated exchange between Rusk and Gromyko in December involved the former promising a 'real scrap', if Hanoi and Beijing did not allow their neighbours to live in peace.[25] On 3 February 1965, the CIA reported that some (fairly elderly) Soviet anti-aircraft weapons had been sighted in North

Vietnam. Soviet aid to Hanoi was starting to flow in the wake of clear evidence that communist forces in South Vietnam were making significant military gains. On 1 February, Robert Komer told McGeorge Bundy that 'my hunch is that Soviets have decided we're probably licked in VN, and are climbing on the bandwagon'.[26] Moscow had just announced a high profile trip to Hanoi by Premier Kosygin. Bundy reported to LBJ from Saigon on 7 February that prospects there were 'grim': 'without a new US action defeat appears inevitable'.[27] On the same day, an artillery attack was launched against a US marine compound at Pleiku, in the central highlands, with a further assault on the coastal Qui Nhon base occurring three days later. On 7 and 8 February (with Kosygin in Hanoi) and on 11 February (with Kosygin in Beijing), the US made retaliatory bombing attacks on the North. On 13 February, LBJ authorised a programme of 'measured and limited' bombing. The ROLLING THUNDER programme proper began on 2 March. The original start was to have been a day earlier. This would have coincided with a major gathering of international communists in Moscow. McNamara warned LBJ against ordering a start to sustained bombing on 1 March: 'That would stir up the Russians and push them closer to the Chinese'.[28]

Pleiku, Kosygin and ROLLING THUNDER

'Pleikus are like streetcars': McGeorge Bundy's remark, made to a reporter some weeks after the incident, seemed to acknowledge that the Pleiku attack was just a pretext for launching sustained bombing; if Pleiku had not come along when it did, another pretext would have done equally well. To a generation, Bundy's remark epitomised the cynicism which led the US into a disastrous war.[29]

In some respects, given the commitments already made in principle to a bombing campaign, the opportunity provided by the Pleiku raid was no doubt too good to miss. The timing of the attack certainly strengthened the case for escalation being prepared by Bundy as he left Saigon for Washington. What, however, of the presence of the Soviet leader in the North Vietnamese capital? Bombing the DRV with Kosygin in residence was bound to provoke Soviet outrage. Ambassador Dobrynin protested on 9 February about 'arbitrary acts' of retaliation. How, he asked, could military action in South Vietnam (presumably by the Viet Cong) 'be the basis for an armed attack on another state?'. On 12 March, he harangued Vice President Humphrey: 'Can you imagine the USSR bombing another country being visited by President Johnson?'.[30]

The US retaliation did not affect the city of Hanoi itself. However, Kosygin's presence there must have added considerably to LBJ's anxieties as he faced what Lady Bird Johnson called the 'tense and shadowed' day of 7 February.[31] After all, there was always the possibility of Soviet retaliation in Berlin. (American officials tended to comfort themselves with the thought that no such action had occurred during the Cuban missile crisis.) In view of all this, it is rather surprising that the first White House meeting, called to discuss the crisis, did not split more drastically on the issue of bombing while Kosygin was in residence. (The meeting began at 7.45 p.m. on 6 February, a short time after the Pleiku attack had commenced in the early hours of 7 February, Vietnam time.) According to William Colby's notes of the meeting, Senator Mansfield opposed the retaliation *per se*, arguing that it would 'assist the healing of the Soviet-Sino split'. Llewellyn Thompson, however – who might have been expected to counsel restraint at least until Kosygin was clear – at first, argued that the Soviets would protest but that 'inaction would be worse'. Even George Ball acquiesced in the retaliation, saying that 'the main problem would be how to handle the publicity and the Kosygin connection'.[32] Vice President Humphrey, who was not present at the initial meeting, led such opposition to the bombing as existed in the Administration. At a National Security Council meeting on 8 February, Ball – in the words of CIA Director John McCone – 'seemed to argue for positive action'. Bundy made it clear that the 'reprisal' for Pleiku would not be one single action – though it would be publicised as such. It would inaugurate 'a continuing series of actions', along the lines of the bombing campaign agreed upon in late 1964. The 8 February meeting agreed that the Soviets should be informed that the attacks would be directed towards targets in the South of the DRV, and out of range of Soviet MIG fighters. According to McCone: 'The President recognized the problem of delaying until after Kosygin left Hanoi but he believed that Kosygin was there to give the North Vietnamese substantial help'.[33]

The question of delaying further bombing until Kosygin was safely back in Moscow was raised at a top-level meeting held on 10 February. (Kosygin left Hanoi for Beijing on 10 February. He travelled to North Korea on 11 February.) Ball, Llewellyn Thompson and Vice President Hubert Humphrey now wished to delay. Rather cavalierly, Bundy remarked: 'We cannot put ourselves in the position of giving the Russians control over our actions by their moving Soviet diplomats from one place to another'.[34] (McCone's notes of the 8 February meeting had criticised Thompson for 'implying that our whole South Vietnamese policy must be governed by what the Soviets say'.)[35] On 10 February, Ball, Thompson and Humphrey were overruled by LBJ.

Not surprisingly, the Pleiku incident has given rise to various conspiracy theories. The simplest of these harks back to Bundy's 'Pleikus are like streetcars' remark. The 'retaliation' for the Pleiku attack unquestionably was little more than a cover beneath which to begin the already agreed escalation strategy. More complex conspiracy theories, however, relate to Kosygin's presence in Hanoi. In order to unravel these theories, it is necessary to examine the purposes of and circumstances surrounding Kosygin's Vietnamese trip.

The trip was certainly the culmination of the rethinking of Soviet policy towards Vietnam which had begun at the time of the Gulf of Tonkin crisis.

The visit was a symbolic affair, designed to advertise Moscow's commitment to the DRV cause. It was also the occasion of an agreement on military aid. Leading military figures in the delegation – notably Marshal Vershinin – were there to discuss deployment of modern, mainly defensive Soviet weaponry: notably, surface-to-air anti-aircraft (SAM) missiles, MIG 15/17 aircraft fighters, armoured personnel carriers, and possibly IL-28 light bombers. (All were subsequently transferred to North Vietnam. Ilya Gaiduk also makes the point that the US military had considered the IL-28s an *offensive* weapon during the Cuban missile crisis.)[36] In explaining the purposes of the visit, Foy Kohler (US Ambassador to Moscow) pointed to the Soviets' 'obvious interest in demonstrating their reliability as socialist ally in face of goading' by China.[37] The CIA's view, before the visit occurred, was that it 'was motivated by growing Soviet concern that both sides in the Indochina conflict may be contemplating actions which could lead to a rapid escalation of the war'.[38] Kosygin was trying to warn *both* sides – and also, presumably, China when he visited there after leaving Hanoi – of the perils of excessive provocation. The aid agreement, in this reading, lent these warnings greater credibility. The Soviets were certainly sending very mixed signals. A *Pravda* article of 31 January actually welcomed LBJ's comments about US–Soviet relations in the 1965 State of the Union Address.[39] On 15 February, a State Department Policy Planning memorandum (drafted by John Huizenga) interpreted the visit in light of a putative commitment by Moscow to a 'middle way' between Washington and Beijing.[40] In April, the CIA judged that Kosygin had wished both to aid *and* warn Hanoi.[41]

At least five conspiracy theories have been developed in connection with the bombing of North Vietnam while Kosygin was visiting Hanoi. The first theory is that the US deliberately acted to quash Kosygin's efforts to urge restraint on Hanoi. In this line of interpretation, the US wished to side-step any suggestion of moving to negotiation. LBJ and his advisers wanted, simply and straightforwardly, to push ahead with the bombing. The suggestion is not (as far as I know) that the US itself was somehow responsible for the Pleiku and Qui Nhon attacks. Rather, the raids were part of an ongoing conflict, and not of a scale demanding immediate retaliation. Moreover, the US had no time to assess the damage and provenance of the Pleiku attack before it hit back. LBJ's response was designed to stop short Kosygin's peace initiative. At the very least, it was designed deliberately to send a clear signal to Kosygin – in a way comparable to that sent by the Gulf of Tonkin Resolution – that Washington saw Moscow's proper role as one of disciplining Hanoi, rather than urging it to negotiate.[42]

The second conspiracy theory is that advanced by LBJ's advisers themselves: that, as Llewellyn Thompson told Ambassador Dobrynin on 7 February, 'this was a deliberate attempt on the part of Hanoi to, as we would put it, "mouse trap" Mr Kosygin'. Thompson's version, as put to Dobrynin, was that Hanoi and Beijing wished 'to say that they had demonstrated that the United States was a paper tiger'.[43] Hanoi felt that the US would not retaliate while Kosygin was in residence. America's spinelessness would be evident. A slightly different tack was taken by Ambassador Kohler on 15 February in his report to Washington. Kosygin was described by Kohler as the 'victim of DRV plot'. If the US retaliated after the Pleiku raid, then the Soviet leader would have to 'fish or cut bait'. He would either have to reveal himself as an objective ally of American imperialism, or make a wholehearted commitment to Hanoi's cause. In any case, the unwanted pressure to negotiate would cease. If the US did not retaliate, Washington would indeed be exposed as a 'paper tiger'.[44] With nothing to fear from the US, Moscow would increase aid to the DRV in the expectation of securing some credit from the inevitable communist victory.

The third, fourth and fifth conspiracy theories may be summarised more briefly. The third is really a variant on the Hanoi 'mouse trap' idea. The CIA report of 9 April referred to the opinion being voiced by Soviet officials that 'the Chinese had inspired the Viet Cong raid [on Pleiku] in order to embarrass Kosygin and disrupt Soviet–US relations'.[45] The fourth theory involves a Russian, rather than a Chinese, plot. R. B. Smith suggests that Moscow may have been a party to the Pleiku attack. The Soviets wished to portray the deployment of SAM missiles and other military equipment as a direct response to American aggression. They may also 'have regarded the American attacks as a useful means to remind Peking of its ultimate dependence on Moscow in any major global confrontation'.[46] Finally, there is the possibility, raised for example by John Prados,[47] that Pleiku was purely a Southern Viet Cong operation, designed not only to 'mouse trap' Kosygin, but also to manipulate Hanoi.

The first conspiracy theory – Pleiku as an excuse for Washington to kill Kosygin's peace mission – has some force. George M. Kahin points out that Washington had every reason to expect a brisk resumption of communist hostilities after the ending in early February of the Tet (Vietnamese New Year) cease-fire. He quotes Allen S. Whiting, Far Eastern Research Director at State, to the effect that Bundy was expecting a major raid while he was in Saigon. Kahin also establishes that Bundy knew the dates of the Kosygin trip before arranging his own visit – in effect, a final assessment before beginning the bombing programme – to South Vietnam.[48] One line in Colby's notes on 6 February also seems to indicate the possibility of a conspiracy to bomb while Kosygin was in Hanoi: LBJ, according to Colby's record, 'emphasized the necessity . . . to permit Kosygin the belief that he had been mouse-trapped by the North Vietnamese'.[49] Against this line of conspiracy theorising, it should be pointed out that the US could only guess at the real purpose of Kosygin's visit. Washington cannot have known exactly what was being discussed. As the CIA later concluded, Kosygin seems to have been in Hanoi to talk war *and* peace. Pleiku was not a minor incident. The raid was carried out by around 300 Viet Cong sappers, operating with covering fire. A simultaneous attack was made on the nearby US II Corps headquarters. In what was the start of a major communist offensive, nine Americans were killed. Bundy himself visited the Pleiku compound: David Halberstam reported on the emotional intensity of Bundy's response. Also worthy of note is that fact that De Soto patrols, intelligence-gathering missions off the North Vietnamese coast, were suspended in order *not* to raise tension as Kosygin visited Hanoi. In a sense, Pleiku was a pretext – a 'streetcar' – to set in motion a previously agreed programme.[50] However, the balance of the documentary record suggests that post-Pleiku 'reprisals' began in spite of, not because of, Kosygin's presence in Hanoi.

The second, North Vietnamese 'mouse-trapping' conspiracy theory is highly persuasive, though unproven. In 1997, General Dang Vu Hiep, NLF political officer in the region in 1964, denied any 'mouse-trapping'.[51] Chinese complicity was possible, though the leading academic study of Beijing's involvement in the war finds no evidence of it.[52] Russian complicity seems very unlikely, and was discounted by the CIA's assessment.[53] South Vietnamese manipulation of Hanoi also seems unlikely. A Hanoi Politburo meeting of January 1965 had enthusiastically backed a renewed NLF guerrilla campaign. It would have been rather unlikely – as Washington appreciated – that a figure like Le Duan, the Politburo member responsible for coordinating the NLF, would have been ignorant of the Pleiku operation.[54]

The Soviet official response to the bombing rapidly developed into a major propaganda campaign against US militarism. On 27 February, before the actual start of ROLLING THUNDER, Kosygin forecast that the Vietnam War would 'spread beyond its present boundaries' unless Washington curbed its aggression. On 23 March, Brezhnev spoke of the many Soviet 'volunteers' who had gone to fight in Vietnam. The prospect of actual Soviet military intervention was raised by commentators like Drew Pearson and by the US academic Hans Morgenthau, following a visit to Moscow. In April, *Pravda* published a joint Moscow–Hanoi statement to the effect that Soviet citizens might be encouraged to go to Vietnam as military volunteers. Soviet cosmonaut Yuri Gagarin was reported in early 1966 as 'admitting' that Soviet forces were fighting in Vietnam. By late 1965, the Soviet press was regularly condemning the putative 'Johnson Doctrine' of global domination by the US.[55]

Moscow's propaganda campaign and talk of 'volunteers' should be seen in the context of the competition with China. Far from healing the Sino-Soviet split, ROLLING THUNDER appeared to exacerbate it. Brezhnev's reference to 'volunteers' may have been a direct response to Beijing's accusation that Moscow's racism prevented it from sending Russian men to protect its 'yellow brothers'.[56] Ambassador Kohler interpreted the 'volunteers' remark as a reference to Soviet technicians, working on the SAM sites.[57] Significant amounts of Soviet aid to the DRV war effort began to flow in March 1965. China refused to grant an air corridor to facilitate a Soviet airlift, though Beijing did cooperate in transporting Russian aid through its territory. Quiang Zhai concludes that stories of China actually sabotaging shipments of Soviet aid are probably not particularly reliable. Nevertheless, Hanoi learned in this period that the Moscow–Beijing rivalry need not always work to its advantage. The rivalry effectively prevented the DRV from developing an integrated logistical support system.[58]

The first US aircraft to be shot down from a SAM site, staffed by Soviet technicians, was an F-4, downed on 24 July. Two days later, LBJ ordered air strikes on two SAM sites. Johnson characteristically fretted over the implications of killing Russian technicians. Rusk advised that 'nothing be said about the Russians being there'. Johnson's worries were resolved in a rhetorical question: 'Are we going to sit and sit and let them knock down our planes?'. The Presidential instinct for compromise resulted in attacks being made on two of seven identified sites. The operation was a fiasco. One of the chosen sites was a dummy and the other merely a temporary position for mobile SAM equipment. Six US F-105s were lost.[59]

The 1965 escalation decisions

Washington policy-makers generally did not share the perception that the USSR was likely in 1965–66 to intervene directly in Vietnam. Official Washington was well aware of the 'grandstanding' dimension to Soviet public attitudes. Moscow's interest in the Vietnam bombing, for example, contrasted sharply with an apparent lack of concern over the more clandestine US 1965 air campaign in Laos.[60]

Nonetheless, anticipated Soviet reactions to escalation were never far from the thoughts of those Americans who made the key decisions of 1964–65. At one level, the CIA consistently advised that Moscow, whatever it said publicly, was cautious about its Vietnam involvement. On 11 February 1965, for example, the CIA concluded: 'Although the Soviets would perceive military risks in more direct involvement, they would expect to be able to keep these at a tolerable level and far from the Soviet homeland'.[61] Mac Bundy told Senator Mansfield during the Pleiku crisis that US intelligence was clear that Moscow did not wish to sacrifice détente to any desire to become directly involved in Vietnam.[62] As the bombing intensified, the CIA began to speculate on the possibility of a direct confrontation with China, and the implications for Russia of the 1950 Sino-Soviet Friendship Treaty. However, in April 1965, the CIA reported: 'The USSR is less concerned than the other Communist states to defeat the US in South Vietnam'. Russia was mainly bothered that Beijing would claim credit for any NLF victory.[63] As he made his final determination to commit mass ground troops in July 1965, LBJ was given intelligence advice to the effect that Moscow might increase pressure on Berlin, but would most probably respond simply in terms of a general increase in military spending.[64]

LBJ constantly sought reassurances about the Soviet response to escalation. On 17 February, he asked General Eisenhower about the prospects of China and Russia entering the war. Ike responded that 'if they threaten to intervene we should pass the word back to them to take care lest dire results occur to them'. The US should be prepared to face off Soviet threats to Berlin.[65] Some of LBJ's advisers certainly did think that escalation could lead to a war with Moscow. On 18 June 1965, George Ball wrote to Johnson that 'if our air attacks threaten the total destruction of the North Vietnamese economy, Red China can hardly help but react'. In this event, 'our best Soviet experts do not believe that the Soviet Union could stand down' if the US 'became involved directly with the Chinese'.[66] Famously, at the 25 July meeting at Camp David, Clark Clifford declared: 'Russia and China don't intend for us to win this war'.[67]

Johnson proceeded with the air and ground escalation against the background of reasonably reassuring intelligence estimates of the possibility of fighting a geographically limited conflict. Memories of Chinese intervention in the Korean War recurred frequently during the 1965 escalation debates. LBJ seemed to reassure himself that, if there were no actual ground invasion of the DRV, all would be well. On 20 July, Robert McNamara argued that 'so long as we do not invade North Vietnam, do not sink a Chinese ship and, most important, do not strike China', Beijing would not intervene directly. However, with increased DRV infiltration into the South, there would be pressures on Washington to 'counter-invade' the North, 'acceding to these pressures could bring the Soviets and the Chinese in'.[68]

LBJ was beset by doubts. In May 1964 he had told Richard Russell that Moscow *would* ultimately back Beijing against the US: 'They wouldn't forsake that Communist philosophy'.[69] As the final point of the decisional process was reached in July 1965, Johnson agonised over the dangers of nuclear war. He told Eisenhower that 'State Department people' regarded the Pentagon as 'taking too much chance on bringing China and Russia in'.[70] He quizzed Generals Earle Wheeler (chairman of the Joint Chiefs) and Harold Johnson (Army Chief of Staff) about this fear. 'If we come in with hundreds of thousands of men', asked LBJ, 'won't this cause them to come in (China and Russia)?'. With General Johnson replying in the negative, LBJ continued: 'MacArthur didn't think they would come in either'. The General said that Korea was not comparable to Vietnam, but that, if China did come in, 'we have another ball game'.[71]

The decisions were excruciating for the President, with the apparent inexorability of the decisional outcome compounding his agony. LBJ, the great controller, most certainly did not feel in control of events. Lady Bird recorded her husband on 8 July as saying: 'Vietnam is getting worse every day'. The

President had 'the choice to go in with great casualty lists or to get out with disgrace'.[72]

Accounts of LBJ's decisions to Americanise the war generally, and correctly, emphasise his domestic concerns: to find a middle way between advocates of restraint and of aggression; to avoid 'disgrace'; to deflect criticisms of his Administration in order to protect the Great Society. In the last analysis, however, the decisions were made on the basis of the prior (and largely unexamined) commitments to anti-communist containment, America's mission to protect freedom, and the Munich analogy. Johnson and his advisers kept returning to these concerns. On 30 June, for example, Mac Bundy reminded LBJ that the US was 'responding to the call of a people under Communist assault'.[73] If LBJ wished to have his faith in containment reaffirmed, he needed to look no farther than his Secretary of State. In comparison with most of the Vietnam advisers, and indeed with Johnson himself, Rusk was a rock of certainty. 'If the communist world', he declared on 21 July 1965, 'found out that the United States would not pursue its commitment to the end, there was no telling where they would stop their expansionisms'.[74] In this formulation, various communisms – Soviet, Chinese, Vietnamese – were, in the final decisional analysis, just aspects of this threatening 'communist world'.

Prospects for negotiations

Secretary Rusk, perhaps more securely than LBJ himself, retained throughout his life a firm allegiance to the ideas of the domino theory and globalised containment – ideas rooted in the invocation of a, more or less unified, threat posed by the 'communist world'. Yet Rusk and Johnson also appreciated that there was a Sino-Soviet split and that there were complex divisions and distinctions within world communism. The two trends of thought were not necessarily irreconcilable: Rusk and Johnson saw the intra-communist splits as akin to dissension within a family which might, if exposed to extreme stress, eventually come together. Yet foundational beliefs – about the potentially unified threat of international communism, about the geopolitical necessity of retaining commitments to South Vietnam – tended to undermine the possibility of exploiting Moscow's apparent desire for peace as a way of achieving a settlement in Vietnam.

In February 1965, Rusk explained to Congressional leaders that the US did not wish to provoke Moscow unnecessarily over Vietnam: 'This is one of the reasons we haven't taken this question to the Security Council of the United Nations. We don't want to force them into the role of an advocate, when it might be they might wish to be somewhat more in the role of the middleman'.[75] Between 1964 and 1966, even as Moscow became more committed to Hanoi, Washington retained the view that the Soviets could act as middlemen. In February 1965, General Maxwell Taylor, then serving as US Ambassador

in Saigon, joined other regional US ambassadors in support of a Soviet intercession. It was 'important', according to the ambassadors, 'that Soviets receive
accurate indications that we would not oppose continuing Soviet role in
DRV . . .'.[76] Here was a leading US decision-maker actually writing in favour
of the involvement of America's main Cold War enemy!

There were, however, major difficulties with the Soviet intercessionary 'middleman' idea. As we shall see below, not only was Moscow often unwilling to
perform the role, Hanoi also often took little notice when it did. There was
also the fundamental difficulty, described above, of perceiving of the Soviet
Union as a US ally, at least in a limited sense, rather than as part of the threatening 'communist world'. At the most obvious level, of course, there was the
problem of finding common ground for a settlement. Frederik Logevall has
made a persuasive case to the effect that the US turned deliberately aside from
various hints and initiatives from Moscow between 1963 and 1965. In late
1963, the US rejected the idea of a conference to settle the future of Cambodia. In May and August 1965, a Laotian conference, supported by Moscow,
was similarly rejected. In both instances, the US objected to the principle of
neutralisation of these countries. (In the case of Laos, it would have been
'reneutralisation', following the original Laotian neutralisation in 1962.)
Washington felt, argues Logevall, that not only had the Laotian experiment
of 1962 been a failure, but that further neutralisations would lead to calls for
the same principle to be applied in Vietnam. (The Laotian neutralisation, of
course, provided the background to the opening of the Ho Chi Minh trail, the
DRV's main supply route to the South, through Laos and Cambodia. US soldiers called the trail 'The Averell Harriman Freeway', after the leading US
negotiator at the 1962 Geneva Conference.)[77] The campaign to reconvene the
Geneva Conference on Vietnam was joined by France, UN Secretary General
U Thant and, only a little less enthusiastically, by Lord Harlech, the British
Ambassador to Washington. In July 1965, the USSR stated clearly its
support.[78]

The US was certainly guilty of giving conflicting signals about its desire to
negotiate. Anatoly Dobrynin later recalled a meeting in March 1965 when he
had been informed by Vice President Humphrey that the US would accept any
government in South Vietnam 'even if it eventually turned socialist'. The US
was only concerned not to 'give in to Beijing's pressure'.[79] Moscow at this time
would almost certainly have backed a settlement which allowed the US to dis-
engage without immediate humiliation. The problem for the US, however, was
– whatever Humphrey said in March 1965 – the prospect of a communist,
reunified Vietnam in the medium term, presumably following national elections. For its part, Hanoi was unwilling to give the US an opportunity to shore
up even a transitional government in the South, strengthening popular
anti-communism by an investment programme. Dobrynin later commented:
'Hanoi stubbornly refused to accept this kind of gradual settlement and to

halt its military operation to unify the whole of Vietnam under the banner of socialism'.[80]

For Washington, as it went to war in 1965, neutralisation of Vietnam represented a ceding of the South. Hanoi could not be trusted. In February 1964, Rusk and LBJ discussed a French suggestion to neutralise the country. The Secretary commented: 'in probing that point with the Russians, it's been very clear that the Communist side is not about to neutralize North Vietnam'.[81] As Humphrey did indicate to Dobrynin, the US certainly also wished to avoid any humiliating concessions, especially when, as in 1965, the communists seemed to be winning. On 21 February, Rusk told Lord Harlech that 'London and Moscow must not believe that embarking on the Co-Chairman process' (to reconvene the 1954 Geneva conference) 'would be accompanied by a unilateral cease-fire by the US'. (Moscow had already made it clear that reconvening Geneva, while the US was bombing the North, was out of the question.)[82] Mac Bundy continually emphasised that the US should negotiate only from a position of strength.

Diplomatic exchanges between Moscow and Washington, over the issue of negotiations, centred on three 1965–66 initiatives: the MAYFLOWER bombing pause; the Averell Harriman – Kosygin conversations of July 1965; and the 1965–66 Christmas bombing pause.

John Colvin, the British Consul in Hanoi, later recalled the view of Scherbakov, the Soviet Ambassador, that the DRV 'probably would negotiate if there were to be a halt in the bombing'.[83] Over two months into the full ROLLING THUNDER campaign, LBJ decided to initiate a pause. Moscow was asked to deliver a message to Hanoi. The role was rejected. When Ambassador Kohler met Soviet Deputy Foreign Minister Nikolai Firyubin, he was told: 'I am not a postman'.[84] (The message informed Hanoi that air attacks would be suspended from 12 May; if North Vietnamese-inspired military action were significantly reduced during the pause, progress towards negotiation might ensue.) Kohler eventually had the message handed to an employee at the North Vietnamese Embassy in Moscow. Bundy reported on 13 May that 'the whole Soviet Government is embarrassed by the notion of admitting it has any middle-man's role with respect to Hanoi'.[85] In fact, the whole affair was bungled; it was, as McNamara later admitted 'a propaganda effort' by the US.[86] Discussions with former Hanoi diplomats in the 1990s revealed the extent of the DRV's reluctance to be seen by China to be negotiating with Washington, especially with Moscow acting as intermediary.[87] Moscow's behaviour presumably indicated its low estimate of the chances for any success for the MAYFLOWER effort, as well as a sensitivity to being seen to be acting as Washington's 'postman'.

That Moscow was not entirely uninterested in a 'middleman' role was evident in its arrangement of a meeting for 14 May between Pierre Salinger, Presidential press secretary at the start of the Johnson Administration and now a private visitor to the USSR, and two officials. Salinger was told of Soviet interest in a peace scheme that excluded – in the words of Kohler's report on the meeting – 'the possibility of American military presence in South Vietnam after neutralist-type government agreed on'.[88] Yugoslavia was suggested as a suitable initial go-between, but with unofficial (and deniable) Soviet involvement. This apparent opening was shut off by Foreign Minister Gromyko when he met Rusk in Vienna on the following day. George Ball told LBJ that his best guess was that the Russians 'had talks with the North Vietnamese Ambassador in Moscow and cold water was thrown on' the Salinger discussions.[89] Rusk reported to LBJ on 16 May that there was clearly 'nothing on the Russian side to cause us to hold off bombing', which quickly resumed.[90]

The MAYFLOWER debacle increased the level of distrust between Moscow and Washington. Considering a June bombing pause, Mac Bundy noted that such a pause might give the Soviets some leverage for urging peace on Hanoi, but as for the Soviet commitment – 'Very doubtful, on the evidence of May'.[91] At a lunch given for George Kennan at Spaso House (Ambassador Kohler's residence in Moscow), Gromyko complained that LBJ was following in Vietnam the policies associated with Barry Goldwater. The May episode had been 'insulting'. However, Gromyko did not rule out Soviet intercession and confirmed that Moscow still valued détente in bilateral US relations.[92]

The Averell Harriman dialogue with Kosygin was the result of various initiatives within the Administration, designed to keep open the prospect of Soviet mediation. Harriman himself, veteran diplomat and now being used as a peace ambassador by LBJ, emerged as the most visible proponent of working with Moscow. He was supported by Chester Cooper and James Thomson of the NSC staff, both of whom lobbied for a reconvening of the Geneva conference.[93] LBJ, however, was also advised by the CIA that the US should only bargain from strength – when 'we have demonstrated we can stop and turn back VC/DRV attacks'.[94] McNamara weighed in on Harriman's side, urging that the way forward was to persuade Moscow that the US recognised the Soviet need to assert its leadership of world communism.[95]

The eventual meeting with Kosygin followed complex exchanges, wherein Moscow expressed a willingness to mediate but also threatened 'in low key' to put pressure on Berlin if the US remained 'unyielding'.[96] In his first conversation with Harriman (held in Moscow on 15 July) Kosygin offered a vigorous, if standard defence of the communist cause in Vietnam: 'the South Vietnamese would fight with bamboo sticks, if necessary, against the current regime there'. US policy, said Kosygin, only served to 'prove the Chinese point that war is inevitable'. Harriman stressed LBJ's sincerity in wanting to negotiate and 'assured Kosygin that the US will not stand by and see country after country fall under Peiping's heel'.[97] The second Harriman-Kosygin conversation, on 21 July, produced a clearer Soviet line on the way to negotiations. The Soviet leader stated that a settlement would be possible 'on the basis of the retention of the 17th parallel' (in other words, involving some kind of recognition for South Vietnam). The US should, said Kosygin, move to issue counterproposals to Hanoi's Four Points.[98] (The Four Points, issued in April 1965, demanded the exit of the US military from the South, no foreign alliances pending reunification, recognising interim NLF authority in South Vietnam, and reunification on a basis of Vietnamese self-determination. To a few Americans, notably George Ball, the points seemed to offer some hope of curbing Soviet and Chinese influence over a reunified Vietnam.)[99] Harriman reported that Kosygin had indicated Moscow's willingness to accept a divided Vietnam. In the second conversation, Kosygin's 'biggest concern', according to Harriman, was 'the embarrassing position the Soviets are caught in. And he wants a settlement'.[100]

The conversations, much to Harriman's consternation, came to naught. Analysing them for Rusk on 22 July, Thomas Hughes, State's Director of Intelligence and Research, noted Kosygin's 'omission of a demand for cessation of bombing and his abstention from any threat of greater Soviet involvement'. However the contrast between the first and second conversations, the linking of issues of progress on disarmament to loosening on Vietnam and continuing public hostility to Washington all pointed to Soviet unreliability and to attempts to manipulate the West.[101] In any case, by this time, the escalation decisions were almost complete. LBJ had accepted the CIA – Mac Bundy line that, if there were to be negotiations, they must reflect a position of strength on the ground. Washington, of course, was also concerned that a failure to show strength would encourage independent approaches to Hanoi from Saigon. Rusk apparently did muse on the possibility of 'dickering' with the Four Points, and contacts were made with (a generally stonewalling) Dobrynin.[102] The Secretary of State told Congressional leaders on 27 July that 'there was no real reason for a basic difference between the US and USSR on Vietnam, but that Moscow had no real influence on the ground'.[103] (This was on the day after the ill fated SAM site attacks!) From LBJ's viewpoint, Harriman's Moscow adventure seems to have been a characteristic, almost pantomimic 'final, final' probing before the 28 July announcement of huge troop increases.

It now seems rather extraordinary that the July escalations were accompanied by a renewal of optimism in Washington. On 30 July, McNamara argued that 'the bombing program offers the Soviet Union an opportunity to play a role in bringing peace to Vietnam by gaining credit for persuading us to terminate the program'.[104] The Secretary's logic seemed rather convoluted in face of the rising international protest against ROLLING THUNDER. By August, the Administration was seriously considering another pause. CIA assessments argued that the Soviets were still interested in mediation, despite the widening of targets in the US bombing campaign.[105] Various hints from Moscow – for example, through Dobrynin, via remarks made by Gromyko to Rusk in

September, and from comments made to *Foreign Affairs* editor, Hamilton Fish Armstrong, in November[106] – seemed to suggest that McNamara's optimism was justified. Gromyko reassured Rusk: 'if Hanoi come to a conference at which the Soviet Union and the United States were present . . . Peiping would not use force to prevent it'.[107] On 27 November, Bundy informed LBJ of 'growing evidence that we can count on quiet but strong Soviet diplomatic support in pushing Hanoi toward the conference table during another pause'.[108] Rusk argued at an 18 December meeting that the US should try to create an obligation on Russia's part to intervene during a pause: 'If we pause, they will owe us something'. He agreed with McNamara that a pause would also help widen the Sino-Soviet gap. LBJ's final comment at the meeting revealed the doubts and uncertainty which accompanied every stage of his Vietnam decision-making: 'You say the Russians won't and can't do any more unless we stop bombing. And they probably won't do anything'.[109]

The pause lasted, eventually, for 37 days from 24 December. It developed into a major 'peace offensive' with US envoys being sent around the world. Harriman visited eleven countries, though not the Soviet Union 'because they might be willing to do something quietly but not otherwise'.[110] Moscow's quiet diplomacy during the pause amounted to little more than the encouragement of contacts between Hanoi and the Polish Foreign Ministry, and a visit to the DRV by Soviet Communist Party Secretary Alexander Shelepin. The CIA, commenting on Shelepin's trip in January 1966, assumed that it did involve some genuine effort to promote negotiations. The US 'peace offensive' had, according to the CIA, been met with caution by Moscow, but not with the customary 'sharp, negative reaction'.[111] If Shelepin was advancing to Hanoi the case for negotiations, he was not successful. His mission was also routinely condemned by Beijing.[112] Shelepin certainly did not go to Hanoi as in any sense an envoy of Washington. In fact, he actually agreed a new aid package, with (in George Ball's account) 'a substantial component of military assistance'.[113]

Washington felt that it had been doubly deceived by Moscow: concerning both the degree of Soviet commitment to mediate, and the objective prospects for peace. The resentful mood was increased as the CIA reported in January 1966 on the possibility of Moscow deploying nuclear missiles in North Vietnam. The CIA speculated that the Soviets were considering such deployments in the event of the war developing into a 'stalemate', in which the US might actually tolerate nuclear missiles in the DRV. The main inhibition to these deployments might be Soviet fears of 'being at the mercy of Chinese supply lines'.[114]

The disappointment of, and American sense of betrayal associated with, the 1965 Christmas bombing pause were to cast long shadows over subsequent efforts to secure peace via Soviet diplomacy. Johnson later blamed the Russians for having 'sold' the idea of a 'long pause' to Mac Bundy, and subsequently to McNamara.[115] LBJ certainly felt that Moscow had retreated perfidiously from what Dobrynin had 'told us' about the possibilities of negotiation.[116] Moreover Washington's view on this was compounded by its judgment that the US had now moved a long way towards Kosygin's July suggestion to Harriman that a clear, negotiating response be made to Hanoi's Four Points. On 3 January 1966, the State Department emulated President Woodrow Wilson in issuing its own, fourteen point negotiating plan. This plan incorporated one key shift in the US position. As LBJ declared in his January 1966 State of the Union Address, in seeking to begin negotiations under the rubric of the 1954 Geneva Agreement, the US would now consider the 'views of any group'. This was a clear reference to the NLF. Hanoi stuck fast to the Four Points.

LBJ had some reason to feel let down by Kosygin. Yet, by the same token, there was a strong element of empty gesture in the entire US 'peace offensive'. Chester Cooper later described its purpose as 'improving the American image rather than finding the key to actual negotiations'.[117] Moscow no doubt also discerned this. Not all US decision-makers welcomed Soviet involvement. Commenting on the Shelepin trip to Hanoi, for example, Maxwell Taylor noted the danger of the US becoming 'trapped into premature negotiations'.[118] Rusk was less suspicious, but always recognised the possibility of Moscow being 'immobilised' by Beijing.[119] LBJ's own comments to the National Security Council on 5 January 1966 also appeared to underline the rather empty, ritualistic character of the 'peace offensive':

> We have a better basis to call on the US people not only for their sons, but also for their treasure. Americans feel better if they know we have gone the last mile even if we have grave doubts about doing so.[120]

It is important to bear in mind that the US interest in using Soviet mediation in Vietnam always involved a degree of ambivalence. Perceptions of the quasi-monolithic 'communist world' continued to affect American commitments – not least LBJ's commitment – in this area. However, the major impression gleaned from the wide range of Washington documents of this period is not one of US officials being excessively suspicious of Soviet intentions in Vietnam. On the contrary, it is of perceptions of the prospects for Russian mediation actually bolstering Washington's brittle confidence. One underlying, if unexamined, assumption of these years of escalation in Vietnam was that if the going became extremely tough, Moscow might show the way to peace.

Notes

1 I. V. Gaiduk, *The Soviet Union and the Vietnam War* (Chicago, Dee, 1996), p. 4.

2 *FRUS, 1964–1968*: Volume XXVII: *Mainland Southeast Asia; Regional Affairs* (Washington DC, US Government Printing Office, 2000), pp. 130–1 (27 May 1964).

3 R. D. Schulzinger, *A Time for War* (New York, Oxford University Press, 1997), p. 152.

4 When exactly the decision for war was made remains a matter of acute controversy. For varying views, see D. M. Barrett, *Uncertain Warriors: Lyndon Johnson and His Vietnam*

Advisers (Lawrence, University Press of Kansas, 1993), ch. 2; L. Berman, *Planning a Tragedy: The Americanization of the War in Vietnam* (New York, Norton, 1982), chs. 2–3; L. C. Gardner, *Pay Any Price: Lyndon Johnson and the Wars for Vietnam* (Chicago, Dee, 1995), ch. 11; D. E. Kaiser, *American Tragedy: Kennedy, Johnson and the Origins of the Vietnam War* (Cambridge, Massachusetts), Harvard University Press, 2000), chs. 10–13; F. Logevall, *Choosing War: The Lost Chance for Peace and the Escalation of the War in Vietnam* (Berkeley, University of California Press, 1999), ch. 11; J. M. Newman, 'The Kennedy-Johnson Transition: The case for policy reversal', in L. C. Gardner and T. Gittinger (eds.), *Vietnam: The Early Decisions* (Austin, University of Texas Press, 1997), pp. 158–77; B. Van De Mark, *Into the Quagmire: Lyndon Johnson and the Escalation of the Vietnam War* (New York, Oxford University Press, 1991).

5 Gaiduk (*The Soviet Union and the Vietnam War*, p. 19) plays down the significance of Khrushchev's fall. But see also R. B. Smith, *An International History of the Vietnam War: Volume 2, The Struggle for South-East Asia, 1961–65* (London, Macmillan, 1985), pp. 349–55.

6 Gaiduk, *The Soviet Union and the Vietnam War*, pp. 8–9. See also I. V. Gaiduk, 'Developing an alliance: The Soviet Union and Vietnam, 1954–75', in P. Lowe (ed.), *The Vietnam War* (London, Macmillan, 1998), pp. 133–51, at p. 143.

7 *FRUS, 1964–1968*: Volume XIV: *The Soviet Union* (Washington DC, US Government Printing Office, 2001), p. 31 (19 Feb. 1964).

8 Quoted in L. C. Gardner, 'Fighting Vietnam: The Russian-American conundrum', in L. C. Gardner and T. Gittinger (eds.), *International Perspectives on Vietnam* (College Station, Texas A and M University Press, 2000), pp. 23–57, at pp. 26–7.

9 See E. E. Moise, *Tonkin Gulf and the Escalation of the Vietnam War* (Chapel Hill, University of North Carolina Press, 1996). R. B. Smith (*An International History . . . : Volume 2*, p. 293) suggests that Moscow may have been informed in advance of the attack on the *Maddox*.

10 *FRUS, 1964–1968*: Volume 1: *Vietnam, 1964*, p. 635 (5 Aug. 1964).

11 Ibid., pp. 636–8 (5 Aug. 1964).

12 Ibid., p. 648 (7 Aug. 1964).

13 Moise, *Tonkin Gulf*, p. 238.

14 I. V. Gaiduk, 'Turnabout? The Soviet policy dilemma on the Vietnamese conflict', in Gardner and Gittinger (eds.), *Vietnam: The Early Decisions*, pp. 207–18, at p. 217.

15 See G. H. Chang, *Friends and Enemies: The United States, China, and the Soviet Union, 1948–1972* (Stanford, Stanford University Press, 1990), pp. 262–9.

16 Chen Jian, 'China and the Vietnam Wars, 1950–75, in Lowe (ed.), *The Vietnam War*, pp. 152–80, at p. 164. See also Xiaoming Zhang, 'The Vietnam War, 1964–1969: a Chinese perspective', *Journal of Military History*, 60:3 (1996) 731–62.

17 Kaiser, *American Tragedy*, p. 327.

18 M. R. Beschloss (ed.), *Taking Charge: The Johnson White House Tapes, 1963–1964* (New York, Simon and Schuster, 1997), p. 293 (21 March 1964).

19 *FRUS, 1964–1968*: Volume III: *Vietnam, July–December 1965* (Washington DC, US Government Printing Office, 1996), p. 140 (13 July 1965).

20 Ang Cheng Guan, 'The Vietnam War, 1962–64: the Vietnamese communist perspective', *Journal of Contemporary History*, 34:4 (2000) 601–18, at 615.

21 *FRUS, 1964–1968*: Volume I: *Vietnam 1964*, pp. 643–4 (6 Aug. 1964).

22 R. K. Brigham, *Guerrilla Diplomacy: The NLF's Foreign Relations and the Vietnam War* (Ithaca, Cornell University Press, 1999), p. 64.

23 R. A. Garson, 'Lyndon B. Johnson and the China enigma', *Journal of Contemporary History*, 32:1 (1997) 63–80, at 83.

24 *FRUS, 1964–1968*: Volume XXX: *China* (Washington DC, US Government Printing Office, 1998), p. 185 (15 July 1965).

25 *FRUS, 1964–1968*: Volume I: *Vietnam 1964*, p. 991 (9 Dec. 1964).

26 *FRUS, 1964–1968*: Volume II: *Vietnam, January–June 1965* (Washington DC, US Government Printing Office, 1996), p. 118.

27 Cited, Berman, *Planning A Tragedy*, p. 43.

28 M. R. Beschloss (ed.), *Reaching for Glory: Lyndon Johnson's Secret White House Tapes, 1964–1965* (New York, Simon and Schuster, 200), p. 195 (1 March 1965).

29 See, e.g., D. Halberstam, *The Best and the Brightest* (New York, Random House, 1972), p. 533.

30 *FRUS, 1964–1968*: Volume XIV: *The Soviet Union*, pp. 234, 258.

31 Beschloss (ed.), *Reaching for Glory*, p. 174.

32 *FRUS, 1964–1968*: Volume II: *Vietnam, January–June 1965*, p. 159.

33 Ibid., p. 193–5. See also H. H. Humphrey, *The Education of a Public Man* (Garden City, Doubleday, 1976), p. 318.

34 Ibid., p. 215; Gardner, *Pay Any Price*, p. 168.

35 Ibid., p. 194.

36 *The Soviet Union and the Vietnam War*, p. 40.

37 *FRUS, 1964–1968*: Volume XIV: *The Soviet Union*, p. 238 (11 Feb. 1965).

38 *FRUS, 1964–1968*: Volume II *Vietnam, January–June 1965*, p. 119 (1 Feb. 1965).

39 See ibid., p. 121.

40 *FRUS, 1964–1968*: Volume XIV: *The Soviet Union*, p. 245.

41 Ibid., p. 280 (9 April 1965).

42 See G. McT. Kahin, *Intervention: How America Became Involved in Vietnam* (New York, Knopf, 1986), pp. 275–80.

43 *FRUS, 1964–1968*: Volume II: *Vietnam, January–June 1965*, p. 173.

44 *FRUS, 1964–1968*: Volume XIV: *The Soviet Union*, p. 241.

45 Ibid., p. 280.

46 Smith, *An International History . . . : Volume 2*, pp. 268–70.

47 J. Prados, *The Blood Road: the Ho Chi Minh Trail and the Vietnam War* (New York, Wiley, 1999), p. 131. Also, Logevall, *Choosing War*, p. 325.

48 *Intervention*, p. 277.

49 *FRUS, 1964–1968*: Volume II *Vietnam, January–June, 1965*, p. 159.

50 See K. Bird, *The Color of Truth: McGeorge Bundy and William Bundy: Brothers in Arms* (New York, Simon and Schuster, 1998), p. 309 (on the 'streetcars' remark) and p. 307 (Halberstam).

51 Prados, *The Blood Road*, p. 131.

52 Quiang Zhai, *China and the Vietnam Wars, 1950–1975* (Chapel Hill, University of North Carolina Press, 2000), p. 133.

53 *FRUS, 1964–1968*: Volume II: *Vietnam, January–June, 1965*, p. 245: 'The recent VC attacks and US/GVN reprisals probably cut across Soviet calculations'.

54 See W. J. Duiker, *US Containment Policy and the Conflict in Indochina* (Stanford, Stanford University Press, 1994), p. 337.

55 See D.S. Papp, *Vietnam: The View from Moscow, Peking, Washington* (Jefferson, McFarland, 1981), pp. 59–67; D. Pike, *Vietnam and the Soviet Union* (Boulder, Westview, 1987), pp. 80–1; I. V. Gaiduk, 'Soviet policy toward US participation in the Vietnam War, *History*, 33:1 (1996) 40–54, at 51.

56 Pike, *Vietnam and the Soviet Union*, p. 79.

57 Gaiduk, *The Soviet Union and the Vietnam War*, p. 37.

58 Zhai, *China and the Vietnam Wars*, pp. 150–1. Mao, who tended to prioritise the Soviet rivalry, clashed with those, like Deng Xiaoping, who favoured cooperating with Moscow over aid to the DRV (see W. J. Duiker, *China and Vietnam: The Roots of Conflict* (Berkeley, Institute of East Asian Studies, 1986), p. 48).

59 *FRUS, 1964–1968*: Volume III: *Vietnam, June–December, 1965*, pp. 241, 243, 257.
60 See R. Warner, *Back Fire: The CIA's Secret War in Laos* (New York, Simon and Schuster, 1995), p. 156.
61 *FRUS, 1964–1968*: Volume II: *Vietnam, January–June, 1965*, p. 246 (11 Feb. 1965).
62 Ibid., p. 209 (9 Feb. 1965).
63 Ibid., p. 596 (21 April 1965).
64 *FRUS, 1964–1968*: Volume III: *Vietnam, June–December, 1965*, pp. 229–30 (Special National Intelligence Estimate, 23 July 1965).
65 *FRUS, 1964–1968*: Volume II: *Vietnam, January–June, 1965*, pp. 300, 305.
66 *FRUS, 1964–1968*: Volume III: *Vietnam, June–December, 1965*, p. 19.
67 See C. Clifford, *Counsel to the President: A Memoir* (New York, Random House, 1991), p. 420.
68 *FRUS, 1964–1968*: Volume III: *Vietnam, June–December, 1965*, p. 178.
69 Beschloss (ed.), *Taking Charge*, p. 368 (27 May 1964).
70 Beschloss (ed.), *Reaching for Glory*, p. 384 (2 July 1965).
71 *FRUS, 1964–1968*: Volume III: *Vietnam, June–December, 1965*, p. 215 (22 July 1965).
72 Beschloss (ed.), *Reaching for Glory*, p. 390.
73 Gardner, *Pay Any Price*, p. 237.
74 Berman, *Planning A Tragedy*, p. 110.
75 Gardner, 'Fighting Vietnam', p. 30 (25 Feb. 1965).
76 See Gaiduk, *The Soviet Union and Vietnam*, p. 32.
77 Logevall, *Choosing War*, pp. 87, 146, 214, 354, 364; N. B. Hannah, *The Key to Failure: Laos and the Vietnam War* (Lanham, Madison Books, 1987); *FRUS, 1964–1968*: Volume XXVIII: *Laos* (Washington DC, US Government Printing Office, 1998), pp. 362–75.
78 Logevall, *Choosing War*, p. 191.
79 A. Dobrynin, *In Confidence* (New York, Times Books, 1995), p. 138.
80 Ibid.
81 Beschloss (ed.), *Taking Charge*, p. 210 (1 Feb. 1964).
82 *FRUS, 1964–1968*: Volume II: *Vietnam, January–June, 1965*, p. 344. See L. B. Johnson, *The Vantage Point*, (London, Weidenfeld and Nicolson, 1971), p. 579.
83 J. Colvin, *Twice Around the World* (London. Cooper, 1991), p. 53.
84 *FRUS, 1964–1968*: Volume II: *Vietnam, January–June, 1965*, p. 650.
85 Ibid., p. 651.
86 Gaiduk, *The Soviet Union and Vietnam*, p. 46.
87 R. S. McNamara, J. G. Blight and R. K. Brigham, *Argument Without End: In Search of Answers to the Vietnam Tragedy* (New York, Public Affairs, 1999), p. 263.
88 *FRUS, 1964–1968*: Volume II: *Vietnam, January–June, 1965*, p. 662 (15 May 1965).
89 Ibid., p. 663.
90 Ibid., p. 665. See also Dobrynin, *In Confidence*, p. 138.
91 *FRUS, 1964–1968*: Volume III: *Vietnam, June–December, 1965*, p. 22 (19 June 1965) (original in brackets).
92 Ibid., pp. 52–3 (Kohler, 26 June 1965).
93 Ibid., p. 73 (29 June 1965).
94 Ibid., p. 88 (30 June 1965).
95 Ibid., p. 97 (1 July 1965).
96 Ibid., p. 146 (CIA, 15 July 1965).
97 Ibid., pp. 147–52.
98 Gardner, 'Fighting Vietnam', p. 33.
99 Gardner, *Pay Any Price*, p. 206.
100 *FRUS, 1964–1968*: Volume III: *Vietnam, June–December 1965*, p. 180 (23 July 1965).
101 Hughes, 'Kosygin's second conversation with Harriman', NSF: CF: Europe and the USSR: USSR, box 221, 22 July 1965.

102 Gardner, 'Fighting Vietnam', p. 33; Dobrynin, *In Confidence*, p. 139.

103 *FRUS, 1964–1968*: Volume III: *Vietnam, June–December, 1965*, p. 262.

104 Ibid., p. 283.

105 Ibid., p. 411 (22 Sept. 1965).

106 Gardner, *Pay Any Price*, p. 274.

107 *FRUS, 1964–1968*: Volume III: Vietnam, June–December, 1965, p. 428 (30 Sept. 1965).

108 Ibid., p. 583.

109 Ibid., pp. 666–9.

110 Gaiduk, *The Soviet Union and Vietnam*, p. 83 (Harriman, 28 Dec. 1965).

111 *FRUS, 1964–1968*: Volume IV: *Vietnam, 1966* (Washington DC, US Government Printing Office, 1998), p. 94 (20 Jan. 1966).

112 See Zhai, *China and the Vietnam Wars*, p. 165.

113 *FRUS, 1964–1968*: Volume IV: *Vietnam, 1966*, p. 133 (25 Jan. 1966).

114 NSF: CF: Europe and USSR: USSR, box 221, CIA Special Memorandum, 17 Jan. 1966 (folder, 'USSR: Memos XI').

115 LBJ to Richard Nixon, *FRUS, 1964–1968*: Volume VI: *Vietnam, January–August 1968* (Washington DC, US Government Printing Office, 2002), p. 896 926 July 1968).

116 Gardner, 'Fighting Vietnam', p. 35.

117 C. L. Cooper, *The Lost Crusade: America in Vietnam* (New York, Dodd, Mead, 1970), pp. 292–3.

118 Meeting Notes File, box 1, Cabinet room meeting, 21 Dec. 1965.

119 Office of the President File, box 13, meeting in Cabinet room, 27 Jan. 1966 (Valenti notes).

120 'Summary notes' of 555th NSC meeting, 5 Jan. 1966, NSC Meetings File, box 2.

5

The Vietnam War, 1966–69

This chapter will review the convoluted history of the various peace initiatives of the later Johnson years. Interaction between the superpowers was a vital aspect of this story. By mid to late 1966, the USSR was providing the majority of North Vietnam's military assistance. On 1 June 1966, President Johnson was advised by the CIA and defence intelligence that Moscow was 'by far the major source of military equipment for North Vietnam', having supplied between 70 and 95 per cent of the total for the previous year.[1] Moscow also had emerged as North Vietnam's main diplomatic sponsor. The Soviets were by now acting as representatives of the Northern regime, especially towards the United Nations, but also in diplomatic contact with a range of Western countries.[2] In such circumstances – and also, given the hopes of eventual Soviet mediation which (as we saw in Chapter 4) attended even LBJ's 1965 escalation decisions – it seemed natural for America to look to the Kremlin as a broker of peace. If Moscow was bankrolling Hanoi, then, so some Washington decision-makers reasoned, the Soviets could force its ally into negotiation. Moscow would, it was true, exact a 'price' (as the US Ambassador to Laos put it in June 1966) for opening itself up to Chinese charges of colluding with Washington.[3] Washington needed merely to find out what 'price' Moscow had in mind, and within any reasonable limits, to pay it.

The reader will be unsurprised to be told that matters were not so simple. Moscow's attitudes towards Hanoi were complex and difficult to interpret. Moscow's control over the DRV, despite the importance of the Soviet military sponsorship, was not complete. In the minds of many American decision-makers, not least in the mind of LBJ himself, trust in Moscow's good faith had ebbed significantly since late 1965. Let us begin this chapter by looking more closely at the President's state of mind in 1966–67.

LBJ, Moscow and peace negotiations

The various peace feelers of 1966–67 foundered on the rocks of mutual mistrust, abetted by a fair degree of mutual misunderstanding. Each side – Washington and the Vietnamese communists – suspected that, at bottom, its opponent was requiring unconditional surrender. The American search for peace was also compromised by a manifest unwillingness or inability to coordinate military and diplomatic activities.[4] Responsibility for such coordination rested ultimately with the President, and Johnson's state of mind and lack of resolution over the peace initiatives certainly contributed to that failure.

With the resumption of bombing in January 1966, Johnson's outlook seems to have darkened. He ended the debate in the Cabinet Room over bombing by reminding his associates that he had been the 'first Congressman to speak up for the Truman Doctrine'. He was 'not happy about Vietnam but we cannot run out – we have to resume bombing'. Concerned by CIA speculation about the possibility of Moscow siting long-range missiles in North Vietnam, LBJ nevertheless reaffirmed that 'I don't want war with Russia and China'. Yet he would not 'back out – and look like I'm reacting to the Fulbrights'.[5] Lady Bird Johnson had watched anxiously as her husband agonised over what to do if 'nothing, nothing, nothing comes out of the peace offensive'.[6]

After January 1966, the President's attitude towards the peace agenda continued to be agonised and hesitant, even schizophrenic. Johnson did seriously wish to negotiate. Henry Kissinger, who was involved in the diplomacy which led to the 1968 Paris peace talks, recalled LBJ's 'eagerness to start negotiations' as 'palpable to the point of being self-defeating'.[7] (Kissinger saw Hanoi as continually delaying in order to extract concessions.) Lady Bird, in a 1989 interview, remembered the President as harbouring 'almost a little boy sort of hope . . . for peace'.[8] LBJ did not see the war as being won by military means alone. This, after all, was Lyndon Johnson, former master of the Senate, the experienced discoverer of common cause in the midst of political strife. Yet he was continually torn in different directions – unwilling to be seen to respond to Robert Kennedy and 'the Fulbrights', paralysed by conflicting advice over Hanoi's war aims, uncertain about the appropriate balance between diplomatic and military pressure, and (particularly after the failed 1965 Christmas bombing pause) undecided about the possibility and/or desirability of Soviet mediation.

By the time of the 31 March 1968 speech, announcing Johnson's exit from the Presidential race, there is virtual unanimity that LBJ was 'worn to a frazzle' and undergoing a severe 'personal crisis'.[9] However, even before the Tet offensive of February 1968, Johnson was showing signs of extreme unhappiness, chronic overwork and decisional irresolution. Other Chief Executives in a similar condition might have sought comfort in alcohol. It is a measure of Johnson's rather extraordinary personality that, in January 1967, White House aides became alarmed that the President was *not* drinking. Joseph Califano interpreted Johnson's sobriety – LBJ had previously been an enthusiastic devotee of 'Cutty Sark' whisky – as an indication of the President's extreme anxiety, evident in his fear of not being in control in an emergency.[10]

Johnson's personal crisis – 'breakdown' is probably too strong a term – led him into ever wilder denunciations of opponents of the war. Eric Goldman records Johnson as condemning anti-war Senators as 'crackpots' who had 'just plain been taken in'. It was 'the Russians who are behind the whole thing'.[11] Again, Johnson was nothing if not inconsistent. In October 1967, he told journalist Robert Manning that it was important 'not to get the country on an anti-communist binge because it would tear up' progress towards détente.[12] However, Johnson's tirades against the Soviet-inspired anti-war protest were not mere random slips of judgement. They testified to Johnson's emotional need to blame the old enemy, communism, rather than seriously to address the concerns of protesters. In October 1967, he told Congressional leaders 'that he did not want to be like a McCarthyite, but this country is in a little more danger than we think'.[13] In the same year, he was recorded as worrying aloud about the children of anti-war Senators dating officials at the Soviet Embassy.[14] (To be fair to LBJ, senior staff in his Administration also found it very difficult to believe that oppositionism was spontaneous and not inspired by Moscow).[15]

Turning back to the early part of 1966, Johnson's attitude towards the possibility of Soviet mediation was affected not only by his near-paranoid notions of Moscow's role in stoking up anti-war protest, but also by the hard line being argued by Walt Rostow. According to Rostow, 'Russian leverage on Hanoi depends mainly on *our* persuading Hanoi that negotiation is the best course'. The National Security Adviser was advising an escalation of the air war, with 'precision bombing' targeted at North Vietnam's oil supplies. Only the US, through military pressure '– not Moscow – can push them over the hump into negotiations'. He told LBJ in April 1966: 'I believe the Russians would fully understand and accept this course; although they are keeping their oar in Hanoi as a contingency . . .'.[16] Rostow's hard line was strongly supported by the US Ambassador in Saigon, Henry Cabot Lodge.[17] It was also backed by Thomas Hughes, intelligence analyst at the State Department. Hughes wrote in August 1966 that the Soviet leaders seemed not 'to have thought much beyond' the benefits accruing from sponsorship of Hanoi – mainly embarrassment to the US and the chance to rebut Chinese charges of revolutionary backsliding. They needed to consider the 'time when their willingness to hitch their cart to Hanoi's horse may lead them into a direct confrontation with us that can no longer be glossed over . . . Perhaps the time has come to get that message across more clearly'.[18]

Leading the case for recruiting Moscow as soon as possible to the cause of mediation was peace ambassador Averell Harriman. LBJ and Rusk received a stream of communications from Harriman, urging the immediate engagement of the USSR in 'constructive action', probably centred around diplomacy at the UN. Harriman ruminated on some kind of comprehensive Soviet-American deal, whereby US concessions in Europe might be traded for Moscow's good offices in Vietnam.[19] In October 1966, Harriman told LBJ and Rusk that 'the only real chance now to induce Hanoi to negotiate a settlement depends on the influence Moscow is willing to exert'. He argued that the Kremlin was weary of the war and quoted a remark made to him by Kosygin in July 1965 to the effect that the conflict in Vietnam 'only helps the Chinese'.[20]

Averell Harriman felt, correctly, that he did not enjoy Johnson's full confidence. Harriman also regarded Rusk as far too cautious in his attitude towards Soviet mediation, despite the Secretary of State's willingness to raise with Ambassador Dobrynin the possibility of a new Geneva Conference on the future of Indochina.[21] Harriman was supported by Llewellyn Thompson, who advised Johnson in July 1966 that the Soviets 'stand to lose' by the war 'in almost any outcome'. The US could escalate the war in the South of Vietnam without running any risk of Soviet retaliation, but 'any dramatic step-up' in terms of air attacks or blockades in the North (as advocated by Walt Rostow) would involve 'real danger'.[22]

Though Rusk, LBJ himself, and especially Walt Rostow, were cautious about the possibility of repeating what they saw as the humiliation of Christmas 1965, it should be emphasised that none of the key decision-makers ever ruled out a major mediatory role for Moscow. Even Rostow, for example, was prepared to explore with the President the possibility of inviting Moscow to repeat its mediation of the Indo-Pakistan conflict. A draft letter was actually composed by Rostow in August 1966, congratulating Kosygin on the 1965 Tashkent mediation and hinting that something similar might be attempted in Vietnam.[23]

Johnson still, as he had put it in March 1965, did not know 'what the hell to do'.[24] His decisions, to combine further escalation with various, and sometimes rather ambivalent, peace feelers, reflected the complex pressures on him. Harriman was encouraged by LBJ's attitude, telling Robert McNamara in May 1966 that the President 'hopes for some settlement, and gave me the impression he didn't see any value in escalation'.[25] The following month saw Johnson deciding to authorise air attacks on North Vietnamese petroleum depots.

MARIGOLD to SUNFLOWER

Between the Summer of 1966 and the Spring of 1967, a direct US–Soviet dialogue, primarily via Dobrynin and Gromyko, did proceed, involving a possible Soviet role in securing peace in Vietnam. There were also two further, shadowy, initiatives – codenamed MARIGOLD and SUNFLOWER – which involved the Soviet Union tangentially at first, but eventually more directly. (The more direct phase of Soviet involvement, the talks in London in February 1967 between Kosygin and British Prime Minister Harold Wilson, will be discussed separately, in the next section of this chapter.)

The dialogue with Gromyko built on the contacts established between the Soviet Foreign Minister and Ambassador Foy Kohler in the Summer of 1965. Gromyko clearly wished to maintain a dialogue with the US over the war, and

Washington received a stream of hints and suggestions to the effect that some kind of mediation via Moscow might be feasible.[26] According to Ambassador Dobrynin, Gromyko 'always favored improving relations with Washington', and was not set against a Soviet mediatory role in Vietnam. However, the Soviet Foreign Minister was also a conservative and cautious figure, concerned with 'never allowing himself to overstep major ideological barriers'.[27]

The most significant conversations with Gromyko occurred in September–October 1966, when the Kremlin veteran made his annual visit to the US for the UN General Assembly. Dean Rusk's September conversations with Gromyko were widely interpreted – especially by the optimistic Harriman – as possibly presaging a breakthrough. Rusk reported a calmness and feeling of promise surrounding the exchanges.[28] However, there was little obvious agreement. Gromyko maintained that the US had 'made no effort to make its proposals acceptable to the other side'. America 'did not even stop the bombing', Rusk declared that America was 'ready to discuss peace now or at any other time, but we could not be indifferent to the presence of large numbers of regular North Vietnamese soldiers in South Vietnam'.[29]

The tone, rather than the substance, of these conversations certainly encouraged Rusk. He told a South Vietnamese delegation on 5 October that, 'if they were acting on their own', the Soviets would be prepared to 'see the matter settled on the basis of the status quo ante at the 17th Parallel'. The problem, as Rusk saw it, was that Chinese accusations of US–Soviet collusion were pushing Moscow towards the rejection of compromise and mediation.[30] On 10 October, LBJ himself met Gromyko and Dobrynin in Washington. Before the meeting, not only Harriman but also Walt Rostow pressed on LBJ the desirability of a mediatory role for Moscow. At the meeting, Johnson emphasised the 'great responsibility' of both powers for securing peace. The US was sincere in wanting a settlement: 'If the United States wanted victory over North Viet Nam, we could achieve it, but our aim is not that but to settle the problem'. Gromyko accused Johnson of setting terms for negotiations which amounted to a demand for North Vietnamese capitulation. The Soviet Union, according to Gromyko, 'did not engage in negotiations'; however, he 'did not deny that they had some influence among their own friends but the position of the United States made it more difficult for the Soviet Union to use this influence'. The 'first of first steps' must be to stop the bombing. LBJ responded that he did not doubt the Soviets' 'good faith', but maintained that an unconditional, unreciprocated bombing halt was unacceptable. Johnson pointed out that the communists in Vietnam 'had killed more of our soldiers with mortars and bombs than we had killed in the North by aerial bombardment'. However, the US was 'ready to talk without conditions at any time and any place'. Gromyko wanted LBJ to issue a fixed timetable for US troop withdrawal. Following the talks, he issued to reporters an upbeat account of his exchanges with the American President.[31]

Between September 1966 and the early months of 1967, the US Administration made various moves towards establishing some kind of procedure (if not exactly a timetable) for mutual de-escalation in Vietnam, including American troop removal, as recommended by Gromyko. LBJ issued a vague statement at the Manila conference in October 1966 to the effect that the US would withdraw six months after the confirmation of an end to the communist violence in South Vietnam. The US also adopted its 'Phase A/Phase B' formula for de-escalation. This was made public by Arthur Goldberg, US Representative to the United Nations, on 22 September 1966. Washington would 'order a cessation of all bombing' of North Vietnam 'the moment we are assured, privately or otherwise, that this step will be answered promptly by a corresponding and appropriate de-escalation on the other side'.[32]

The LBJ–Gromyko conversation and these various efforts to suggest possible de-escalatory procedures took place against the background of the unfolding MARIGOLD peace initiative. This involved a network of Polish and Italian diplomatic contacts. At MARIGOLD's heart was the possibility of linking Hanoi's agreement to recognise an independent, non-communist, South, with the establishment by Washington of a de-escalatory timetable. The initiative opened up major rifts in Washington over the possibility of fruitful negotiation with Hanoi. Even the generally sceptical Walt Rostow, however, felt that Soviet influence might be a positive force in pushing forward the MARIGOLD initiative. He wrote in November 1966 that 'the net influence of the Soviet Union and Eastern Europe on Hanoi is probably towards a negotiated end to the war'.[33] As will be noted further below, in early November, Washington acceded to a British initiative and allowed George Brown (London's Foreign Minister) to raise the 'Phase A/Phase B' issue directly with the Soviet leadership.

As far as MARIGOLD was concerned, Moscow certainly was aware of, and indeed almost certainly approved, the Polish initiative. Hopes crashed, however, with the ordering of US air strikes on North Vietnam on 2–4 and 13–14 December 1966. Hanoi's representatives failed to attend a prearranged meeting in Warsaw on 5 December. Despite the raids, Washington attempted to keep the process alive by involving the USSR more directly. On 6 December, LBJ wrote to Kosygin. He described his Manila statement as a direct response to Gromyko's prompting in September. Johnson noted recent Soviet exchanges with Ambassador Foy Kohler: 'It is clear that we both agree on the most important objective – that the fighting should be brought to an end as quickly as possible'. Peace might come either via negotiations – 'by direct contact, through an intermediary, or by means of a formal conference' – provided Hanoi recognised the independence of the South. Another scenario for ending the war might involve 'a simple tapering off of military action on both sides'. The US requested Soviet cooperation.[34]

The second round of US bombing, 13–14 December, effectively closed off immediate prospects for such cooperation, finally terminating MARIGOLD.

According to Robert McNamara, a senior group of advisers – McNamara himself, Nicholas Katzenbach, Llewellyn Thompson and US Ambassador to Poland, John Gronouski – attempted to delay the air raids, already postponed from November. 'But Johnson, still influenced by the after effects of the (1965) Christmas bombing pause, felt postponement would be interpreted as weakness'.[35] Soviet spokesmen delivered a series of optimistic messages about the Polish initiative, but blamed the US bombing for its failure.[36] In late December, Washington worked on another letter to Kosygin, promising that Llewellyn Thompson, the new Ambassador to Moscow, would make constructive and flexible suggestions for Soviet mediation. This letter, which emanated from a State Department group headed by Averell Harriman, appears not to have been sent.[37]

Soviet interest in mediation was not killed by the collapse of MARIGOLD. Indeed, it was Moscow itself which sparked the succeeding initiative, codenamed SUNFLOWER. One strand of the SUNFLOWER process involved direct contacts between Washington (primarily through John Guthrie, the American Charge d'Affaires) and the North Vietnamese Embassy in Moscow. McNamara later recalled: 'the Russians came to the US, and said that they would be willing to put a proposal to the Vietnamese. The Russians said they believed such a proposal would lead to serious talks. So we put a proposal in Moscow to the Vietnamese representative there'.[38] The 'proposal' was a version of the 'Phase A/Phase B' formula, originally announced by Ambassador Goldberg in September 1966, and transmitted to Moscow by British Foreign Secretary George Brown in November. In early January 1967, a Soviet diplomat, Alexander Zinchuk, reported that there were 'forces for moderation in Hanoi – forces who think they cannot win the war and that a compromise must be made at some point'.[39] On 28 January, Hanoi's Foreign Minister, Nguyen Duy Trinh, indicated that talks could commence if the US announced an unconditional bombing halt. Hanoi was no longer insisting on prior US recognition of a communist role in any future South Vietnamese government. By this time, speculation about some kind of US–North Vietnamese mutual de-escalation, probably brokered by Moscow, had become febrile. The precise terms for the de-escalation, however, were very unclear. LBJ did not help to clarify matters by announcing in a 2 February press conference that 'almost any step' on Hanoi's part might trigger American reciprocation.[40]

'Phase A/Phase B': Washington, Hanoi and London

When George Brown met the Soviet leadership on 25 November 1966, he presented the 'Phase A/Phase B' formula as follows: 'The order of events would therefore be: phase A, stop the bombing, while phase B, which would follow, would be the execution of the other agreed measures of de-escalation by both sides'.[41]

Brown's role as a go-between to Moscow was not regarded in Washington as a key, central aspect of the MARIGOLD initiative. William Bundy on 10 November expressed doubts whether 'the Soviets had anything new to say to George Brown about Vietnam'. Harriman suggested that Kosygin and Gromyko 'might be interested in trying out some ideas in their talks with Brown'.[42] Brown, however, was not apprised by Washington of the main, Polish dimension to MARIGOLD. When Brown and British Prime Minister Harold Wilson discovered, in January 1967, the full extent of MARIGOLD, there ensued the first of a series of intensely emotional Anglo-American rows over the Vietnam peace process. The British, according to Brown, had not been able to deal effectively and informedly with Moscow: 'It is not surprising that the Russians were so puzzled'.[43]

US unwillingness to embrace London as a full partner in negotiations with (or via) Moscow was traceable to a number of factors in the complex US–UK relationship at this time: distrust of, even contempt for, the mediation and high diplomatic pretensions of Harold Wilson; a simple caution about using inter-mediaries with Moscow; above all, the effects of the complex, and shifting power relations between London and Washington at this time.[44] These tensions came together in, and probably shaped decisively, the major failure of US–Soviet diplomacy in respect of the Vietnam War – the London 'Phase A/Phase B' negotiations of February 1967.

The events of what London referred to as 'Kosygin week' were extraordinarily complex and are still open to a number of interpretations. A bare narrative will best advance the current discussion.

Kosygin's visit to London began on 6 February 1967. Harold Wilson, overseen by Chester Cooper (appointed by LBJ to act as US liaison), presented to Kosygin a version of the 'Phase A/Phase B' proposal. North Vietnamese de-escalation would follow a US bombing halt. Wilson suggested that London could exercise a positive influence on Washington, just as Moscow could positively pressure Hanoi: 'Her Majesty's Government could deliver theirs'.[45] Wilson, and to some degree Cooper, were encouraged by Kosygin's attitude. Despite receiving a rather negative telegram from LBJ overnight, Wilson pressed home the de-escalation plan on 7 February. Cooper informed Washington that Moscow was indeed interested in a formulation whereby Phases A and B would be 'kept apart'.[46] Washington and Hanoi, with Soviet mediation, would, in effect, secretly make a bargain to de-escalate, consequent on the US bombing halt.

On 7 February in Washington, at the Tuesday luncheon foreign policy meeting, LBJ and his senior advisers effectively reversed Wilson's understanding of the 'Phase A/Phase B' formula. The reversal – a bombing halt would now follow a guaranteed and verified termination of North Vietnamese troop infiltration into the South – was contained in a letter sent directly to Ho Chi Minh. The sending of the letter was the culmination of an extended debate on how to proceed, and was also probably influenced by a major row between LBJ and Robert Kennedy on the best road to peace in Vietnam. Meanwhile, Cooper and Wilson worked on a text for Kosygin to take back to Moscow. Johnson expressed his concern, following a speech by Kosygin at the London Guildhall that the Soviet leader had 'got Wilson aboard'.[47] On Friday 10 February, London received the message that the US would 'order a cessation of bombing of North Vietnam as soon as they are assured that infiltration from North Vietnam to South Vietnam has stopped' – the bombing would stop only after a verified end to infiltration.[48] Cooper was told that the position now being taken by Washington was in line both with the letter to Ho Chi Minh, and with American reactions to massive North Vietnamese troop movements towards the South. (During this period, bombing was halted as a gesture towards the Tet Vietnamese holiday.) Brown and Wilson gave vent to their feelings of betrayal to US Ambassador David Bruce, while Washington pondered whether to try to salvage something positive from the contact with Kosygin. Dean Rusk, for example, advised LBJ that the US should hold off bombing for the time being, since 'there remains an outside chance that Kosygin will get some reply from Hanoi'.[49] At this time, Rostow saw a '15 per cent chance, 15 to 20, I'd say, that something will emerge in the next weeks or months'.[50] On 11 February, Johnson made his worries about Bobby Kennedy explicit in a telephone call to his National Security Adviser: 'I'd just as soon not have a damn bit of connection to London, and the better – the easier the better, because the first thing you'll have, Bobby will have arranged the thing in London'. He continued that he 'wouldn't be a bit surprised to see that leak tomorrow – that he worked this all out with Wilson'.[51] Kosygin, who was visiting Scotland on 11 February, was given a revised version of the 'Phase A/Phase B' proposal. Wilson and Cooper attempted to gain diplomatic ground by, in effect, offering Kosygin an extension of the Tet bombing halt. In Washington, only Vice President Hubert Humphrey seriously argued for an extended bombing halt in order to keep the momentum of Wilson's initiative going. Bombing resumption, and Hanoi's rejection (received on 15 February) of the terms set out in LBJ's letter to Ho Chi Minh, marked the collapse of Wilson's residual hopes for a breakthrough.[52]

The whole affair was redolent of bureaucratic misadventure and linguistic imprecision in regard to the de-escalation timetable. Benjamin Read, Executive Secretary at the State Department, recalled the various transatlantic understandings of the 'Phase A/Phase B' timetable as 'hopelessly garbled'.[53] Harold Wilson regarded his initiative as having been undermined by Walt Rostow. From the point of view of US–Soviet relations, what stands out from the events of 'Kosygin week' really was the uncertainty of LBJ's commitment to Russian intercession. Whatever the particular problems between London and Washington, Moscow could only emerge from the whole affair with the view that LBJ's commitment to a Soviet-mediated peace was uncertain, confused and subject to sabotage from within the Presidential inner circle.

1967

Kosygin's reaction to the failures of February 1967 included a message to Llewellyn Thompson to the effect that American unreliability was playing into the hands of Beijing. The 'net result' of the 'Phase A/Phase B' debacle was that the 'Chinese view has triumphed, and the Chinese can now say that all those efforts were nothing but a masquerade'.[54] Unsurprisingly, the months after February 1967 were taken up with military, rather than diplomatic, affairs. Dobrynin was reported in April as saying that 'many members of government were convinced that we were not ready for negotiations but were bent on achieving a military victory'.[55] Despite Soviet scepticism, Harriman continued to urge the case for joint Moscow–Washington mediation. Official Washington debated whether the fact of increased Soviet military aid to Hanoi made the possibility of Russian mediation more or less likely. A Special CIA Estimate in May argued that Moscow had 'concluded that for the time being they have no alternative but to help Hanoi carry on the war'.[56]

Debates nevertheless continued in Washington about the possibility of re-engaging Moscow, and certainly about the need to influence what appeared to be a major review of policy towards Hanoi on the part of the Soviets.[57] Llewellyn Thompson argued that the possibility of successful Soviet mediation continued to be compromised by the rivalry with China. In fact, as Thompson informed Eugene Rostow on 8 May, 'neither the Soviets nor the North Vietnamese hold the key to this situation'. Moscow did 'not want to take the blame for any settlement that would be acceptable to us, as this would greatly enhance the standing of the Chinese Communists in the whole area at their expense'. As for the North Vietnamese, they 'will not want to pull the rug out from under the Viet Cong'. So many of 'our peace moves' had 'coincided with an escalation of our attacks against North Vietnam' that Moscow was genuinely uncertain 'if our peace intentions are not a cover for actions designed to achieve a military victory'.[58] George Brown was again allowed to take a message to Moscow in May. He was requested by Dean Rusk 'to press the Soviets to find out how the North Vietnamese leadership would react to a number of US proposals that included a combination and modified versions of earlier initiatives'.[59] By the end of May, as part of the process that culminated in the Glassboro summit, LBJ was again appealing for a concerted US–Soviet effort to bring a negotiated settlement to Vietnam. Discussions between Walt Rostow and LBJ, however, indicated the strength of Llewellyn Thompson's point about the perceived (and, indeed, actual) ambivalence of US peace moves. Rostow anticipated some joint peace initiative on Vietnam coming from the Glassboro summit. He was also clear that any such initiative would not impair the US military effort. He told LBJ on 11 June: 'If we undertake a peace gambit with the USSR . . . in the days ahead, as I would be inclined to do, we must do it against the background that some time during July we may have to up the ante in Viet Nam: with respect to troops and, even, with respect to bombing'.[60] Looking forward to Glassboro on 17 June, Harriman informed Johnson that Kosygin did want peace, but was very sensitive to the accusation, orchestrated of course by Beijing, 'that they are conniving with the United States'.[61] Two days later, the President treated Senator Fulbright to a frank verdict on Kosygin's potential as a peace broker. Reviewing the London episode of February, LBJ called the 'Wilson–Kosygin deal' a 'pure phony'. The Soviet leader was 'not going to get back in there unless he can deliver something, and I don't think he's quite ready to deliver it now because I don't think he has that horsepower with North Vietnam'.[62]

A position paper, prepared for LBJ at Glassboro, summarised recent events: 'Since Kosygin's talks with Wilson during the February truce the Soviets have indicated we should expect them to take no further efforts to facilitate communications with Hanoi'. Moscow's position was that only 'permanent and unconditional bombing cessation' could lead to negotiations. Kosygin was expected to 'put on an angry, perhaps brutal, display' at the United Nations; however, 'he may be prepared for more dispassionate private discussions', especially in view of a recent US decision to moderate the bombing of Hanoi itself.[63] At the UN, Kosygin repeated the insistence that the US should stop bombing unconditionally and at once. Immediately before the summit, however, McGeorge Bundy gave his view that 'there is more prospect of Soviet help on Vietnam than they have ever given (though much less than Averell Harriman thinks)'.[64] Walt Rostow reported that, according to private Soviet sources, the demand for a 'permanent' bombing halt was being dropped. LBJ must make clear, however, that the US 'cannot accept a stoppage of bombing simply for the possibility of talks'.[65] A CIA report informed LBJ that the President should be aware of Kosygin's problems in keeping in step with the Kremlin consensus on Vietnam. During Kosygin's 'February visit to London . . . he seems to have been a bit too free-wheeling to suit both Brezhnev and Podgorny'.[66] Rusk, who was prepared to join Harriman in encouraging LBJ to press Kosygin for progress on Vietnam, reported on 22 June that Gromyko was giving few signs of eagerness to intercede. The Soviet Foreign Minister told Rusk that Moscow 'could not conduct negotiations for Hanoi'.[67]

In line with Gromyko's comment, Kosygin actually made contact with Hanoi during his first day of talks at Glassboro. The Soviet leader summarised Hanoi's position: 'Stop the bombing and they would immediately go to the conference table'. He again made the point that America in Vietnam was helping China 'in achieving their very worst designs'. Johnson responded that Beijing 'represented the very greatest danger to both countries at present'. The

US would be prepared to withdraw from South Vietnam if it had 'an agreement providing self-determination for the people of South Viet-Nam'. Kosygin urged that Washington establish direct contact with North Vietnam, but promised to relay LBJ's comments to Hanoi. This LBJ-Kosygin initiative, which appears to have sparked no interest from North Vietnam, envisaged discussions following on immediately from a bombing halt, provided Hanoi did not take precipitate military advantage. Kosygin failed to give a direct undertaking that Moscow would assist the US in organising the negotiations.[68] He urged Johnson 'to end this obnoxious war and start negotiating at once'. LBJ responded by invoking the memory of the Korean War, which had seen intense and prolonged fighting continuing alongside negotiations. Kosygin's appeal for peace on 23 June at Glassboro combined a rhetorical flourish with an unflattering description of countries, like the United Kingdom, which had been involved as putative peace intermediaries. 'At several different times in the past', declared Kosygin, the President had sought an intermediary between the US and North Viet-Nam and had even considered using the offices of some second rate countries, which carried no weight in the world, but here and now there was an opportunity to engage in direct negotiations with Hanoi. LBJ should grab it.[69]

The Glassboro conversations on Vietnam became the basis for LBJ's 'San Antonio formula', delivered in September 1967. The US position now was that negotiations, following a bombing halt, need not be conditional on Hanoi accepting South Vietnamese self-determination. During the later months of 1967, prospects for Soviet mediation seemed slight. Walt Rostow advised LBJ on 23 September that the USSR 'would be delighted to have the war go on quietly and peacefully (for us) in the South without bombing the North'.[70] According to the CIA, control of South Vietnam was not a vital Soviet interest. However, Soviet policy was currently (September 1967) driven by the desire not to be seen as the 'appeaser' of Washington.[71] In October, Dean Rusk gave his candid view that the Russians had 'given up any attempt to influence Hanoi'.[72] In November, Zbigniew Brzezinski, then working for the State Department Policy Planning staff, wrote that Moscow was beginning to see the benefits of the conflict: problems in the NATO alliance, a lessening of Chinese hostility to Moscow and domestic splits in the US.[73] A State Department analysis in December reported Ambassador Dobrynin as saying that Moscow's attitude towards the war was 'hands off'. The Soviets were held to suspect that 'we really do not want peace'.[74] Johnson attempted to reassure both himself and opinion in Congress, emphasising the degree of distance between Moscow and Hanoi – not 'hands off', certainly, but not unswerving support either. The President told a dinner group of Democratic Congressmen on 2 November that the USSR supplied Hanoi 'just like you'd supply your brother. That doesn't mean that she's out there with her guns shooting at us herself. And that's a lot of difference'.[75] Only a month later, however, Johnson was telling Harriman that it might be best to give up on negotiations and just 'hold on until the Communists gave in'.[76] Rather than giving in, of course, Hanoi began a massive new offensive.

1968: the Tet offensive and the Paris talks

In January 1968, prior to the Tet offensive, Ambassador Thompson reported from Moscow that 'so long as the situation does not get out of control', there was little incentive for the Soviets to pursue a settlement.[77] Moscow's attitude at this time was certainly not 'hands off'. Towards the end of 1967, Moscow agreed a new aid package for Hanoi. The new understanding was linked directly to the Tet offensive, launched on 30 January 1968.

Preoccupied with the *Pueblo* crisis, the Johnson Administration failed to make a sure-footed response to the concerted attack on South Vietnam's cities. The attack was devastating, both to the US political and public opinion, and to the North Vietnamese themselves, who eventually suffered huge losses. In the drama of the period between 30 January and LBJ's 31 March speech, announcing not only his leaving of the Presidential race but also a new negotiations initiative, the US–Soviet dimension of the Vietnam conflict was overshadowed. Again, however, as in 1965, anticipated Soviet reactions figured largely in the internal debates about how to respond to Tet. At a 9 February meeting with the Joint Chiefs of Staff, LBJ raised the possibility of sending major reinforcements, backed up by an actual declaration of war. Although the CIA advised that neither the Soviets nor the Chinese wished to increase their commitment to the war, Dean Rusk advised against what would be 'a direct challenge to Moscow and Peking in a way we have never challenged them before'.[78]

The final decision was, of course, for a new version of the 'middle way': an element of de-escalation, a newly invigorated search for a negotiated peace, a continued military commitment to South Vietnam. The widespread dissatisfaction with LBJ's 'middle way' was brought home to the President when he boarded the aircraft carrier, *Constellation* on 17 February. According to speechwriter Harry McPherson, Johnson overheard a pilot, recently returned from the war: 'I've seen the god-damned Russian freighters sitting there, and the supplies stacked along the wharves. I can't hit them. It might start a wider war. Well, the war is too wide for me right now'.[79]

The 31 March speech was discussed in advance of its actual delivery with Ambassador Dobrynin. LBJ urged Dobrynin to work, building on the spirit of Glassboro, towards achieving a negotiating role for Moscow. The USSR, LBJ insisted, 'should be aware, however, that the US was not going to pull out of Vietnam'. Only five per cent of Americans wanted that. The US was prepared to halt bombing in ninety per cent of the territory of North Vietnam. Attacks below the 20th parallel would continue, to protect US personnel.

Dobrynin was assured there was no 'firm' time limit on the bombing cessation.[80] LBJ told Senator Fulbright that the offer gave Moscow 'a chance . . . to
show some responsibility'.[81]

The Soviets appear to have been opposed to any North Vietnamese hopes
that victory might be achieved without negotiations. However, they were also
suspicious of LBJ's new turn for peace. Dobrynin informed Harriman that the
mistrust engendered by the failure of 'Kosygin week' in London had not disappeared. For the Soviet Ambassador, LBJ was making 'an obvious appeal to
the Soviet government to help end the military conflict in Vietnam, yet essentially on the President's terms'.[82]

LBJ's main tactic was to attempt to convince Moscow that it had a shared
interest in checking (as he told Dobrynin on 31 March) China's 'aggressive
ambitions'. A wider regional war, serving Chinese interests, would be the price
of failing to reach a settlement in Vietnam. Harriman detected signs of hope
from Dobrynin: 'if we left North Vietnam alone, they were not as concerned
about events in South Vietnam'.[83]

Hanoi's swift acceptance of LBJ's offer to negotiate seems to have taken
Moscow by surprise. State Department analysts on 3 April argued that 'even
if Moscow had not counseled Hanoi's response to the President's speech, the
North Vietnamese at least knew they could count on full Soviet support'.[84]
Moscow offered assistance over the issue of choosing a venue for the talks.
The initial choice of Warsaw was unacceptable to Johnson. On 3 May, LBJ
announced that talks would begin in Paris shortly. This announcement followed Soviet pressure on Hanoi. As the Soviet Embassy in Hanoi put it:
'Without acting as an official mediator, the Soviet Union rendered an important service for the two sides to sit down at the negotiating table and open
official talks'.[85]

US–Soviet interchanges during the early period of the talks oscillated
between frankness and the repetition of entrenched positions. On 13 May,
Assistant Secretary of State William Bundy and Dobrynin had a wide-ranging
discussion of the prospects for peace. Bundy expressed concern that Hanoi
might simply be using the talks for military advantage, but accepted the Soviet
view that any 'absolute' commitment to halting military movement was unrealistic. Dobrynin reported North Vietnamese doubts about American good
faith and declared that 'there were many in Hanoi who, if the talks did not
go well, would become receptive to the Chinese argument that they were a
mistake to begin with'.[86] A more formal encounter on 17 May between State
Department personnel and Deputy Soviet Foreign Minister Kuznetsov pro-
gressed little beyond the communist view that progress depended on the US
renouncing all 'acts of war'. Dean Rusk noted the danger of the Paris talks
becoming mired at 'the level of fantasy', with Hanoi 'saying that there were
no [North Vietnamese] forces in the South'. 'Perhaps the US should add to the
fantasy by saying there were no US forces in the South'.[87]

Averell Harriman, now heading the US delegation in Paris, maintained direct contact with Moscow's Ambassador in the French capital, Valerian Zorin, with a view to keeping Soviet pressure on Hanoi. (Harriman saw Zorin as a conservative Stalinist, and at one stage actually asked Dobrynin that Zorin be replaced.) On 5 June, following a meeting between Kosygin and Hanoi delegation head Le Duc Tho, a letter was received in Washington from the Kremlin. Kosygin urged LBJ to undertake 'a full cessation ... of bombardments and other acts of war in relation to' North Vietnam.[88]

Kosygin's letter exposed deep divisions in Washington. Dean Rusk, Walt Rostow and (increasingly) LBJ himself saw it merely as a restatement of North Vietnam's 'fantasy' position: the kind of unhelpful, formal argument that Kuznetsov had presented to Rusk in May. LBJ wrote later: 'What was Moscow saying now that it had not said two and a half years earlier?'[89] The US had observed a bombing halt in December 1965, but had simply allowed Hanoi to take advantage. As Rostow informed LBJ in July, the letter was an 'opening'[90], but this was 'high-risk poker'. Accession to Kosygin's request might even lead to war with the Soviets: 'we would have to resume bombing if Moscow could not deliver Hanoi and that might make trouble with Moscow'.[91] Rusk argued that Hanoi must, at the very least, promise 'something concrete' in response to a US bombing halt.[92] Moscow was 'unable to tell us what would happen if we stopped the bombing'.[93]

Clark Clifford, now Secretary of Defense, opposed the Rostow-Rusk line. He interpreted Kosygin's letter as a direct offer: Moscow would *ensure* that progress was made, if only the US stopped all bombing. On 9 and 11 June, Clifford 'proposed that we take an action in Vietnam – perhaps lowering the level of the bombing of the North – based *directly* on the Soviet message, making clear to both Moscow and Hanoi that if there was no corresponding action by the North Vietnamese our action would be terminated'.[94] Kosygin, according to Clifford, 'honestly wants war to end'.[95] Johnson's reply to Kosygin contained a promise to cooperate, but only if 'you are in a position to tell us privately and with precision that there would be no adverse military consequences to our own and allied forces as a result' of (an apparently unconditional) bombing halt.[96]

LBJ's response was intended as a way to keep Kosygin's initiative alive, while recognising the dangers identified by Rostow and Rusk. Again, it was Johnson's familiar version of the 'middle way'. Presidential doubts were buried in Johnsonian bluster. He told Richard Nixon in June that the US was 'very close to winning' in Vietnam; Clifford was admonished to the effect that 'being soft' would not bring peace.[97] However, in Moscow it was regarded as little short of an outright rejection. Dobrynin told Harriman on 22 June that 'we had missed an opportunity'. (Harriman replied that 'the stakes were too serious to take such a risk'.)[98] Several senior figures in Washington agreed with Dobrynin. Rostow told LBJ in July that Llewellyn Thompson and Charles

Bohlen 'feel a certain regret that we did not pick up Kosygin's message, institute a total bombing halt, and then lean very heavily on the Soviet Union to
produce results'.[99]

Bohlen and Thompson continued to press for a bombing halt and for a
more active response to Moscow. A CIA report in mid-July offered a cool
verdict on the prospects. In an analysis passed to LBJ by Richard Helms, John
Huizenga of the Office of National Estimates concluded that 'the Soviets
clearly do not have significant influence on Hanoi's policy'. It would be naive
to suppose, argued Huizenga, that 'the outcome Moscow will be working for'
would be anything other than 'one satisfactory to the Hanoi leadership'. Nevertheless, Moscow was clearly engaged in 'some diplomatic activity in the ante-
rooms of the Paris talks'.[100] At this stage, LBJ and Rostow certainly considered
a more positive, direct response to the Kosygin letter. Johnson's mental and
emotional condition at this time was one of turmoil. His main concern in
regard to Soviet policy, of course, was the proposed arms summit, rather than
the recruitment of Moscow to the cause of Vietnamese peace. On 30 July, the
day of a rather hard-line press conference on the war, Johnson complained
privately that 'the International Communists have a movement under way to
get me to stop the bombing'.[101]

The Soviet invasion of Czechoslovakia in late August delayed, rather than
demolished, LBJ's move to a more compliant position on the bombing. The
decision of 31 October to halt bombing completely was the product of intense
US–Soviet diplomatic interaction. In early September, Dobrynin informed Walt
Rostow that, in the event of a halt, Hanoi 'would negotiate seriously'.[102] On
2 October, Dean Rusk made a virtually direct request for Soviet assistance,
noting that the Russians 'were probably the best informed people in the world
as to the negotiating situation since they were getting detailed information
from both sides'.[103] Following contacts between US representative Cyrus Vance
and the Soviet Embassy in Paris, Dobrynin offered Washington on 14 October
the possibility of 'speedy progress'.[104] On 25 October, Rostow reported to the
President on a recent exchange with Dobrynin. The Soviet Ambassador had
been informed that 'the leaders of Hanoi should seize the moment'. The US
was prepared to halt bombing without specific North Vietnamese assurances
that no military advantage would be taken. Dobrynin declared that a breakthrough was likely in Paris.[105] Later on 25 October, Johnson received another
letter from Kosygin, this time emphasising the need to move beyond 'third-
rate details' and end all bombing. Johnson, encouraged by reports that North
Vietnam was finding it difficult to regroup militarily following the Tet Offensive losses, decided to comply. A major problem – far more than a 'third-rate
detail' – involved the reluctance of the Saigon government to participate in the
talks.[106]

The Johnson era expired amid continued wrangling between Washington
and Saigon, and with the US military pressing for bombing resumption and

for American occupation of the demilitarised zone. With Soviet diplomatic assistance, however, the procedural path towards substantive talks was eventually cleared. Commenting later on Moscow's role during this period, Cyrus Vance noted: 'We made clear to the Russians what we had told the North Vietnamese, and we asked the Soviets to let us know whether it was clear in their minds that the North Vietnamese understood what had been said and what was expected of them'.[107]

It would be four more years before the US military withdrew from Vietnam. US–Soviet cooperation clearly had been an important factor in starting the talks, and in keeping the possibility of a diplomatic solution in the minds of the North Vietnamese. There was little sign, however, of any real Soviet commitment to peace. With talks finally underway, Moscow appeared to be reassured that a wider, regional conflict, serving Chinese interests, was unlikely to break out in the immediate future.[108] For the time being, Moscow seemed happy to enjoy the peripheral benefits of the continuing American commitment to Southeast Asia, while awaiting signs of intent from the incoming Nixon Administration.

Notes

1 *FRUS, 1964–1968*: Volume IV: *Vietnam, 1966* (Washington DC, US Government Printing Office, 1998), p. 432.
2 See I. V. Gaiduk, *The Soviet Union and the Vietnam War* (Chicago, Dee, 1996), pp. 75–80.
3 *FRUS, 1964–1968*: Volume IV: *Vietnam, 1966*, p. 463 (Sullivan to George Ball, 29 June).
4 See R. S. McNamara, *In Retrospect* (New York, Times Books, 1995), p. 252.
5 Office of the President File, box 13, 'Meeting in Cabinet room, 27 Jan. 1966' (Valenti notes). On the CIA and Soviet missile estimates, see NSF: CF: Europe and USSR: USSR, box 221, CIA, 20 Jan. 1966, 'Communist reaction to the US peace offensive'. See also L. C. Gardner, 'Fighting Vietnam: the Russian–American conundrum', in L. C. Gardner and T. Gittinger (eds.), *International Perspectives on Vietnam* (College Station, Texas A and M University Press, 2000), pp. 23–57, at p. 37.
6 Quoted in F. E. Vandiver, *Shadows of Vietnam: Lyndon Johnson's War* (College Station, Texas A and M University Press, 1997), p. 164.
7 H. Kissinger, *Diplomacy* (New York, Simon and Schuster, 1994), p. 663.
8 Vandiver, *Shadows of Vietnam*, p. 264.
9 Clark Clifford and Douglass Cater, quoted in M. Small, *Johnson, Nixon and the Doves* (New Brunswick, Rutgers University Press, 1988), p. 136.
10 J. A. Califano, *The Triumph and Tragedy of Lyndon Johnson* (New York, Simon and Schuster, 1991), p. 121.
11 E. R. Goldman, *The Tragedy of Lyndon Johnson* (New York, Harper and Row, 1969), pp. 590–1.
12 Quoted in C. DeBenedetti, 'Lyndon Johnson and the antiwar opposition', in R. A. Divine (ed.), *The Johnson Years: Volume Two: Vietnam, the Environment and Science* (Lawrence, University Press of Kansas, 1987), pp. 23–53, at p. 37.
13 Quoted in T. Wells, *The War Within: America's Battle with Vietnam* (Berkeley, University of California Press, 1994), p. 207.
14 D. Halberstam, *The Best and the Brightest* (Greenwich, Fawcett Crest, 1972), pp. 757–8.

15 See Wells, *The War Within*, pp. 206, 210. LBJ told Richard Nixon in July 1968 that he
    believed Moscow was behind the anti-war campaign (see *FRUS, 1964–1968*: Volume VI:
    Vietnam, January – August 1968 (Washington DC, US Government Printing Office, 2002),
    p. 895 (26 July 1968)).
16 *FRUS, 1964–1968*: Volume IV: *Vietnam, 1966*, pp. 330–31 (5 April 1966).
17 See ibid., p. 433 (undated).
18 *FRUS, 1964–1968*: Volume XIV: *The Soviet Union* (Washington DC, US Government Print-
    ing Office, 2001), p. 411 (6 Aug. 1966).
19 See Gardner, 'Fighting Vietnam', p. 39.
20 Harriman to LBJ and Rusk, 3 Oct. 1966, NSF: CF: Vietnam, box 212.
21 Gardner, 'Fighting Vietnam', p. 40.
22 *FRUS, 1964–1968*: Volume XIV: *The Soviet Union*, p. 405 (15 July 1966).
23 Gardner, 'Fighting Vietnam', p. 38.
24 M. Beschloss (ed.), *Reaching For Glory* (New York, Simon and Schuster, 2001), p. 216 (Lady
    Bird Johnson's taped diary, 7 March 1965).
25 *FRUS: 1964–1968*: Volume IV: *Vietnam, 1966*, p. 405 (29 May 1966).
26 See I. A. Gaiduk, 'Soviet policy towards US participation in the Vietnam war', in W. L. Hixson
    (ed.), *Leadership and Diplomacy in the Vietnam War* (New York, Garland Publishing, 2000),
    pp. 132–46, at p. 142.
27 A. Dobrynin, *In Confidence* (New York, Times Books, 1995), p. 131.
28 See *FRUS, 1964–1968*: Volume XIV: *The Soviet Union*, p. 419 (22–24 Sept. 1966).
29 *FRUS, 1964–1968*: Volume IV: *Vietnam, 1966*, p. 664 (24 Sept. 1966).
30 Ibid., p. 702.
31 Ibid., pp. 716–21. See also Gardner, 'Fighting Vietnam', p. 41.
32 See G. C. Herring (ed.), *The Secret Diplomacy of the Vietnam War: The Negotiating Volumes
    of the Pentagon Papers* (Austin, University of Texas Press, 1981), p. 389.
33 *FRUS, 1964–1968*: Volume IV: *Vietnam, 1966*, p. 875 (28 Nov. 1966).
34 Ibid., pp. 907–8.
35 McNamara, *In Retrospect*, p. 289.
36 Ibid., p. 250; Gaiduk, *The Soviet Union and the Vietnam War*, pp. 92–3.
37 Gardner, 'Fighting Vietnam', p. 42.
38 R. S. McNamara, J. C. Blight and R. K. Brigham, *Argument Without End: In Search of
    Answers to the Vietnam Tragedy* (New York, Public Affairs, 1999), p. 289.
39 NSF: CF: Vietnam, boxes 143, 147, 148, folder, 'MARIGOLD II', 'McNaughton-Zinchuk
    lunch', 3 Jan. 1967. See also Harrison Salisbury, Oral History (LBJ Library).
40 NSF: CF: Vietnam, box 137, folder, 'Memos/Bombing Halt', 'press conference, 2 Feb. 1967'.
41 NSF: CF: UK, box 210, telegram, 27 Nov. 1966.
42 *FRUS, 1964–1968*: Volume IV: *Vietnam, 1966*, p. 823 (10 Nov. 1966).
43 PREM 13 1917, telegram, Brown to Rusk, 4 Jan. 1967 (Public Records Office, London).
44 For background, see J. Dumbrell, *A Special Relationship: Anglo-American Relations in the
    Cold War and After* (Basingstoke, Macmillan/Palgrave, 2001), especially ch. 4; J. Dumbrell,
    'The Johnson Administration and the British Labour Government: Vietnam, the Pound and
    East of Suez', *Journal of American Studies*, 30:2 (1996) 211–31.
45 FCO 15 633 (PRO).
46 NSF: Files of W. W. Rostow, 'Marigold-Sunflower', box 9, Cooper to Rusk and Harriman,
    7 Feb. 1967.
47 *FRUS, 1964–1968*: Volume V: *Vietnam, 1967* (Washington DC, US Government Printing
    Office, 2002), p. 109.
48 NSF: CF: Vietnam, box 256, 'Sunflower DOUBLE PLUS', Rostow, 'For the President's diary'.
49 NSF: CF: Vietnam, box 251, 'Sunflower 2', Rusk to LBJ, 11 Feb. 1967.
50 *FRUS, 1964–1968*: Volume V: *Vietnam, 1967*, p. 122 (11 Feb. 1967).

51 Ibid., p. 124.

52 For a fuller, documented account of these events, see J. Dumbrell and S. Ellis, 'British involvement in Vietnam peace initiatives, 1966–1967: marigolds, sunflowers and "Kosygin week"', *Diplomatic History*, 27:1 (2003) 113–49.

53 Read, Oral History, pp. 10–12 (tape 2). See also *FRUS, 1964–1968*: Volume V: *Vietnam, 1967*, pp. 150–161. A strong element of cynicism and scepticism about Kosygin's mediation is evident in the LBJ–McNamara and LBJ–Rostow exchanges. Ambassador David Bruce was described by LBJ as wanting 'to be a Goddamned peace-maker' (ibid., p. 154, 123 Feb. 1967).

54 Quoted in Gardner, 'Fighting Vietnam', p. 44.

55 *FRUS, 1964–1968*: Volume XIV: *The Soviet Union*, p. 478 (telegram from Moscow Embassy, 24 April 1967).

56 Ibid., p. 482 (4 May 1967).

57 See Gaiduk, *The Soviet Union and the Vietnam War*, pp. 113–20.

58 *FRUS, 1964–1968*: Volume V: *Vietnam, 1967*, p. 395.

59 Gaiduk, *The Soviet Union and the Vietnam War*, p. 120.

60 *FRUS, 1964–1968*: Volume V: *Vietnam, 1967*, p. 472.

61 Ibid., p. 521.

62 Ibid., p. 523 (19 June 1967).

63 NSF: CF: Europe and USSR: USSR, box 229, folder, 'Hollybush I', 11 June 1967.

64 *FRUS, 1964–1968*: Volume XIV: *The Soviet Union*, p. 499 (21 June 1967).

65 Ibid., p. 501 (21 June 1967).

66 NSF: CF: Europe and USSR: USSR, box 230, folder, 'Hollybush', 15 June 1967 (CIA).

67 *FRUS, 1964–1968*: Volume XIV: *The Soviet Union*, p. 505.

68 Ibid., pp. 523, 530–33, 539, 550.

69 *FRUS, 1964–1968*: Volume V: *Vietnam, 1967*, p. 548 (23 June 1967).

70 NSF: CF: Europe and USSR: USSR, box 224, 'memos xvi', 23 Sept. 1967.

71 *FRUS, 1964–1968*: Volume XIV: *The Soviet Union*, p. 590 (28 Sept. 1967).

72 *FRUS, 1964–1968*: Volume V: *Vietnam, 1967*, p. 838 (3 Oct. 1967).

73 NSF: NSC Meetings File, box 2, folder, 'vol 4', Brzezinski to W. H. Roche, 'China, the Soviet Union and Vietnam', 27 Nov. 1967.

74 *FRUS, 1964–1968*: Volume XIV: *The Soviet Union*, pp. 605–6 (11 Dec. 1967).

75 Quoted in Gardner, 'Fighting Vietnam', p. 52.

76 *FRUS, 1964–1968*: Volume V: *Vietnam, 1967*, p. 1092 (2 Dec. 1967).

77 *FRUS, 1964–1968*: Volume XIV: *The Soviet Union*, p. 625 (11 Jan. 1968).

78 Quoted in R. Dallek, *Flawed Giant* (New York, Oxford University Press, 1998), p. 507. See also *FRUS, 1964–1968*: Volume VI: *Vietnam: January – August, 1968*, p. 291 (CIA, 1 March 1968).

79 H. McPherson, *A Political Education* (Boston, Houghton Mifflin, 1988), p. 426.

80 *FRUS, 1964–1968*: Volume XIV: *The Soviet Union*, p. 641 (31 March 1968).

81 *FRUS, 1964–1968*: Volume VI: *Vietnam, January – August, 1968*, p. 499 (1 April 1968).

82 See Gaiduk, *The Soviet Union and Vietnam*, p. 148; Dobrynin, *In Confidence*, p. 171.

83 NSF: Files of W. W. Rostow, box 11, 'memo of conversation, 1 April 1968'. LBJ to Dobrynin, as note 70.

84 Quoted in Gaiduk, *The Soviet Union and the Vietnam War*, p. 150.

85 Ibid., p. 154.

86 NSF: CF: Europe and USSR: USSR, box 225, folder, 'memos 19', 'luncheon conversation, 13 May 1968'.

87 Ibid., 'memorandum of conversation, 17 May 1968'.

88 NSF: Files of W. W. Rostow, box 10, Rostow to LBJ, 5 June 1968 (enclosing the Kosygin letter).

89 L. B. Johnson, *The Vantage Point* (London, Weidenfeld and Nicolson, 1971), p. 510.
90 *FRUS, 1964–1968*: Volume VI: *Vietnam, January – August 1968*, p. 850 (12 July 1968).
91 NSF: Files of W. W. Rostow, box 10, folder, 'Kosygin (3)', Rostow to LBJ, 14 July 1968.
92 Quoted in Gaiduk, *The Soviet Union and the Vietnam War*, p. 165.
93 *FRUS, 1964–1968*: Volume VI: *Vietnam, January – August, 1968*, p. 903 (26 July 1968).
94 C. Clifford, *Counsel to the President* (New York, Random House, 1991), p. 547.
95 *FRUS, 1964–1968*: Volume VI: *Vietnam, January – August, 1968*, p. 771 (9 June 1968).
96 NSF: Files of W. W. Rostow, box 10, folder, 'Kosygin (3)', LBJ to Kosygin, 11 June 1968.
97 *FRUS, 1964–1968*: Volume VI: *Vietnam, January – August, 1968*, pp. 900 (26 July 1968) and 776 (9 June 1968).
98 NSF: CF: Europe and USSR: USSR, box 229, folder, 'Dobrynin conversations 2', 'memorandum of conversation, 22 June 1968'.
99 NSF: Files of W. W. Rostow, box, 10, folder, 'Kosygin (3)', Rostow to LBJ, 12 July 1968.
100 *FRUS, 1964–1968*: Volume XIV: *The Soviet Union*, pp. 661–2 (15 July 1968).
101 Quoted in Gardner, 'Fighting Vietnam', p. 56.
102 *FRUS, 1964–1968*: Volume XIV: *The Soviet Union*, p. 699 (10 Sept. 1968).
103 Ibid., p. 730.
104 Quoted in Gaiduk, *The Soviet Union and the Vietnam War*: p. 180.
105 *FRUS, 1964–1968*: Volume XIV: *The Soviet Union*, p. 742.
106 See ibid., pp. 744–5; G. C. Herring, *LBJ and Vietnam: A Different Kind of War* (Austin, University of Texas Press, 1994), pp. 171–7.
107 Vance, Oral History, p. 21.
108 See Gaiduk, 'Soviet policy towards US participation in the Vietnam War', p. 145.

6

Cuba

LBJ, Latin America and communism

This chapter will explore the extent to which the US in the 1960s, faced by the continuing defiance of Fidel Castro's regime in Cuba, saw Soviet influence in the Caribbean as a force for stability and discipline. In postulating elements of partnership in US–Soviet relations, it is important to appreciate the ambivalence of American attitudes and the divisions of opinion in official Washington. A CIA report of January 1968 concluded that the notion of 'a world-wide Soviet triumph' had 'long since lost much of its substance and virtually all its immediacy'.[1] Yet it was still difficult to believe that the Soviets had entirely discarded hopes of recruiting the lands of the rising peoples to a revolutionist path. Eugene Rostow, serving LBJ as Under Secretary of State for Political Affairs, warned in May 1967 of a 'renewal (or should I say intensification?) of Soviet adventurism in the many soft under-bellies of the world'.[2]

During the Johnson era, of course, the US had its own, local, 'soft underbelly'. Castro's nationalist revolution of 1959 (against the US-backed regime of Fulgencio Batista) had turned leftward after 1960. The expropriation of foreign property on the island, and the associated economic warfare with the US, encouraged a new closeness between Havana and Moscow. Under the implicit bargain made in 1960–61, Havana gained a protector and underwriter for the revolution. Moscow obtained a propaganda – to a lesser degree, a strategic – prize: an ally, possibly a surrogate, in America's backyard. Nikita Khrushchev's decision to withdraw Soviet offensive missiles, following the 1962 Cuban crisis, seemed to Castro a betrayal of the bargain. In 1963, as LBJ succeeded Kennedy, communist Cuba stood still in defiance of the US: a mixture of national embarrassment and security threat. Before examining the development of LBJ's policy towards Cuba and its Soviet ties, it is the intention now to consider Johnson's approach to Western hemispheric issues, his legacy from Kennedy, and the continuing effects of the 1962 Cuban missile crisis.

Lyndon Johnson was a US president who had once taught at a Mexican-American grade school in Cotulla, Texas, where Hispanics – he recalled – were treated 'just worse than you'd treat a dog'.[3] According to Ralph Dungan, who worked on Latin American issues for JFK, Johnson had 'kind of a romantic Tex-Mex view of the region'.[4] He seems to have shared with Thomas Mann, fellow Texan and Johnson's first State Department leader on Latin America, a simplistically racialised view of how to treat America's Southern neighbours. Describing the Mexican-Americans he had known in the Texas of his youth, LBJ recollected: 'They'll come right into your yard and take it over if you let them. But if you say to 'em right at the start, "hold on, just wait a minute", they'll know they're dealing with somebody who'll stand up. And after that you can get along fine'.[5] (LBJ frequently recycled his anecdotes and analogies. His remarks here recalled his famous advice to treat the Russians like a bully on the front porch.) Thomas Mann's assessment of 'my Latinos' has become something of a classic of stereotypical 'othering' by an American official: 'They understand only two things – a buck in the pocket and a kick in the ass'.[6]

Johnson inherited the Kennedy commitment, embodied in the Alliance for Progress, to meshing US Western hemispheric security interests with the encouragement of political and economic (particularly land) reform. Under LBJ, the Alliance for Progress foundered. JFK supporters – notably Bobby Kennedy and Arthur Schlesinger Jr – blamed the appointment of Mann as 'Mr Latin America' in the new Administration. To Schlesinger, Tom Mann was 'a colonialist by mentality and a free enterprise bigot'.[7] Mann's December 1963 appointment (as Assistant Secretary for Latin America and Coordinator of the Alliance for Progress) has, in fact, cast a long shadow over subsequent interpretations of LBJ's policies in the Western hemisphere. The appointment was actually the culmination of organisational changes, begun by JFK and designed to consolidate bureaucratic authority over regional policies. Mann was not an especial pal of LBJ and had been appointed by Kennedy as Ambassador to Mexico. In March 1964, Mann informed Latin American chiefs of mission that anti-communism, rather than democracy-promotion, should guide US aid policies. Leaked to the *New York Times*, and dubbed the 'Mann Doctrine', this injunction unquestionably gave out signals that Washington was unlikely to fret overly about the democratic credentials of the (increasingly militarised) regional governments. LBJ's National Security Action Memorandum 297, issued in April 1964, required Latin American military aid to be geared towards 'internal security missions'.[8] The early Johnson years in particular did see a newly explicit emphasis on the anti-communist (particularly anti-Soviet) and pro-free enterprise strand within the Alliance for Progress. In January 1965, Dean Rusk urged regional allies to avoid diplomatic and consular contacts with the USSR. Any expansion of the Soviet diplomatic presence would 'only confirm their arrogant assumption that Free World governments are gullible and lacking in toughness . . .'.[9] In 1964, Johnson declared in public that he had concluded 'that you could take all the gold in Fort Knox and it would just go down the drain in Latin America, unless the private investor . . .

could have some confidence that he could make his investment and it would not be confiscated . . .'.[10] In early 1964, LBJ set up a Business Group for Latin America, chaired by David Rockefeller, to develop policies for the private sector under the Alliance for Progress aegis. (Rockefeller had been part of JFK's team which coordinated the Alliance in its early stages, but had publicly criticised its lack of commitment to the role of private capital.)

Johnson had no wholehearted personal commitment to the Alliance for Progress, an initiative which after all, would always be seen as a child of Camelot. Yet the Alliance's loss of direction was not entirely the fault of the Johnson Administration. Particularly with the level of funding voted to it by Congress, the Alliance for Progress, even had JFK lived, was unlikely to have successfully squared the circle of security and reform. Efforts made by the Johnson team to foster regional economic integration may even be seen as injecting new life into the Alliance in the late 1960s. It is also sometimes forgotten that Mann served only until 1966. His successors, Lincoln Gordon and Covey Oliver, were not in the same mould as ther predecessor.[11]

As his 1965 Johns Hopkins University speech (on US investment in Vietnam) showed, LBJ was not hostile to the big-spending internationalist reformism which had inspired at least one element of the Alliance for Progress. In Latin America, however, fear of 'Castroite subversion' tended to trump the commitment to democratic reform. Sovietised communism, not military dictatorship, appeared the main threat to the 'democracy' whose importance he extolled to Dean Rusk in 1963: 'This hemisphere is where we live. These people are our neighbors. If we can't make it work here, where we live, how can we expect to make it work anywhere else?'.[12]

Johnson's attitudes towards Cuba were affected not only by these general perceptions about the hemisphere and its inhabitants; but also by pragmatic considerations about the possible domestic repercussions of giving ground to Castro, and about the dangers of actually invading the island.

For LBJ, the contest with Cuba's leader was highly personal. When Castro ordered the shutting off of water supplies to the US base at Guantanamo (on the Eastern tip of Cuba) in 1964, Johnson interpreted it as a deliberate and personal provocation: Castro 'had decided, perhaps with Soviet encouragement, to take the measure of the new President . . . , to push me a little and see what my response would be'.[13] At the time of the Dominican Republic crisis, LBJ complained to Democratic Senator Mike Mansfield about the domestic political risks of allowing Castro to claim regional successes. 'Do we let Castro take over and us move out?' Republicans ('the Dirksens') would 'eat us up if I let another Cuba come in there'.[14] On occasion, Johnson spoke as if Havana, and even Moscow, were just part of a global communist plot: 'They are moving other places in the hemisphere. It may be part of a whole Communistic pattern tied in with Vietnam'.[15] LBJ and Mann continually feared waking up to find 'another Cuba' lying on America's hemispheric doormat. Actual invasion, however, was best avoided. Memories of the disastrous 1961 invasion by US-sponsored Cuban exiles remained with LBJ. He insisted to Senator Fulbright in December, 1963: 'No, I'm not getting into any Bay of Pigs deal'.[16] Johnson's patience, however, was not inexhaustible. Regarding the 1965 invasion of the Dominican Republic, LBJ told Abe Fortas: 'I don't *want* to be an intervener. But I think Mr Castro's done intervened pretty good . . .'.[17] He commented 'That's right' in response to the following comments, made in June 1965, by Secretary McNamara: 'I went through the Bay of Pigs, and I'm responsible in part for that. And we were wrong not because we did what we did. We were wrong because we failed'.[18]

Washington's developing policy towards Havana was conditioned not only by recollections of the 1961 Bay of Pigs invasion, but also by the continuing backwash from the 1962 missile crisis. To Johnson's relief, U-2 overflights of Cuba revealed no sign of Soviet strategic missiles. At his first Presidential briefing on Cuba, Johnson was told by McGeorge Bundy that a primary American objective was 'to ensure that there is no reintroduction of offensive missiles'. Bundy reported that Cuban overflights had revealed no such missiles and that 'big withdrawals' of Soviet troops had taken place.[19] CIA reports periodically confirmed the apparent absence of offensive missiles, despite occasional newspaper reports to the effect that the Soviets were reintroducing them. (Such reports generally emanated from Cuban exiles in Florida). LBJ was assured that Moscow did not wish to repeat the 1962 confrontation. CIA Director Richard Helms reported in March 1967: 'We do not believe that the Soviets will again try to turn Cuba into a strategic base of their own, as in 1962'. Moscow wished to avoid 'another grave confrontation with the US'. In any case, the build-up of a strategic nuclear force in the USSR itself, according to Helms, made Cuba less important to Moscow than in 1962.[20]

Aside from missiles and the putative Soviet fear of sliding back into confrontation, the 1962 crisis cast another shadow over US policy towards Cuba later in the decade: this time, in the form of JFK's undertaking not to invade. This undertaking had formed part of the resolution of the crisis, and appeared in the 28 October correspondence with Moscow. JFK's promise was hardly absolute. It was clearly tied to the removal of missiles. On 21 November, he wrote to Khrushchev that 'there need be no fear of any invasion of Cuba while matters take their present favorable course'.[21] At a press conference on the previous day, Kennedy had stated that 'if Cuba is not used for the export of aggressive Communist purposes, there will be peace in the Caribbean'.[22] Khrushchev attempted to convert this into a blanket undertaking, informing JFK on 11 December 1962: 'We believe that the guarantees for non-invasion of Cuba given by you will be maintained and not only in the period of your stay in the White House, that, to use an expression, goes without saying'.[23] The Johnson Administration, however, certainly did not see itself as bound by any absolute commitment not to invade. Reintroduction of Soviet missiles or sustained 'export of aggressive Communist purposes' would cancel the force of JFK's undertaking. Indeed, one reason why Johnson was so concerned about Cuban subversion in Latin America was precisely because clear evidence of such activity would increase the domestic pressure on the President to invade.[24]

Johnson's ambivalence about invasion was, in fact, made evident in the very first days of his Presidency. He told Deputy Soviet Chairman Mikoyan on 26 November 1963 that 'the United States was not planning to invade Cuba'.[25] Two days later, however, LBJ informed CIA chief McCone that, although there must be no repetition of the Bay of Pigs, 'the Cuban situation was one that we could not live with and we had to evolve more aggressive policies'. LBJ and McCone also discussed the possibility of invasion on 30 May, when the CIA chief argued that any invasion should be conducted with the support of regional allies in the Organisation of American States – 'otherwise it would involve confrontation with Khrushchev'. McCone (in his own record of the meeting) 'stated that if the action was a Hemispheric action I didn't see that the USSR could do much about it'. Johnson 'agreed'.[26] A State Department assessment of 1966 dismissed JFK's 'no invasion' pledge as little more than a device used by Khrushchev 'to placate Castro' after the 1962 climbdown.[27]

The US, the USSR and Cuba: 1963–65

The most dangerous issue in US-Cuban relations during the Johnson years involved the possibility of a shootdown, with Soviet-supplied surface-to-air (SAM) missiles, of an overflying American U-2 aircraft. The U-2 overflights, of course, were yet another legacy of the 1962 Cuban missile crisis. In July 1964, Gordon Chase, deputy to McGeorge Bundy and Cuba specialist on the NSC staff, described the legal basis for the US spy flights as 'somewhat shaky' and urged that the issue be kept out of the World Court.[28] The purpose of the flights was primarily to check on possible Soviet missile deployments. Bromley Smith, NSC Executive Secretary, reported to Bundy in March 1964:

> The Russians should continue to be held responsible for Castro's conduct in con-
> nection with those aspects of the Cuba missile crisis which are still with us. Our
> surveillance arises out of Khrushchev's failure to get Castro to accept on-site inspec-
> tion in Cuba.[29]

Before proceeding with the issue of U-2 overflights, it is important to consider the general atmosphere surrounding US–Cuban relations in the two years or so following Kennedy's death. The most obvious initial area of tension involved the possibility of Cuban involvement in the assassination itself. The Guantanamo water supply mini-crisis of February 1964 was easily resolved, but indicated the potential for problems in the US–Cuban cohabitation. More fundamentally, however, the context for US–Cuban–Soviet relations was set by American reactions to Castro's 1964 'peace offensive', together with LBJ's attitude towards the continuation of CIA-directed covert operations against the Cuban regime.

Johnson's worries about the Cuban connections of Lee Harvey Oswald were voiced during his meeting with Mikoyan on 26 November 1963. The Soviet Deputy Chairman replied that Fidel Castro was 'a great humanitarian', who had shown sincere regret over JFK's death. When LBJ referred generally to 'Castro-promoted subversion', Mikoyan countered that 'a small nation like Cuba' was not capable of subverting anyone.[30] As indicated in Chapter 2, Johnson seems to have retained some suspicion that Cubans were involved in the assassination. (Later conspiracy theories, of course, tended to implicate anti-Castro Cuban exiles, incensed at JFK's 'no invasion' pledge, rather than Castroites.) LBJ continued to give private voice to the idea that CIA plans to kill Castro had provoked the murder of Kennedy. Johnson certainly feared a Cuban attempt against his own life. In the early days of his Presidency, however, he was content to finesse the issue, deflecting any pressure for a retaliatory invasion of Cuba.[31]

In regard to the Kennedy assassination, LBJ seems to have thought in terms of a Cuban, rather than a Cuban–Soviet conspiracy. He also occasionally speculated on the possibility of Vietnamese involvement. In general, however, the President tended to interpret Cuban actions in terms of Soviet power projection. As indicated above, he detected Moscow's hand in the 1964 Guantanamo water supply affair. Interestingly, a CIA report of March 1964 interpreted the water cut-off as a direct Cuban action. It was a retaliation – the 'least hard' retaliation easily available to Castro – for the detention in Florida of Cuban fishermen, who had strayed into US waters. At the time, Cuban leaders, according to the report, actually enjoyed Moscow's discomfiture in the face of a new US–Cuban confrontation: 'Nikita [Khrushchev] must be soiling himself with fright'.[32] The crisis was resolved by LBJ's decision to effectuate a contingency plan to import water and to commence seawater treatment. Apart from two fishermen, who chose to remain in Miami, the Cubans held in Florida were released fairly quickly.

The first fifteen or so months of LBJ's Presidency were, in fact, taken up by a detailed attempt to rethink policy towards Cuba. As in so many other areas, the Kennedy legacy here was very ambiguous. The Kennedy era saw a sustained commitment to covert operations, sabotage and attempts to assassinate Castro. As LBJ himself later put it: 'We had been operating a damned Murder Inc. in the Caribbean'.[33] However, in January 1963, McGeorge Bundy and Gordon Chase launched an initiative which was designed to open a personal dialogue with Castro, with a view to securing US–Cuban accommodation on terms acceptable to Washington. These initiatives – which involved William Attwood (adviser to Adlai Stevenson, US Representative at the UN), Lisa Howard of the American Broadcasting Company and the French journalist, Jean Daniel – reached a hiatus with JFK's death. Attwood became Ambas-

sador to Kenya. However, the initiatives involving Howard were resumed and
continued intermittently through 1964, with briefings being relayed via Adlai
Stevenson. At LBJ's first Cuba briefing (19 December 1963), Bundy reported
on the 'very tenuous, sensitive, and marginal contacts' with Castro. The US,
according to Bundy, was 'essentially faced with a decision as to whether or
not we are prepared to listen to what Castro has to say'. A year later, Bundy
and Chase arranged, through Lisa Howard, a meeting between Democratic
Senator Eugene McCarthy and Cuban leader Ernesto 'Che' Guevara. The
possibility of American recognition for the regime was discussed in these
meetings.[34]

LBJ's willingness to listen to Castro was based on a slightly paradoxical
American understanding of the relationship between Havana and Moscow.
Chase reported in April 1964 that Castro was 'very uneasy' about his grow-
ing dependency on Moscow. He was worried about a possible Moscow–
Washington deal being made over his head. He also regarded, following the
Cuban missile crisis, any Soviet guarantees to Cuba as virtually worthless.[35]
The US should even prepare itself for a possible 'Castro decision to eject the
Russians'. Chase also felt that Moscow might leave of its own accord:

> A Soviet decision to quit Cuba cannot be dismissed categorically in view of such
> factors as (1) the lack of real Soviet progress in making Cuba a 'show piece' (2) the
> obvious US determination to make Cuba a 'dead end' (no more Cubas will be per-
> mitted) (3) the magnitude of Soviet aid to Cuba, and (4) the extent of the USSR's
> own present economic problems.[36]

Under this interpretation, Castro was engaged in a deliberate 'peace offensive',
designed to secure a *modus vivendi* with Washington in anticipation of the
day when Moscow's support had either disappeared or severely diminished.
The US should respond positively, albeit with a strong commitment to securing an accommodation on *American* terms.[37] Castro's flexibility – the Guantanamo water incident notwithstanding – was seen to be evident in public
statements concerning the possibility of negotiating over expropriated US
assets. In an interview with the *New York Times* journalist Richard Eder in
July 1964, Castro even stopped condemning the Alliance for Progress as a tool
of American imperialism, and offered the initiative his limited support.[38]

An alternative view of the possibility of accommodating Castro emphasised
the degree to which the 'peace offensive' actually emanated from Moscow,
rather than from the Cuban regime's desire to free itself from Soviet dependence. A CIA report in February 1964 noted how Moscow had been working
'to defuse the Cuban situation'.[39] In March, the CIA opined that Castro had
been told during his second visit to Moscow (January 1964) that there was a
US–Soviet 'accord' on Cuba and that the Cuban leadership should work to
'consolidate' the accord.[40] In January 1964, the CIA described Castro's Cuba
as 'still a dangerous involvement of Soviet interests in an exposed position,

and the USSR still desires to stabilize Cuban–American relations'.[41] The Eder interview was generally interpreted by American Havana-watchers as reflecting Soviet pressure to move towards normalisation of relations with the US.[42]

The key question, of course, was: normalisation on whose terms? We will return to the possibility of accommodation, and its implications for US–Soviet relations, at the end of this chapter. As it was, LBJ, slowly and indecisively, decided against accommodation. The decision was partly linked to US reluctance to abandon covert operations, the second strand of the JFK legacy. At the first Presidential briefing on Cuba after the assassination, Desmond Fitzgerald of the CIA outlined plans to attack the Matanzas power plant. (The plan was rejected, with Llewellyn Thompson arguing that an 'attack on a big Cuban target could give Castro important leverage in his negotiations for more Soviet aid'.)[43] Low-level CIA sabotage and 'dirty tricks' persisted during the Johnson years. The CIA may, for example, have planted a cache of Cuban weapons which were found in Venezuela in December 1963. According to Warren Hinckle and W. J. Turner, the 'Cuba Project' – an undercover CIA operation that began in 1959 – 'slumbered' after 1963.[44] LBJ had little appetite for daredevil assassination plots and, in April 1964, issued an instruction to abandon such activity. Yet at least one Cuban would-be assassin, employed by the CIA, remained operative until early 1966. In December 1967, W. G. Bowdler, who by then was Cuba specialist on Walt Rostow's staff, described how the CIA was 'revamping the Cuban operation'. Since the 1961 invasion, the CIA had worked from a 'not well camouflaged establishment in Miami', geared to 'stimulating Castro's overthrow from the outside with propaganda, infiltrators, supplies, etc'.[45]

LBJ's decision to reject the Bundy–Chase accommodation strategy involved a clear commitment to isolating Castro from other regional governments in the Organisation of American States (OAS), and to enforcing and extending the 'Free World' trade embargo on Cuba. The economic quarantine on Cuba, of course, contrasted sharply with LBJ's economic bridge-building to Russia and the East European communist satellites. This contrast pointed up the peculiar propinquity, and domestic political sensitivity, of communist defiance of the US in the Caribbean. The isolation-embargo approach, as Morris Morley has argued, exemplified the post-1962 move away from the failing 'insider' strategy of destabilisation and assassination.[46] The new 'outsider' policy, in isolating Cuba economically and politically, was still designed to lead to the final extinction of the regime – possibly as a result of the Soviets losing patience, possibly as an outcome of popular discontent in Cuba itself, possibly as part of some kind of US deal with Moscow. In the short to medium term, however, the 'outsider' strategy was bound to increase Cuban reliance on the USSR.

LBJ's decision to order the invasion of the Dominican Republic in April 1965 marked the symbolic end of the 1963–65 US–Cuban accommodationist dialogue. Washington's rejection of the Cuban 'peace offensive' had been signalled well before the invasion (for example, in a hostile State Department statement issued following Castro's interview with Richard Eder). Though some 'accommodationist' sentiment had begun to surface in Congress, notably in the person of Senator Fulbright, Johnson perceived the likely domestic opposition to accommodation as intense. The establishment of an accommodationist dialogue with Castro would (in LBJ's view) pose major problems, and was certainly not something to be attempted during the Presidential election year of 1964. Typically, LBJ did not entirely turn his back on accommodation. The CIA certainly developed the view in 1965, following the resignation from his official posts of Ernesto 'Che' Guevara, that the Cuban revolution had grown out of its heroic phase, and that Castro was moving to a 'more cautious position on exporting revolution'.[47] Some signs of accommodation were also apparent in a dialogue between Washington and Havana, brokered by the Mexican government, over liberalising the exit of US citizens from Cuba to the United States.[48] Nevertheless, though it occasionally signalled that concessions on the embargo might be considered, the US stubbornly stuck to its broad strategy. For LBJ, isolation and embargo appealed to the Presidential fondness for the 'middle way': in this case, a middle way between accommodation and the tough line being advocated by Thomas Mann.

In early 1964, at the height of the policy rethink, Mann clearly identified the only acceptable goal as the elimination of Castro: 'The simple fact is that Castro represents a successful defiance of the United States, a negation of our whole hemispheric policy of almost a century and a half'. Castro was, continued Mann, a model for other countries. The model must not be allowed to continue in existence: 'Until Castro did it, no Latin American could be sure of getting away with a communist-type revolution and a tie-in with the Soviet Union'. The US could deal safely with Castro provided Moscow were reminded of the 'grave risks' of meddling. The 'best hope for a favorable resolution of the cold war' was for Moscow 'to decide once and for all that world revolution is a luxury that it simply cannot afford'. Quashing Cuba would demonstrate to the Soviet leadership 'that big gains could not be made in the Western hemisphere 'at relatively little cost'. In the final analysis, Cuba was not 'a Soviet vital interest'. Mann reviewed a range of policy options and argued the need for a 'satisfactory peg' – the Venezuelan arms cache was a possibility – on which to hang a practical case for decisive action. A 'satisfactory peg' – a pretext for invasion – could be manufactured if one failed to present itself.[49] Soon after Mann's analysis was written, General Maxwell Taylor raised the prospect of invasion in the context of the apparent failure of the 'insider' strategy: 'little remains which offers promise of real effectiveness . . . short of a blockade or an ascending scale of military action up to or including invasion'.[50]

At last we return to the U-2 overflights. In the early LBJ years, this was the issue which seemed most likely to precipitate a major US–Cuban–Soviet crisis. Johnson's understanding of the dangers and problems associated with the over-flights led directly into his advocacy of the 'middle way' of isolation and embargo. In April–May 1964, LBJ was warned that a U-2 shootdown was imminent – with 'odds . . . no better than even'.[51] The USSR strongly protested the overflights. Khrushchev told Johnson that they were 'illegal' and a 'viola-tion of the UN Charter'.[52] US discussion centred on the issue of whether Russians or Cubans were in control of the SAMs. Gordon Chase actually suggested that Cuban personnel might 'over-run the few Russians on the sites' and use the equipment to attack US planes.[53] Secretary McNamara raised the prospect of sending dummy aircraft or crewless 'drones' in order to cause Castro to exhaust his weaponry.[54] (The Washington discussions of April–May 1964 indicated how little impression was being made by Castro's putative 'peace offensive'. Chase was implicitly arguing that possible Cuban aggres-sion, rather than flexibility, was a reason for moving to accommodation.) By the summer of 1964, with the SAM system operational, and the Russians apparently still in control, tension declined. From Washington's viewpoint, Soviet installation of the SAM system was part of the price being paid by Moscow to compensate Castro for retreating during the 1962 missile crisis. In July, Castro appeared to acknowledge that the Russians had extracted a pledge from him not to use the SAM missiles unless Cuba were directly attacked.[55] In January 1965, George Denney told his State Department boss, Dean Rusk, that Castro had, in effect, yielded to Soviet pressure: 'Castro, doubtful of the support he might receive from the new Soviet hierarchy in a showdown with the US about the overflights, has decided to put the issue on ice'.[56]

The American faith in the moderating force of Soviet influence over Cuba led to some excruciating ironies. In so far as Washington desired Soviet forces to retain physical control of the SAM sites, the US was actually hoping for an indefinite Russian military presence on the island. From Johnson's viewpoint, the apparent resolution of the overflight crisis seemed to lessen the case for either of the 'extreme' positions (direct action possibly culminating in inva-sion, or accommodation) on offer. It consolidated his natural inclination to the 'middle way' of isolation and embargo.

The US, the USSR and Cuba: 1965–69

OAS support for the American invasion of the Dominican Republic in April 1965 further isolated Castro's regime within Latin America. (The OAS had already voted, in July 1964, to break diplomatic and economic ties with Cuba, following the discovery of the Venezuelan arms cache.) The US policy of iso-lating Cuba began to assume extreme proportions. In early 1965, Washington actually objected to a Cuban football team being transported by air to play in Haiti.[57]

US–Cuban relations after 1965 centred mainly on issues of putative Cuban sponsorship of hemispheric revolutionary movements. The U-2 overflight issue sank into the background. In October 1967, however, the CIA actually warned that Castro was contemplating the invasion of the US Guantanamo base. The Cuban leader wished to 'force the Soviet Union to take a stronger position vis-a-vis the United States' and to 'inspire revolutionary emulation' through-out the region. An invasion would distract attention from the 'catastrophic' economic situation in Cuba.[58] The CIA even suggested that Moscow might encourage such an attack in order to divert the US from its commitments in Vietnam. Even so, the CIA saw such a course of events as rather unlikely, par-ticularly given the conservative, cautious instincts of the Soviet leadership. Moscow would not relish the creation of a situation which would almost cer-tainly veer out of Russia's control.[59]

Even as the CIA warned of a possible assault on Guantanamo, the US assessment of the Cuban security threat became affected by the death of 'Che' Guevara (9 October 1967). Guevara was killed by a Bolivian military battal-ion, supported by American Green Berets and CIA personnel. On the day of Guevara's death, Walt Rostow informed LBJ that it seemed likely that the Bolivian battalion, 'the one we have been training' had 'got Che Guevara'.[60] CIA assessors reported that Che's mission to export revolution to Bolivia had been opposed by Moscow. A 1968 CIA assessment noted that leadership had stabilised following Guevara's departure from Cuba. The period since 1966, according to this November 1968 assessment, had seen a consolidation of power between Castro and the military. The US policies of isolation and embargo had succeeded in weakening the regime. However, the island was stable. The Committees for the Defence of the Revolution were successful instruments of popular mobilisation. Castro's caution in respect of agricultural collectivisation had also contributed to social stability. The Cuban Commu-nist Party, according to the CIA, was a personal Castro vehicle, not an ideo-logical Marxist movement nor a bureaucratised instrument of power. The CIA also noted Castro's social conservatism. Extraordinarily, Cuba's young men had recently been ordered by their hairy leader to shave off their beards![61] In 1968, the CIA also reported on the purge of Cuban Communist Party 'micro-factions' (old, pre-Castro, pro-Soviet communists). Walt Rostow regarded the purge as a 'new low in Cuban–Soviet relations'. He concluded, however: 'The Soviets have put up with Castro's defiance before and are likely to do so again'.[62] According to the CIA, 'Castro poses problems for the Soviets, but it is too dangerous for them to try to eliminate him'.[63]

A combination of US preoccupation with Vietnam and Soviet immobilism in the Caribbean produced a situation of relative equilibrium in US–Cuban relations in the later Johnson years. William Walker goes so far as to suggest that, by 1968, Fidel 'became mostly a nuisance factor'.[64] (His comment was a deliberate echo of Senator Fulbright's 1964 remark: 'Castro is a nuisance but not a grave threat' to the US.)[65] Cuba's nuisance value was picked up in a 1968 report on Cuba's involvement with the US radical left. Castro's social conservatism did not prevent him, according to Thomas Hughes (State Department Director of Intelligence and Research), establishing links with the Black Panthers and student leftists. Members of (the anti-Soviet) Students for a Democratic Society were said to have established 'summer camps' in Cuba in 1968: 'SDS members will undoubtedly be indoctrinated on the fine points of violent revolution'.[66] During this putative 'nuisance' period, US–Soviet exchanges over Cuba tended to the status of shadow boxing. As indicated below, Soviet spokesmen offered uneasy and unconvincing defences of Cuban efforts to export revolution. Alternatively, US and Soviet interlocutors raked over old scores. At the 1967 Glassboro summit, for example, Kosygin denied – at least as LBJ told the story to Eisenhower – ever supporting the placing of offensive missiles on Cuba: 'I tried to keep Khrushchev from doing it, and when he did it I made him back up and get out'.[67]

Hemispheric subversion and Soviet–Cuban relations

What made Cuba more than a nuisance were Castro's commitment to international revolutionism, and the fact of Soviet power projection so close to the US. The two factors in a sense, of course, pulled in different directions. Moscow generally opposed Castro's adventurism. It supported the Latin American Communist parties, many of whom were following popular front strategies and tended (as had the Cuban Communist Party before 1959) to condemn the Castroites as 'voluntarists' and adventurers. Thomas Hughes wrote in 1967: 'It appears that Moscow is engaged in an effort to show its interest in Latin America and the revolutionary struggle there, without actually committing itself to give material assistance to Latin American guerrillas'.[68] The CIA reported that, when Kosygin visited Havana after the 1967 Glassboro summit, Fidel had been told to back away from regional revolutionism. Kosygin, in turn, was accused of leading a country which had 'turned its back upon its own revolutionary tradition'.[69]

In 1970, Dean Rusk judged that one major, positive effect of the policy of 'circumscribing' Castro was a decline in the status of Castroism as an 'exportable commodity'.[70] Central to the project of containing Castroism, of course, was the putative need for decisive action when Washington sniffed the spoor of Cuban sponsorship of political unrest. When anti-American rioting began in Panama in January 1964, Thomas Mann pointed to 'Castro agents' controlling events.[71] (LBJ reacted to the Panama crisis with a mixture of firmness and hints that concessions would be made as Panama and the US looked to renegotiate the 1903 Canal Treaty.) When a military 'golpe', or coup, was mounted against leftist Brazilian President Joao Goulart on 31 March 1964, the US provided a naval show of force to support the militarists. In August of the previous year, US Ambassador Lincoln Gordon had warned of a 'substantial imminent danger' of communist takeover in Brazil.[72] American priorities in the Dominican Republic crisis of April 1965 were, as Rusk put it, 'restoration of law and order, prevention of a possible Communist takeover, and protection of American lives'.[73] (A military government had taken over from the Juan Bosch regime in 1963. In late April 1965, constitutionalists began a revolt against the military regime led by Donald Reid Cabral.) Two days after ordering US marines to invade, LBJ spoke privately to Senate Majority Leader Mike Mansfield: 'The Castro forces are really gaining control . . . The big question is, Do we let Castro take over and us move out?'.[74] He told Abe Fortas: 'Our choice is whether we're going to have Castro or intervention . . . I think the worst domestic political disaster we could suffer would be for Castro to take over'.[75]

In the Panamanian and Dominican Republic episodes – a little less so in the Brazilian example, where 'orthodox' communism was more of an issue – discontent was equated with Castro. What H. W. Brands has called 'the American fixation on Castro' made it difficult for the Administration to understand, much less to respond in any appropriate way to, the popular discontents of Latin America. (As Brands points out, however, the 'Castro-as-devil theme' did play well in terms of US domestic politics.)[76] Two questions spring to mind. Was 'Castroite subversion' (as articulated by Washington) anything more than a convenient myth? Presuming that 'Castroite subversion' had some substance, how far was Moscow involved?

The Cuban leadership – Guevara always; Castro, usually – saw the exporting of revolution as essential to justify and protect the Cuban revolution itself. At the Tricontinental Conference in 1966, Castro insisted that imperialism be forced 'to fight against each oppressed people, and at the same time, all oppressed people united'. Guevara formulated his theory of creating 'two, three, several Vietnams' in a message sent to the Tricontinental secretariat.[77] In practice, the commitment to replicating Vietnam waxed and waned, as did American anxiety about it. In January 1965, the State Department reported on 'Che' Guevara's tour of Africa, interpreted by Washington as a direct response to Cuba's isolation in the OAS. The trip reflected 'Cuba's estimate that its security is enhanced by being a focal point of world attention'.[78] By April 1965 – at the very time of the Dominican Republic invasion! – the CIA was reporting that 'the appeal of Castroism today is probably less than at any time among the masses in Latin America'. Castro's appeal had declined drastically since the Cuban missile crisis.[79] In October 1966, a CIA report noted that 'the Cuban timetable for revolution in Latin America calls for successful socialist revolutions in one or two countries as model cases by 1970'.[80] By late 1967, with the killing of Guevara and the apparent failure to ignite revolutionary sparks, the CIA guessed that Castro 'must now be having serious doubts about these prospects'. CIA analysts proclaimed the revolutionary diaries of Guevara, recovered from Bolivia, a 'story of failure'.[81] For Thomas Hughes at State, Che's death was 'a serious setback for Fidel Castro's hopes to foment violent revolution in "all or almost all" Latin American countries'.[82]

The CIA's frequently negative assessments of Cuba's subversive potential contrasted sharply with LBJ's public denunciations of Castro's foreign meddling. In his 1964 State of the Union Address, for example, Johnson used considerable rhetorical licence to link infiltrators 'in Hanoi and Havana, who ship arms and men across international borders to foment insurrection'.[83] Unquestionably, Cuba did supply training and arms to revolutionaries, both in Latin America and Africa. Concrete evidence, however, was always very difficult to find. As to Castro actually *directing* revolutionary activity, even leading Presidential advisers like McGeorge Bundy had their doubts. On 30 April 1965, shortly before LBJ was due to speak live on television about the Dominican Republic invasion, Defense Secretary McNamara warned him that the CIA had not 'shown any evidence that I've seen that Castro has been directing this . . .'.[84]

However sensitive its nose for regional 'Castroism', Washington was aware that Cuban adventurism was not entirely identifiable with *Soviet* power. As we have seen, Washington was well aware that Moscow was eager to restrain Cuba's foreign adventures. Indeed, it can be argued that the real issue for Washington was Castro's symbolic defiance of the US, regardless of the role of the USSR. However, in practical terms at least, without Soviet backing, Cuba was hardly a credible sponsor of international insurrection. Thomas Hughes argued in 1966 that Cuba has 'limited ability to aid revolutions on its own'.[85] It also should not be forgotten that official Washington had not entirely abandoned the notion that Cuba was little more than a cat's paw of Soviet subversion. This view was implicit in the remarks of Eugene Rostow, quoted at the beginning of this chapter. A 1965 State Department report described Cuban regional subversion as operating 'with Soviet acquiescence, if not encouragement'.[86] These ideas of Cuba as a Soviet surrogate could take both simple and sophisticated forms. For some American analysts, for example, even if Moscow did wish to restrain Castro, it was not impossible that the Soviets could be cajoled or shamed into changing tack. International revolutionary leadership by Moscow might prove essential in the contest with China. To many observers in the US (and, no doubt, to many in Cuba) it also seemed that the Havana regime depended for its existence on the USSR. Whatever the tensions between Havana and Moscow, Cuban foreign policy – in this rather reductionist analysts – was the servant of the Kremlin.

Most academic accounts of the Cuban–Soviet relationship in the 1960s focus on the concepts of autonomy and dependency.[87] Castro is seen to have been testing the limits of the relationship: refusing, for example, to back the

1963 Test Ban Treaty, or seeking on occasion to position Cuba with non-aligned, 'third force' nations. Castro is also seen as trying, with little success, to play Moscow off against Beijing. All these complexities were elaborated in Washington's own analysis of the Havana–Moscow relationship. Disputes between Cuban and Soviet leaders were reported in great detail by CIA and State Department analysts. Some of these disputes were primarily economic. Moscow saw Cuba as a drain on its budget.[88] Cuba blamed the unreliability of Soviet petroleum supplies for the imposition of petrol rationing in 1967.[89] Others were ideological. The CIA explained in 1967 that the Soviet 'theory of revolution calls for all forms and methods of struggle' rather than the 'dogmatism' of Castro, Beijing and (theorist of Cuban-style revolution) Regis Debray.[90] (From the Cuban standpoint, of course, 'orthodox' communism – with its insistence upon waiting for the objective conditions for proletarian revolution – was itself a dogmatism). The conservative style of the post-Khrushchev Soviet leadership, in particular, put Moscow and Havana on a path of collision. In November 1967, Brezhnev declared: 'Bolsheviks have always proceeded from the fact that socialist revolution is not . . . a conspiracy of a group of heroes'.[91] (Here Brezhnev was again echoing the criticisms of Castroite 'voluntarism' made by the pre-1959 Cuban Communist Party.) Sometimes the disputes were personal. The CIA reported that, during Kosygin's post-Glassboro trip to Havana in 1967, 'Fidel Castro's attitude was at first so contemptuous that he refused to meet privately with Kosygin'.[92] When Castro snubbed the 50th anniversary celebrations of the Bolshevik Revolution – he sent a 'third team' of diplomats to Moscow – the CIA saw the Soviets as 'close to losing their patience'. According to CIA analysts: 'Brezhnev thinks that Castro is some kind of idiot and Castro probably isn't very fond of Brezhnev either'. Brezhnev made public remarks about Cuba being an 'expensive friend'.[93] Castro's public support for the Soviet invasion of Czechoslovakia in August 1968 has often been interpreted as a surrender to Moscow, made in the face of economic need for aid and the failure to spread revolution in Latin America.[94] Castro's position here was actually quite complex. He denounced the 'unhealthy' slide of the Czech communists towards capitalism, but also criticised the USSR for showing similar tendencies.[95] His public support for the invasion can also be seen as understandable veneration for the Brezhnev Doctrine – at least in so far as the Doctrine involved the willingness of Moscow to intervene militarily on behalf of troubled allies. (In Cuba's case, troubles would emanate from Washington, rather than domestic counter-revolutionaries and 'capitalist roaders'.) The CIA, however, saw it rather differently. An Intelligence Information Cable of 26 August 1968 argued that the invasion was 'deplorable' to Havana. It was seen as an example of US–Soviet collusion, setting dangerous precedents. For Cuban officials, 'Soviet intervention, which reflects an arrangement with the United States, gives the United States a pretext for invading Cuba'.[96]

American analysts in the Johnson years generally saw the Soviet commitment to Cuba as indefinite and as essential to the survival of Castro's regime.
The Cuban leader's flirtations with Beijing and with non-alignment were unrealistic and almost certainly bound to fail. Castro might try to emulate Albania,
or Yugoslavia. Such a development would, however, involve extreme danger
to the survival of his revolution: 'a high faith in his own skill and rectitude
might blind Castro to the costs and risks of defying the Soviets'.[97] Implicit in
analyses such as this was the prospect, if Castro overplayed his hand, of Soviet
acquiescence in an American invasion.

Conclusion

The most significant conclusion to emerge from this discussion is the degree
to which Moscow acted (from Washington's viewpoint at least) as a force for
stability in the Caribbean in the 1960s. The operation of this role was
complex, and American understanding of it always likely to be undercut by
the traditional fears of Soviet expansionism. The close Cuba–Soviet alliance
of the 1970s, in the era of acknowledged détente, was to cause major problems for US foreign policy, particularly in Africa. However, there is no question that the upshot of Johnson's policies of isolation and embargo[98] was to
push Havana into a closer relationship of dependence with Moscow.

Was US–Cuban accommodation feasible? In purely procedural terms, the
answer must be affirmative. The CIA reported in March 1964 that Cuban
Foreign Minister Raul Roa wanted détente with Washington. The Cuban leadership wished to avoid 'Russification'.[99] However, it proved almost impossible to conceptualise the terms for accommodation. In April 1964, Gordon
Chase indicated some of the questions arising if the US was willing to accept
that a Castro regime, without Soviet backing, was 'here to stay'. Should
America 'insist on an end to all Soviet economic assistance to Cuba?'. Should
we 'help the Russians to find a fig-leaf to cover their withdrawal from
Cuba?'.[100] Even more fundamental questions suggest themselves. If, as Thomas
Mann argued, the real problem with Castro was his actual existence, how
could the US accept – even if shorn of Soviet support – that he was 'here to
stay'? Castro's crime was one of double defiance. He had snubbed his nose at
US regional dominance *and* turned to communism. Walt Rostow appeared to
accept the Mann logic in a memorandum delivered to LBJ in October 1967.
The memo referred to Castro's extreme 'cult of personality', to his attempts
to 'form special groupings of communist states with North Vietnam and North
Korea', and to the 'very serious' condition of Cuba's economy. Castro might,
wrote Rostow, turn to Washington. Such a prospect filled him with horror:
'Castro is trying to reduce his dependence on the socialist states and expand
his ties with Western Europe and there is *a danger of his seeking accommodation with the US*' (emphasis supplied).[101]

The pushing together of Havana and Moscow is normally interpreted as an unintended consequence of America's entire post-1959 Cuban policy. In 1962, William Appleman Williams wrote that the 'policy had the practical effect of subverting its own avowed objectives'.[102] In some sense, this holds true also for Johnson's policy. After all, the US, ostensibly concerned to advance the cause of democracy, ended the 1960s as the friend and sponsor of Latin American anti-communist militarism. However, the pushing together of Havana and Moscow – especially if we acknowledge the sophistication of the CIA and State Department analyses quoted above – cannot entirely be regarded as an *unintended* consequence. Washington wished to destroy Castro. Smothering him in the bear-hug of post-Khrushchev Soviet conservatism was a (just about) acceptable alternative.

Notes

1 CIA, 'The USSR: problems, policies and prospects', 9 Jan. 1968, NSF: CF: Europe and USSR: USSR, box 225 (folder, 'Memos XVIII').

2 E. V. Rostow to L. Thompson, 1 May 1967, ibid., box 223 (folder, 'Memos XV').

3 R. Dallek, *Lone Star Rising* (New York, Oxford University Press, 1991), p. 77.

4 Dungan, Oral History, p. 6.

5 R. Dallek, *Flawed Giant* (New York, Oxford University Press, 1998), p. 91.

6 W. LaFeber, *The American Age* (New York, Norton, 1989), p. 575.

7 Quoted in S. G. Rabe, *The Most Dangerous Area in the World: John F. Kennedy Confronts Communist Revolutions in Latin America* (Chapel Hill, University of North Carolina Press, 1999), p. 173.

8 Ibid., p. 184.

9 Ibid.

10 *PPPUS: Lyndon B. Johnson, 1963–64*, Volume 2 (Washington DC, US Government Printing Office, 1965), p. 1465.

11 See Rabe, *The Most Dangerous Area . . .*, p. 177; Covey Oliver, Oral History, p. 15; W. LaFeber, 'Thomas C. Mann and the devolution of Latin American policy', in T. J. McCormick and W. LaFeber (eds.), *Behind the Throne: Servants of Power to Imperial Presidents: 1898–1968* (Madison, University of Wisconsin Press, 1993), pp. 166–203.

12 D. Rusk, *As I Saw It: A Secretary of State's Memoirs* (London, Tauris, 1991), p. 403.

13 L. B. Johnson, *The Vantage Point* (London, Weidenfeld and Nicolson, 1971), p. 187.

14 M. R. Beschloss (ed.), *Reaching for Glory: Lyndon Johnson's Secret White House Tapes, 1964–1965* (New York, Simon and Schuster, 2001), p. 300 (30 April 1965).

15 Ibid., p. 299 (to Abe Fortas, 30 April 1965).

16 M. R. Beschloss (ed.), *Taking Charge: The Johnson White House Tapes, 1963–1964* (New York, Simon and Schuster, 1997), p. 87 (2 Dec. 1963).

17 Beschloss (ed.), *Reaching for Glory*, p. 339 (23 May 1965).

18 Ibid., p. 377 (30 June 1965).

19 'Meeting with the President', 27 Dec. 1963, NSF: Files of McGeorge Bundy, box 19 (folder, 'Vol. 1').

20 W. Rostow to LBJ, 'Report of Soviet strategic missiles in Cuba', 7 March 1967, NSF: CF: Latin America: Cuba, box 19 (folder, 'Bowdler File 2').

21 *FRUS, 1961–1963*: Volume VI: *Kennedy–Khrushchev exchanges* (Washington DC, US Government Printing Office, 1996), p. 223.

22 *PPPUS: John F. Kennedy, 1961* (Washington DC, US Government Printing Office, 1963), p. 515.

23 *FRUS, 1961–1963*: Volume VI: *Kennedy–Khrushchev Exchanges*, p. 228.

24 See Beschloss (ed.), *Taking Charge*, p. 234.

25 *FRUS, 1961–1963*: Volume XI: *Cuban Missile Crisis and Aftermath* (Washington DC, US Government Printing Office, 1996), p. 894.

26 Ibid., p. 896.

27 'Intelligence note', 14 Dec. 1966, NSF: CF: Latin America: Cuba, box 19 (folder, 'Bowdler File 2') (George Denney).

28 Chase to Bundy, 14 July 1964, NSF: CF: Latin America: Cuba, box 29 (folder, 'Cuba Over-flights 2').

29 Smith to Bundy, 17 March 1964, ibid.

30 As note 25.

31 See Beschloss (ed.), *Taking Charge*, p. 87; M. R. Beschloss, *The Crisis Years: Kennedy and Khrushchev, 1960–1963* (New York, HarperCollins, 1991), pp. 682–93; Dallek, *Flawed Giant*, p. 53; J. A. Califano, *The Triumph and Tragedy of Lyndon Johnson* (New York, Simon and Schuster, 1991), p. 295; T. Powers, *The Man Who Kept the Secrets: Richard Helms and the CIA* (New York, Pocket Books, 1979), p. 157.

32 CIA, 'Current thinking of Cuban government leaders', 5 March 1964, NSF: CF: Latin America: Cuba, box 29 (folder, 'Cuba Overflights 1').

33 Dallek, *Flawed Giant*, p. 53.

34 As note 19. See also W. O. Walker, 'The struggle for the Americas: the Johnson Adminis-tration and Cuba', in H. W. Brands (ed.), *The Foreign Policies of Lyndon Johnson: Beyond Vietnam* (College Station, Texas A and M Press, 1999), pp. 61–97, at pp. 69, 76; NSF: Files of Gordon Chase, 'Plank-Chase report on US-Cuban relations', 3 Feb. 1964, box 4; W. Attwood, *The Twilight Struggle: Tales of the Cold War* (New York, Harper and Row, 1987), pp. 255–65; L. Freedman, *Kennedy's Wars: Berlin, Cuba, Laos and Vietnam* (Oxford, Oxford University Press, 2000), pp. 244–5.

35 Chase to Bundy, 20 April 1964, NSF: CF: Latin America: Cuba, box 18 (folder, 'Chase File').

36 Chase, 'US Policy toward Cuba', April 1964, NSF: CF: Latin America: Cuba, box 29 (folder, 'Cuba-US Policy, vol. 2').

37 Ibid.

38 M. Halperin, *The Taming of Fidel Castro* (Berkeley, University of California Press, 1981), p. 97.

39 CIA, National Intelligence Estimate, 19 Feb. 1964, *FRUS, 1964–1968*: Volume XIV: *The Soviet Union* (Washington DC, US Government Printing Office, 2001), p. 27.

40 CIA, 'Current thinking of Cuban government leaders', 5 March 1964, NSF: CF: Latin America: Cuba, box 29 (folder, 'Cuba overflights 1').

41 CIA National Intelligence Estimate, 27 Jan. 1965, *FRUS, 1964–1968*: Volume XIV: *The Soviet Union*, p. 226.

42 Halperin, *The Taming*, pp. 97–110.

43 'Meeting with the President', 27 Dec. 1963, NSF: Files of McGeorge Bundy, box 19.

44 W. Hinckle and W. W. Turner, *Deadly Secrets: The CIA – Mafia War Against Castro and the Assassination of JFK* (New York, Thunder's Mouth Press, 1992), p. 6. See also W. Hinckle and W. W. Turner, *The Fish Is Red* (New York, Harper and Row, 1981); J. G. Blight and P. Kornbluh, *Politics of Illusion: The Bay of Pigs Invasion Reexamined* (Boulder, Lynne Rienner, 1998), p. 117.

45 Bowdler to Rostow, 18 Dec. 1967, NSF: CF: Latin America: Cuba, box 19 (folder, 'Vol. 3'.).

46 M. H. Morley, *Imperial State and Revolution: the United States and Cuba, 1952–1986* (Cambridge, Cambridge University Press, 1987), p. 187. Also, W. I. Cohen, *Dean Rusk* (Totowa, Cooper Square, 1980), p. 227.

47 CIA, 'The fall of Che Guevara and the changing face of the Cuban revolution', 18 Oct. 1965 (Brian Latell) (from P. Kornbluh, 'The death of Che Guevara: declassified', National Security Archive briefing book 5 (available on NSA website)).

48 See N. Miller, *Soviet Relations with Latin America, 1959–1987* (Cambridge, Cambridge University Press, 1989), pp. 114–15.

49 Mann, policy draft for State Department Policy Planning Council, 13 Feb. 1964, NSF: CF: Latin America: Cuba, box 29 (folder, 'US policy, vol. 1').

50 Taylor to LBJ, 21 March 1964, ibid. (folder, 'US Policy vol. 2').

51 Chase to Bundy, 30 April 1964, ibid. (folder, 'Cuba-overflights').

52 Khrushchev to LBJ, 5 June 1964, *FRUS: 1964–1968*, Volume XIV: *The Soviet Union* (Washington DC, US Government Printing Office, 2001), p. 88.

53 Chase to Bundy, 22 April 1964, NSF: CF: Latin America, box 29 (folder 'Cuba-overflights').

54 'Summary Record of NSC Meeting 531', 5 May 1964, NSF: NSC Meetings File, box 1.

55 Halperin, *The Taming*, p. 95. See also State Department 'Intelligence Note', 14 Dec. 1966, NSF: CF; Latin America: Cuba, box 19 (folder, 'Bowdler File 2') (on Castro's *Playboy* interview).

56 Denney to Rusk, 26 Jan. 1965, NSF: CF: Latin America: Cuba (folder, 'Cuba-overflights').

57 See incoming telegram to State Department, 6 Feb. 1965, NSF: CF: Latin America: Cuba, box 18 (folder, 'Cuba country 3').

58 CIA, 'Intelligence information cable', 11 Oct. 1967: NSF: CF: Latin America: Cuba, box 19 (folder, 'Bowdler 3').

59 CIA, 'Intelligence memorandum', 13 Oct. 1967, ibid.

60 Rostow to LBJ, 9 Oct. 1967, in Kornbluh, 'The death of Che Guevara' (as note 47).

61 CIA, 'Intelligence memorandum', 'Stability factors in Cuba', 18 Nov. 1968, ibid. (folder, 'Bowdler 4').

62 CIA, 'Special Report: Political trends in Cuba', 15 March 1968, ibid. (folder, 'Bowdler 3'); Rostow to LBJ, 31 Jan. 1968, ibid.

63 CIA, 'Intelligence information cable', 28 Dec. 1967, ibid.

64 Walker, 'The Struggle for the Americas', p. 85.

65 J. W. Fulbright, *Old Myths and New Realities* (New York, Random House, 1964), p. 25.

66 T. L. Hughes, 'Cuban involvement with the US radical left', 7 Oct. 1968, NSF: Latin America: Cuba, box 19 (folder, 'Bowdler 4').

67 *FRUS, 1964–1968*: Volume XIV; *The Soviet Union*, p. 560 (telephone conversation, LBJ–Eisenhower, 25 June 1967).

68 State Department Research memorandum, 16 June 1967, NSF: CF: Europe and USSR: USSR, box 223 (folder, 'Memos').

69 CIA, 'Intelligence information cable', 17 Oct. 1967, NSF: CF: Latin America: Cuba, box 19 (folder, 'Bowdler 3').

70 Dean Rusk, Oral History, p. 11 (tape 2).

71 H. W. Brands, *The Wages of Globalism: Lyndon Johnson and the Limits of American Power* (New York, Oxford University Press, 1995), p. 31.

72 W. M. Weis, *Cold Warriors and Coups D'Etat: Brazilian–American Relations, 1945–1964* (Albuquerque, University of New Mexico Press, 1993), p. 162.

73 Brands, *The Wages of Globalism*, p. 54.

74 Beschloss (ed.), *Reaching for Glory*, p. 300 (30 April 1965).

75 Ibid., p. 301 (30 April 1965).

76 Brands, *The Wages of Globalism*, p. 32.

77 J. Levesque, *The USSR and the Cuban Revolution* (New York, Praeger, 1978), p. 121.

78 Airgram, State Department to all African posts, 29 Jan. 1965, NSF: CF: Latin America: Cuba, box 18 (folder, 'Cuba Country 5').

79 CIA, Special Report: Subversion in Latin America, 23 April 1965, NSF: CF: Latin America: Cuba, box 31 (folder, 'Cuba-subversion 1').

80 Walker, 'The Struggle for the Americas', p. 82.
81 CIA, 'Weekly summary', 15 Dec. 1967, NSF: CF: Latin America: Cuba, box 37 (folder, 'Che Guevara').
82 Hughes, 'Guevara's death – the meaning for Latin America', 12 Oct. 1967, in Kornbluh, 'The death of Che Guevara' (as note 47).
83 *PPPUS, Lyndon B. Johnson, 1963–64: Volume 1* (Washington DC, US Government Printing Office, 1965), p. 116.
84 Beschloss (ed.), *Reaching for Glory*, p. 302. See also Dean Rusk, Oral History, pp. 5–6 (tape 3, Bundy).
85 State Department, 'Intelligence note', 3 Jan. 1966, NSF: CF: Latin America: Cuba, box 19 (folder, 'Bowdler 1').
86 State Department, 'Summary statement of US policy towards Cuba', June 1965, ibid., box 29 (folder, 'Cuba-US policy 2').
87 See N. Carbonnell, *And the Russians Stayed: the Sovietization of Cuba* (New York, Morrow, 1989); W. Raymond Duncan, *The Soviet Union and Cuba: Interests and Influence* (New York, Praeger, 1985); D. B. Jackson, *Castro, the Kremlin, and Communism in Latin America* (Baltimore, Johns Hopkins University Press, 1969); Levesque, *The USSR and the Cuban Revolution*; Y. Pavlov, *Soviet-Cuban Alliance: 1959–1991* (New Brunswick, Transaction, 1994); P. Shearman, *The Soviet Union and Cuba* (London, Routledge and Kegan Paul, 1987); J. Valenta, 'Cuba in the Soviet alliance system', in G. Fauriel and E. Laser (eds.), *Cuba: the International Dimension* (New Brunswick, Transaction, 1990), pp. 3–39.
88 See State Department, 'Intelligence note', 19 Jan. 1967, NSF: CF: Europe and USSR: USSR, box 223 (folder, 'memos 2').
89 T. L. Hughes, 'What is going on in Cuban-Soviet relations?', 11 Jan. 1968, NSF: CF: Latin America: Cuba, box 19 (folder, 'Bowdler 3').
90 CIA, 'Intelligence information cable', 28 Dec. 1967, ibid.
91 Quoted in CIA, Special memorandum: 'Bolsheviks and Heroes: the USSR and Cuba', 21 Nov. 1967, ibid.
92 CIA, 'Intelligence information cable', 27 July 1967, ibid. (folder, 'Bowdler 2').
93 As note 91.
94 See Levesque, *The USSR and the Cuban Revolution*, pp. 147, 161.
95 Ibid.
96 CIA, 'Intelligence information cable', 26 Aug. 1968, NSF: CF; Latin America: Cuba, box 19 (folder, 'Bowdler 4').
97 As note 91.
98 See Morley, *Imperial State and Revolution*, pp. 373–5 for statistics on the effect of the embargo. Also, D. B. Kunz, *Butter and Guns: America's Cold War Economic Diplomacy* (New York, Free Press, 1997).
99 CIA, 'Current thinking of Cuban government leaders', 5 March 1964, NSF: CF: Latin America: Cuba, box 29 (folder, 'Cuba overflights 1'). See also W. S. Smith, *The Closest of Enemies* (New York, Norton, 1987).
100 Chase to Bundy, 22 April 1964, NSF: CF: Latin America: Cuba, box 18 (folder, 'Bowdler 1').
101 Rostow to LBJ, 11 Oct. 1967, NSF: CF: Latin America: Cuba, box 19 (folder, 'Bowdler 3'). See also D. Bernell, 'The curious case of Cuba in American foreign policy', *Journal of Inter-American Studies and World Affairs*, 36:2 (1994) 65–103.
102 W. A. Williams, *The United States, Cuba, and Castro* (New York, MR Press, 1962), p. 170. See also T. G. Paterson, *Contesting Castro: the United States and the Triumph of the Cuban Revolution* (New York, Oxford University Press, 1994).

7

Crises: the Six Day War and the Soviet invasion of Czechoslovakia

Introduction: a superpower partnership?

The most dangerous US–Soviet confrontation of the Johnson era occurred towards the end of the 1967 Six Day War between Israel and the Arab countries of Egypt, Syria and Jordan. In his memoirs, LBJ recounted how he received a message from the Kremlin on the 'hot line', following the 9 June Israeli invasion of Syria. Aleksei Kosygin threatened Soviet military intervention unless Israel halted its advance.[1] In response, LBJ ordered the American Sixth Fleet, containing two aircraft carriers and then lying in the Eastern Mediterranean, to turn eastwards toward Syria.

The confrontation rapidly fizzled out, with Israel, having already made major territorial gains, deciding to sign a peace accord. Yet, as CIA Director Richard Helms later testified, LBJ's instruction to the Sixth Fleet was an occasion of considerable danger.[2] Meeting Israeli Foreign Minister Abba Eban shortly after the conflict, Johnson described it as 'the most awesome decision' he had made during his Presidency.[3]

The Soviet invasion of Czechoslovakia (on 20 August 1968) resembled, as Dean Rusk memorably put it, the slapping of a metaphorical 'dead fish' against the face of America's President.[4] As we saw in Chapter 2, it quashed hopes for an October arms control summit and set back the détente agenda. The Soviet Union was simply unwilling to tolerate Alexander Dubcek's liberal communist regime in Prague, despite the Czech leader's insistence that his country remained a loyal member of the Warsaw Pact. Little appeared to have changed since the USSR's invasion of Hungary in 1956.

A tough, military response by the US to the invasion of 1968 was always extremely unlikely. Some American officials, it is true, did advance the idea – prior to 20 August – that the US might use military force to deter a Soviet intervention. On the evening of the invasion, LBJ told the National Security Council: 'It is one country invading another Communist country. It is aggression. There is danger in aggression anywhere'.[5] There was no question of the US using its military power to settle intra-communist troubles. As Benjamin Read put it on 23 August: 'After careful review, we have concluded that our present course of mobilizing world opinion through the United Nations offers the best hope at this time of influencing the Soviets toward moderation in the present crisis'.[6]

On the face of it, the events of June 1967 and August 1968 might have seemed to indicate the severe limits to any Cold War thaw, and to reveal how dangerous a place the world remained. In his Sixth Fleet decision, Johnson committed the US to a potentially dangerous and very unpredictable course of action. In August 1968, the USSR showed its contempt not only for liberalised communism, but also apparently for good relations with Washington. Contemporary comment, however, tended not to follow this line of interpretation. Even allowing for journalistic ignorance of the detailed superpower interchanges (notably on the 'hot line' in 1967), there was relatively little expressed fear of nuclear conflict. Several commentators argued that both the Six Day War and the Czech invasion revealed high levels of superpower mutual understanding and quasi-partnership.

On 3 June 1967 – a week or so before LBJ's Sixth Fleet decision and two days before Israel inaugurated the Six Day War – *The Economist* led with an article entitled, 'The Small World of LBK'. It pointed to a brief pause in US bombing of North Vietnam, along with superpower efforts to restrain the burgeoning confrontation in the Middle East, as evidence of Johnson and Kosygin ('LBK') working together to contain crises on the interface of their alliance systems.[7] Two weeks later, *The Economist's* tone was slightly less assured. However, its 17 June leader argued that when the Soviets 'have exploited the propaganda advantage of British and American unpopularity in the Arab world, they will probably get down to the serious business of bringing the Middle East under control. To do this they will have to co-operate with the Americans'.[8] *Time* magazine's verdict on the conflict was even more confident that the superpowers were acting in partnership: 'From the first click of the "hot line" to the last circumlocution at week's end, the two great powers carefully and repeatedly affirmed their determination to avoid a big war'.[9]

Fourteen months later, *Time* described the invasion of Czechoslovakia as a 'savage challenge to détente'. Again, however, the tone of its coverage was that the crisis showed how *far* the world was from nuclear war. On 30 August 1968, *Time* described Washington's 'all too apparent awareness that it could do as little in secret as it could openly to save Czechoslovakia from its fate'.[10] To several commentators, the events of August 1968 confirmed their view that the world was being run as a demarcated superpower condominium. Writing in the *New York Review of Books*, Ronald Steel interpreted the crisis as exemplifying a 'system of great power reciprocity'. The Soviets invaded 'after confirming that the gentleman's agreement with the United States on spheres of influence was still valid'. They 'would not have tried to save Castro even had the Bay of Pigs turned into a full-scale American invasion [of Cuba], and the United States has made it clear that it has no intention of intervening in Eastern Europe'.[11]

In the final chapter, some general conclusions on this theme of 1960s super-power partnership – the extent and limits of détente – will be offered. The rest of this chapter will focus on the theme of superpower co-operation – 'LBK' – in the 1967 and 1968 crises.

The Middle East

LBJ, Moscow and the Middle East

As Vice President, Johnson had been mildly critical of the efforts made by the Kennedy Administration to improve relations with the Egyptian regime of Gamal Abdul Nasser.[12] LBJ was regarded by most of his associates as a strong supporter of Israel. He certainly prided himself on his high level of approval among American Jewish voters, and counted Ephraim Evron, an Israeli diplomat working in Washington, as a close personal friend.[13] Johnson inherited from JFK no especially pressing problem directly involving Israel, although Nasser's intervention (made possible by Soviet military aid) in a civil war in Yemen set some Washington alarm bells ringing. LBJ certainly regarded the region as probably the most dangerous in the world. Eugene Rostow actually recalled the President as seeing the Middle East as more hazardous to world peace than the war in Vietnam. It was, in Eugene Rostow's phrase, 'like the Cuban missile crisis, only it goes on all the time'.[14]

Johnson's view was that Israel should be strongly supported, but that the US had to avoid unduly antagonising America's other friends in the region, notably the Shah of Iran. The best way to combat Soviet influence was certainly (as Walt Rostow wrote on 4 June 1967) to 'cut' Nasser 'down to size'.[15] The US had also, however, to cultivate moderate Arab opinion – not only to counteract the Soviets, but also to shore up American oil interests. In February 1965, Johnson defended his policy of sending military aid to King Hussein's regime in Jordan. LBJ told Abe Feinberg, an American contributor to Israeli and Democratic Party causes, that Hussein – 'this little King' – 'has some value to us . . . we ought to keep him as far away from the Soviet (Union) and Nasser as we can'.[16] A memo prepared by Robert Komer in May 1964 seemed to reflect the Presidential thinking: '*The one thing we ask of Israel* is not to keep trying to force us to an all-out pro-Israel policy'. The US had to keep 'a superficial balance' between Israel and the (anti-communist) Arabs.[17]

Soviet policy in the period leading up to the outbreak of the Six Day War was exceedingly difficult for Washington to read and understand. Moscow's aims were clear enough: to extend its influence in the region, to acquire bases to service a permanent Soviet naval presence in the Mediterranean, and to score propaganda points by portraying Israel as the agent of American imperialism. Russia's supply of arms to its regional clients was, however, designed to give Israel's Arab neighbours an edge in terms of weaponry, but certainly not overwhelming superiority. The most thorough study of this phase of Soviet arms supply to the region, published in 1975, concluded: 'The Soviets had given the Arabs the capability to engage in political braggadocio and threat but not some of the means at the Soviet disposal that would have ensured Arab military victory'.[18] Moscow appeared concerned to embarrass the US, and to use the Middle East as a lever in wider international political stakes, rather than to provoke an all-out war between Israel and Egypt. Yet not all signs pointed in the same direction. On 11 May 1967, the Soviet President Podgorny actually informed an Egyptian delegation, headed by Anwar Sadat, that Israel was poised to attack Syria. Podgorny's warning was mischievous, and reflected intense intra-Politburo disagreement over how best to manipulate the regional recipients of Soviet aid. A Soviet foreign policy official interviewed by Alexei Vassiliev recalled major disagreements over Middle East policy at this time. He also remembered that 'Gromyko was afraid that we would get into a clash with the United States and the missile crisis of 1962 would be repeated'.[19] The situation was further complicated by the shifting relationship between Nasser and Moscow. The Egyptian leader was encouraged by the anti-Israeli stance taken by Soviet Defence Minister Andrei Grechko and some other military figures close to Brezhnev. Nasser also wished to act as if Moscow's full support for a war had already been guaranteed. Yet on 25 May, Kosygin – now leading the 'peace party' in Moscow – advised Egypt against starting a direct conflict with Israel.[20] Tension between Nasser and the Syrian military regime, which had broken away from Nasser's United Arab Republic and was now close to Moscow, also added to the regional geopolitical complexity.

President Johnson's handling of the crisis of May 1967 indicated the degree to which the US was unconvinced about the strength of the Soviet commitment to Egypt. Nasser moved troops into the Sinai, bordering Israel, effectively forcing the United Nations force (which had kept peace in the Sinai since 1957) to withdraw. On 22 May, Nasser commenced a blockade of the Gulf of Aqaba – a move condemned by Israel as an 'armed attack' on its sovereignty. LBJ's reaction was to attempt to recruit Moscow to the cause of seeking a diplomatic solution.

At this stage, LBJ was extremely concerned about interconnections between the Middle East and Vietnam. On 24 May, he asked General Earle Wheeler whether it was likely that the 'Soviets had staged this Middle East crisis' in order 'to force us to turn our attention from Vietnam'. Wheeler and CIA Director Helms agreed that there was little 'sign of Soviet calculation'.[21] At one level, and with other considerations notwithstanding, the US Vietnam commitment made any American military intervention in the Middle East extremely unlikely.[22] Senators Stuart Symington and J. W. Fulbright gave Johnson the, no doubt very unwelcome, advice that, since the US could not deal simultaneously with two major regional crises, American forces should quit Vietnam.[23]

Nasser's actions naturally caused disquiet in Washington about Soviet policy aims. Lucius Battle, former US Ambassador to Cairo, wondered 'whether

Nasser either has more Soviet support than we know about, or had gone slightly insane'.[24] The top policy-makers, however, felt that Moscow would co-operate in regional crisis management. Dean Rusk wrote to the US Embassy in Moscow on 19 May, outlining his views on the need for superpower co-operation.[25] LBJ wrote on the same day to Kosygin, complaining about 'harassment of Israel by elements in Syria', but urging Moscow to join Washington in promoting peace, including use of 'our influence over action by the United Nations'. Moscow's response was positive. However, Nikolai Federenko, Soviet Ambassador to the UN, attacked the US for condemning the Egyptian blockade, while America continued to blockade Cuba and to drown 'Vietnam in blood'. Rusk warned Gromyko that Israel could not be expected to back down in direct confrontation, and that the US did not wish it to do so.[26] Johnson's scepticism about UN diplomacy was made clear in private remarks made on 24 May: 'I want to play every card in the UN, but I've never relied on it to save me when I'm going down for the third time'.[27]

At this time, Robert McNamara was concerned about the possibility of Soviet MiG fighter pilots being brought into any regional conflict.[28] Lucius Battle warned of 'a vigorous Soviet effort to turn this crisis into a US–Arab confrontation'.[29] Dean Rusk, however, was more reassuring:

> Privately we find the Russians playing a generally moderate game, but publicly they have taken a harsh view of the facts and have laid responsibility at Israel's door – and by inference at ours. Syria and Cairo say publicly they have Soviet support; but our general impression is that this is somewhat less than complete.[30]

In the period before the onset of war, most American analysts agreed with the Secretary of State. Rusk was advised by George Denney that Moscow, though interested in Middle East 'brinkmanship', would not back any attack by Egypt on Israel.[31] For State's Thomas Hughes, the Soviets seemed to be banking on America's ability to restrain Israel: 'They can derive the political advantages of backing the Arabs while counting on others to keep the crisis controlled'.[32] The CIA judged on 28 May that the 'USSR was not supporting Egypt completely because the USSR would never support the destruction of Israel'.[33]

'Hot line' and confrontation

Any hopes, entertained by Moscow of Washington restraining Israel, were dashed by Tel Aviv's strike against Egypt's air force on the morning of 5 June. A CIA report delivered on that day indicated that 'Israel fired the first shot today'.[34] In fact, by the end of Day One of the war, 298 Egyptian planes had been destroyed.

Academic debate on the outbreak of war has tended to concentrate on the extent of Washington's ability, or willingness, to restrain Israel.[35] McGeorge Bundy, who participated in the so-called 'hot line meetings' at the White House at this time, later recalled the sense of relief at the end of Day One: 'It was in a way reassuring when it became clear that the fighting was the Israelis' idea and that the idea was working. That was a lot better than if it had been the other way around'.[36] From Israel's viewpoint, Washington's fear of superpower conflict in the region had left the American President 'paralyzed'. However, the US was certainly not, as a State Department spokesman declared on Day One, neutral in word and deed.[37] Johnson felt that the events of 5 June rather displayed the limits of his influence over Tel Aviv, and exposed the foolishness of Moscow's reliance on his ability to dictate policy to Israel. After the War, LBJ told Abba Eban: 'The Russians think that the United States has influence with Israel. I don't think that is the case'. He added: 'Israel thinks we have influence with the Russians and that is not the case'.[38]

Contacts between Washington and Moscow began immediately after Israel's strike. Rusk cabled Gromyko, expressing surprise at the attack and stressing the need for superpower co-operation. Kosygin replied on the 'hot line' at 7.47 a.m. (Washington time – LBJ had been informed about Israel's action at 4.30 a.m.). The Soviet leader – in the first ever 'hot line' message relayed during a crisis – called on Washington to work with Moscow to achieve a ceasefire. Seven 'hot line' messages were exchanged during the first two days of war; between 5 and 10 June, twenty messages were exchanged. The severity of the crisis and the novelty of the 'hot line' combined to produce moments of odd humour. At first, the Russians insisted that LBJ should be physically present at the US end of the line before they began transmission. Johnson's first message (at 8.47 a.m. on 5 June) was addressed to 'Comrade Kosygin'. Llewellyn Thompson later explained that the American telegraph operators had asked their Moscow counterparts how to address the Soviet leader: 'They got back the answer "Comrade Kosygin". So the message went'. Not surprisingly, the 'Russians wondered if the President was making a joke, as making fun of them in some way'.[39]

In this early phase of the brief conflict, Washington was supremely, and rather unrealistically, confident of Moscow's desire to achieve a swift peace. Thomas Hughes advised Rusk on Day Two that Soviet support for Egypt and Syria was not 'unreserved'. An extended war 'would raise the specter of Western intervention and eventually pose for the USSR the dilemma of either abandoning the Arabs or else of giving them help of a kind which would involve the Soviets directly'.[40] At a National Security Council meeting held on Day Three, 7 June, Llewellyn Thompson gave his view that 'the end of belligerence should be relatively easy to handle with the USSR'.[41] Nathaniel Davis reported on 'Arab disillusionment with the USSR' and 'Soviet disgust with their Arab clients'.[42]

Yet some obvious differences between the superpowers were evident. LBJ instructed Arthur Goldberg, US Ambassador to the United Nations, to work for a 'ceasefire in place' – allowing Israel, at least for the time being, to retain territory gained during the conflict. Failing that, the US position was that (as of 5 June) Egypt should immediately withdraw from the Sinai and lift the blockade on the Gulf of Aqaba. Moscow initially pressed for an Israeli withdrawal behind 1956 borders. However, as Israel made its concerted advances into Gaza, the Sinai and the West Bank, Moscow's position shifted. On Day Two of the conflict, the Soviets supported a ceasefire in place.

At this time, some of the American decision-makers, notably Walt Rostow, were looking beyond a ceasefire, towards the ever-receding goal of so many subsequent American Administrations: a comprehensive regional settlement, settling Israel's borders, dealing with the refugee crisis, establishing the status of the Palestinians, and regulating the supply of Soviet arms to the region. On 7 June, Rostow argued that Israeli successes would force Moscow to co-operate in the achievement of an acceptable settlement. The Soviets had 'suffered a setback of the first order of magnitude; and they will only react in ways consistent with our interests if the political forces on the spot, as well as the military situation, leave them no other realistic alternative'.[43]

Rostow and the other senior advisers were agreed that the Russians had suffered a massive humiliation. LBJ, however, seems consistently to have been less confident than his advisers that events would pan out to America's advantage. He remarked on Day Three: 'By the time we get through with all the festering problems we are going to wish the war had not happened'.[44] The President later told Abba Eban that the US and Israel 'must not overlook' the Soviet humiliation: 'It constantly prods them to recoup in some way'.[45]

Between 7 June and the US–Soviet crisis of 10 June, Washington was preoccupied with the extraordinary Israeli attack on the US intelligence ship, *Liberty*. The attack was almost certainly made to deny Washington intelligence about Israeli plans to secure the strategic Golan Heights by invading Syria. With Jordan having quit the war on Day Three, and Egypt effectively beaten back on Day Four, Tel Aviv wished to proceed without interference from Washington. Moscow learned officially of the *Liberty* attack via the 'hot line'. LBJ explained to Kosygin that US planes were being deployed to near the Egyptian coast to investigate the attack, not to attack Nasser. Though Israel maintained that the *Liberty* attack was an error, Moscow may have seen it as a final testing of America's patience. Stung by Chinese taunts about Russian quiescence and unreliability, Moscow seems to have decided to raise the stakes in respect of its defence of Syria. When Israel invaded on 9 June, Day Five, Moscow cut off diplomatic relations with Tel Aviv. An unnamed Soviet official later described Gromyko as proposing the diplomatic break 'so as to avoid getting involved in the large-scale military adventure that our "hawks" were insisting on'.[46]

At 8.48 a.m. on Day Six, June 10, Kosygin came on the 'hot line', threatening military action if Israel did not withdraw. The USSR would 'adopt an independent decision' if military action were not halted in the next few hours: 'These actions may bring us into a clash, which will lead to a grave catastrophe'. Israel must cease its fighting – 'if this is not fulfilled, necessary actions will be taken, including military'.[47]

At 9.30 a.m., LBJ assured Kosygin that the US was urging Tel Aviv to accept a ceasefire, and not to advance towards Damascus. At 9.44, Kosygin replied that there was no sign of any Israeli halt 'and that action cannot be postponed'.[48] At 10.50, LBJ reassured Kosygin about an imminent ceasefire, receiving a relatively emollient reply from Moscow at 11.31. At 11.54, in the last of the 'hot line' exchanges, LBJ informed Kosygin that military action was ending, and that the Israelis would not advance to the Syrian capital.

The 'hot line' meeting of 10 June was fraught, and punctuated by frequent exits and entrances – LBJ to oversee the communications with Moscow, Nicholas Katzenbach 'to call in the Israeli Ambassador to put pressure on Israel to accept a cease fire'.[49] The meeting focused on the nature of Kosygin's threat. In Nathaniel Davis' subsequent version of events, there 'was some back and forth about the tenor of the Soviet message, and the danger that the Russians might be testing us out'. Discussion centred on the situation on the ground in Syria and on the likelihood of the Israelis pressing on to Damascus. Llewellyn Thompson said that 'the Syrians were the apple of the Russians' eye' and that Moscow was far more sensitive 'to the plight of the Syrians than to that of the Egyptians'.[50]

The decision to turn around the Sixth Fleet was taken very quickly. According to Richard Helms, it was effectively taken by Thompson and McNamara when LBJ had left the Situation Room.[51] Harold Saunders' account of Helms' recollection is worth quoting fully:

> While the President was out, Secretary McNamara asked whether we should turn the Sixth Fleet around to sail toward the eastern Mediterranean. Thompson and Helms agreed. Helms pointed out that Soviet submarines monitoring the Fleet's operations would report immediately to Moscow, that the task force had stopped circling and had begun heading eastward.
>
> The President returned and McNamara mentioned this possibility. The President said, 'Yes, go ahead and do it'. McNamara picked up a secure telephone and gave the order.

Helms remembered the conversations being conducted 'in the lowest voices he had ever heard in a meeting of that kind'. However, by the end of the morning (and LBJ's 11.54 a.m. message to Kosygin) 'everyone relaxed a bit as it became clear that the fighting was petering out'.[52]

Verdicts on the confrontation and aftermath of the Six Day War

The confrontation of 10 June ran against the grain of American expectations. Only two days previously, the CIA had reported that there was no prospect of Soviet military intervention in the Middle East. Actual, close confrontation, of course, did not occur. Tel Aviv came under intense American pressure to desist. Eugene Rostow and Nicholas Katzenbach told Israeli diplomats in

Washington that world opinion was against Israel, while Moscow was 'busy sabre-rattling'. Israel was warned: 'Our credibility with the Russians is at stake'.[53] A UN ceasefire resolution was accepted, the Israeli advance halted, while Syria and Israel signed a peace agreement on the afternoon of 10 June.

Despite the brevity of the superpower crisis, LBJ certainly, as is evident from his memoirs, saw it as a moment of supreme danger and importance. His worries about the consequences of Soviet humiliation – expressed on 7 June, and also subsequently to Abba Eban – seemed vindicated. President Johnson was profoundly worried throughout the war by the possibility of Soviet intervention. According to Clark Clifford, LBJ's first reaction to hearing of the *Liberty* attack on 7 June was to suspect that it had been made by Soviet forces.[54] The 10 June Sixth Fleet decision was made with full awareness that a direct Soviet intervention was possible, even likely. For Richard Helms and Llewellyn Thompson, the 10 June crisis 'was a time of great concern and utmost gravity'. Thompson concluded 'that this crisis shows how important it was for the President to keep his cool'.[55]

LBJ's response to Kosygin's threat – a mixture of toughness, reassurances to Moscow and increased pressure on Israel – involved the familiar Presidential penchant for compromise. The swift resolution of the crisis, of course, meant that Johnson's 'cool' was never properly put to the test. In the short term, however, his instinct for compromise served him, in this instance, reasonably well. Some of his advisers subsequently talked down the crisis, implying that LBJ was claiming too much credit for what was really a fairly routine matter. McGeorge Bundy later argued that the Israelis never had any intention of advancing to Damascus. In November 1968, Bundy expressed the hope 'that the President will not talk about the 1967 Middle East crisis in terms of its being the most serious crisis of the past two decades'.[56] Nicholas Katzenbach argued that LBJ always knew that Israel would halt its advance. Kosygin also 'wasn't really threatening things'. Rather, he was saying 'Let's get on with it' – he wanted the US and USSR to impose peace.[57] Anatoly Dobrynin later added that the 'Kremlin did not actually plan any definite military action against Israel'.[58] Despite this, the Bundy-Katzenbach implication, that Johnson, Helms and Thompson tended to exaggerate the dangers of the 10 June confrontation, is not persuasive. Bundy and Katzenbach failed to take due account of the inflammatory nature of the region's politics, the extremely unpredictable nature of US–Israeli relations (evidenced, of course, in the *Liberty* attack), and the minatory tone of Kosygin's 'hot line' message.

Immediately following the conclusion of the war, members of the Administration disagreed as to likely future Soviet behaviour. White House aide John Roche urged Johnson to press home the advantage achieved by the Arab–Soviet reversals, criticising Ambassador Goldberg's reconciliatory stance at the UN.[59] Zbigniew Brzezinski, however, warned that the Soviets might become increasingly bellicose in the region, seeking to 'restore their revolutionary credentials'.[60] A State Department telegram to US diplomats of 14 June raised the spectre of Moscow inciting 'Arabs to use Suez Canal and oil to blackmail West', but did not 'rule out eventual Soviet cooling to idea of pouring weapons into area only to have them mishandled and left largely unpaid for'.[61] American intelligence tended to bear out the view that the Middle East crisis of 1967 had indeed been an occasion of utmost gravity. Walt Rostow informed LBJ on 14 August of remarks made by Boris Ponomarev, a Soviet official responsible for relations with European communist parties, to Italian communists. Ponomarev indicated that, in Moscow's view, 'the point of maximum danger' was not Vietnam, but rather the Middle East. 'Soviet military concern previously centered on the United States and West Germany. Now Israel must be included'.[62] A Warsaw Pact chiefs' meeting in Moscow during the Six Day War was also reported as having agreed 'that the Arab world should not be lost either to the West or to Communist China'.[63]

Between June 1967 and the end of Johnson's Presidency, the US and USSR circled one another, vainly asserting that their mutual suspicion should not stand in the way of achieving a regional settlement. Walt Rostow looked to the Glassboro summit, whose main public purpose was to deal with Middle Eastern issues, to advance his goal of a comprehensive settlement. The Glassboro exchanges on the Middle East, despite Kosygin's insistence on Israeli withdrawal from newly conquered territories, did reveal some community of interest between the superpowers. The Soviet leader insisted that he was ready for a renewed war, but that his real goal was peace – 'the path to this goal consisted above all in trust for each other'. The leaders squabbled over who had been responsible for starting the war. According to Kosygin, 'the Arabs were an explosive group of people' who would not accept a settlement which allowed the Israelis to keep the war gains: 'They will fight with their bare hands if necessary'.[64]

Johnson's judgment of Glassboro was that Kosygin was not delivering an ultimatum on the Middle East and that the Soviet leader had 'backed away from the implication that the Soviet Union might itself become involved'.[65] Dean Rusk told British Ambassador Patrick Dean on 29 June that, on Middle Eastern issues, 'we and the Russians were not as far apart as appeared on the surface'.[66]

The upshot of the limited post-Six Day War superpower convergence was the passage, in November 1967, of UN Security Council Resolution 242. The Resolution involved a yoking together of five American principles for peace, enunciated by LBJ in June, and the Soviet demand for Israeli withdrawal. The Resolution called for regional powers to respect the sovereignty and territorial integrity of their neighbours; for a settlement of the refugee problem; free maritime passage through the Suez Canal and Strait of Tiran; an end to the Arab–Israeli state of war; the establishment of clear national boundaries; and Israeli military withdrawal from 'territories' (not '*the* territories') gained in

June 1967. By this time, Moscow was rearming its Arab clients, while pressuring Nasser (in particular) to accept the need for a diplomatic – 'land for peace' – resolution to the regional crisis. The UN Resolution also set in motion a regional negotiating process, co-ordinated by Gunnar Jarring, Swedish Ambassador to the UN.

LBJ is often seen as the US President who presided over a new, intimate 'special relationship' between America and Israel.[67] The more radical Arab nations certainly saw Washington's behaviour as increasing their need for Soviet protection. It should also be remembered that the complete Soviet break with Israel contributed to the accelerating polarisation in the region. Anatoly Dobrynin later argued that Moscow's breaking of diplomatic relations with Israel involved an effective ending of Moscow's ability to work for a regional peace. Even as the region polarised, the objective superpower interest in stability remained.[68] For Nasser, also, the lesson of the Six Day War was certainly not that the future lay with Moscow. Rather the Soviets had let down its allies. The Russian leaders were 'a hopeless case'.[69] Nasser, indeed, attempted to open up a dialogue with Washington – not with LBJ, but with Richard Nixon, following the November 1968 elections.

Throughout 1967, the Johnson Administration worked sporadically for a regional settlement based on Resolution 242. A new Soviet initiative in September produced a burst of diplomatic activity, linked to Johnson's longing for a foreign policy success. From Washington's viewpoint, the Soviet peace initiatives, which called for more or less complete Israeli withdrawals, were simply unsellable to Tel Aviv (as well as being, as Walt Rostow put it, 'generally unacceptable', even to Washington).[70] Washington clearly recognised, however, that superpower interests were running in parallel. Neither Moscow nor Washington wanted a resumed conflict, with all its unpredictabilities. As the CIA argued, 'the risk of Soviet involvement, by accident or miscalculation, might be greater than before'.[71] In September, Nicholas Katzenbach told Dobrynin: 'We believe we have a common purpose with the Soviet Union of getting a settlement and ending a dangerous situation'. Washington was, however, 'reluctant . . . to tell Ambassador Jarring what to do'.[72] It was not simply a matter of having to take account of the UN mediator. Even if they could agree with each other, and despite their mutual concern for predictability, Washington and Moscow could not simply impose a solution on the various parties to the Middle East's conflicts.

Czechoslovakia

The Johnson Administration and Eastern Europe

In mid-1966, the Johnson Administration committed itself to a co-ordinated strategy of bridge-building towards Eastern Europe. The policy emerged from several sources and reflected a variety of motivations. Among these motivations was a desire to revive those earlier 'bridge-building' efforts which had largely expired with the US bombing of North Vietnam in February 1965. The Administration also wished to divert attention from Vietnam, to respond to signs of liberalisation in Eastern Europe, and to contain indiscipline among the Western European allies. General de Gaulle's announcement, in March 1966, that he was going to take France out of NATO's integrated command had – along with West Germany's *Ostpolitik* overtures to the East – created a crisis for the Western alliance. Bridge-building was a way of trying to revive the alliance, making sure that (as Hubert Humphrey put it) 'our wagons are in line'.[73] The policy involved enhanced trade between the US and Eastern Europe as well as increased cultural, diplomatic and other contacts (such as the setting up of the trans-European International Institute for Applied Systems Analysis). Bridge-building, as noted in Chapter 2, ran into problems in Congress. Moscow, for its part, tended to welcome technology transfers and food imports to the USSR from the US. However, the Soviets were also inclined to resent bridge-building to the Warsaw Pact allies as a fairly blatant effort to undermine communist cohesion.

The 1966 bridge-building policy drew on already fairly deep-rooted and sophisticated understandings of the tensions and changes within the Warsaw Pact. A CIA report of March 1964 had pointed to a 'new and less rigid relationship' between Eastern Europe and Moscow. The 'lesser Communist regimes' now recognised their own power and were growing in self-confidence. They were exploiting 'the disappearance, except in the broadest sense, of clearly defined limits set by Moscow of what constitutes acceptable behavior by a Soviet bloc member'. The report noted the differences between 'the Stalinist' leader of East Germany, Walter Ulbricht, and his fellow communist leaders. In Czechoslovakia, the report noted that Antonin Novotny had 'been forced by liberal elements in his party to remove close associates with Stalinist backgrounds, to ease restrictive domestic policies, and to give more latitude to the restive liberals and intellectuals'.[74]

The crucial question, of course, was the degree to which Moscow was prepared to see liberalisation develop. The Soviets wished to channel necessary change. Indeed, the CIA in 1964 suggested that a mature, liberalised 'grouping of independent Communist states' might 'constitute a stronger, more viable system than an empire held in thrall by the Soviet Union'. However, 'de-Stalinization in Eastern Europe' was linked to 'de-satellization' and to a loss of leadership (and vulnerability to criticism and rivalry from Beijing) which Moscow might not be prepared to tolerate.[75]

Washington's East European bridge-building of 1966–68 sought to embed the notion of communist diversity in the international political consciousness. According to Dean Rusk, it was not simply a matter of attempting 'to drive wedges between the smaller countries of Eastern Europe and the Soviet Union'.[76] In fact, the bridge-building policy pulled in different directions. Its economic and financial initiatives sought to disturb the satellites' dependence on Moscow. Yet, so key Washington players argued, the Soviets would only benefit from being relieved of some of the burdens of alliance management and discipline. Bridge-building was thus seen in Washington as part of the process of coming to terms with change in both Eastern and Western Europe. It was part of the agenda, attractive to both superpowers, of channelling change and promoting stability. It was a way of containing German nationalism, by offering the prospect of a changed political environment to the East. In the phrase used by Francis Bator – the White House assistant, of Hungarian background, who was very prominent in the 1966 initiative – it looked to a 'growing out of the Cold War'.[77] The hazards of the policy, however, were also clear. These ranged from the problems of selling it to the US Congress, and from the difficulties of anticipating Soviet reactions, to the danger of heightening expectation and stimulating unrealistic hopes among the East European reformers.

During 1966 and 1967, Administration spokesmen went to rhetorical battle on the subject of bridge-building and communist diversity. LBJ, in the October 1966 address to editorial writers discussed in Chapter 2, called for 'peaceful engagement' to supersede 'co-existence' (both with the USSR and the Eastern European states).[78] Nicholas Katzenbach in December ridiculed those American anti-communists whose 'patriotism exceeds their understanding'. He mentioned a 'lady in New Jersey' who was 'waging a campaign against the import of carrots from Canada on the ground that some of the carrots are communist carrots'. In fact, communism was 'no longer the monolith of Stalin's time'. Now, 'we see Eastern European countries pursuing individual national interest and identity'.[79] In February 1968, Foy Kohler (now Deputy Under Secretary for Political Affairs at State) noted the scale of changes in Poland: 'Collectivization (of agriculture) has been abandoned altogether. A measure of freedom of expression is tolerated'.[80]

Americans were being encouraged to abandon the 'idea that all Communists are devils'.[81] One difficulty here, of course, was the problem of explaining how the recognition of diversity did not extend to Vietnam. (Kohler argued that stout resistance to 'the more radical Communists' – Beijing and some elements even in Moscow – could only further the agenda of détente.)[82] Another issue which bubbled under the surface of these speeches about communist diversity was whether 'peaceful engagement' was not so much a deepening of 'co-existence' as a way of actually *winning* the Cold War. In August, LBJ declared that, despite 'our understanding of the Russian people' (including the American and Russian 'love of story and song'), differing 'principles and differing values may always divide us'.[83] Kohler went further. He argued that the splits within world communism, which began with the Soviet–Yugoslav split of 1948, were transforming the prospects for global politics. Many East Europeans were rejecting communist ideology and 'turning to more pragmatic solutions'. The Russian people, in their turn, were 'increasingly aware of the way we live in the West' and were 'demanding some of the same things for themselves'. The communist rulers were facing 'irresistible pressures' for change. Kohler's implication (which contrasted sharply with some of his reports when he served as Ambassador to Moscow) was that, one day, non-'doctrinal communists' – first in countries like Poland and Czechoslovakia, then in Russia itself – might succeed in effecting a peaceful transition to democratic capitalism. Later in 1968, it became evident that the Soviet Politburo also saw a link between LBJ's 'peaceful engagement', liberalisation in the East European satellites, and a threat to the survival of Soviet communism.

Washington and the 'Prague Spring'

On 5 January, Czech communist leader Antonin Novotny, facing severe internal dissent and economic reversals, was effectively forced out of office, making way for Alexander Dubcek, the Slovak communist leader. The US Embassy in Prague reported that this was the first time ever 'a Communist regime has purged' a top leader 'by bringing popular pressure to bear on him'.[84] Dubcek's rise did not initially cause great alarm in Moscow, though the tactic of allying himself with a mobilised party rank-and-file was soon drawn to the Soviet Politburo's attention.[85] In March, the American Embassy in the Czech capital raised the possibility of Soviet military intervention. The situation had patent echoes of Moscow's military strike against Hungary in 1956. However, so the Embassy advised, it 'can be hoped that lessons were learned on all sides from 1956, and it can be expected that Prague will do its utmost to avoid any high risk foreign policy moves'.[86]

Dubcek was careful to avoid any suggestion that he favoured a foreign policy independent of the Warsaw Pact and Moscow. His internal reforms, however, involved the democratisation of the Czech Communist Party in a way which profoundly challenged the Leninist tradition. As Llewllellyn Thompson reported from Moscow, the 'introduction of democratic processes in Czechoslovakia, even if confined to the party, would threaten to undermine the whole system'.[87] Dean Rusk opened a meeting of the National Security Council in April by suggesting that communism was at the crossroads. The citizens of communist countries had, to the chagrin of their bureaucratic leaders, discovered Western individualism – ironically, just as the US was struggling with Vietnam War protest and black radicalism:

> Our tradition has been individual rights, and we have only recently had to concern ourselves with collective problems. The Communist societies depart from the collective view and are only recently facing the problem of the individual. This produces a pull of attraction to the West.

Bridge-building, according to Rusk, was having an effect: it recognised 'the desire of Eastern European intellectuals to pursue professional contacts with their Western colleagues' and the desire of the East Europeans 'to assert their independence against the Soviet Union'.[88] Writing in May 1968, Nathaniel Davis argued that the Czech liberalisation was a triumph for the White House's policy of reaching out to Eastern Europe. Generalised détente-promotion was sometimes dismissed as being too preoccupied with 'atmospherics' and 'fluff'. Yet contact with the West had re-educated and re-oriented the citizenry of Eastern Europe: 'Czechoslovakia today is an example of psychology producing reality'.[89]

Between March and August 1968, the leading American decision-makers were concerned to rebut Soviet charges that Washington was fomenting Czech defiance of Moscow. It was widely felt that the public denouncement of CIA involvement in Czech reform politics would pave the way for actual Russian invasion. On 22 July, Deputy Undersecretary Charles Bohlen assured Dobrynin that there was 'absolutely no truth' in a recent *Pravda* allegation of a 'NATO Western plot against Czechoslovakia involving the Pentagon and CIA'.[90]

During these months, official Washington debated the likelihood of invasion, considering possible ways to deter it. LBJ's special concern undoubtedly was the effect of an invasion on the arms control process. It was pointed out to the President that, with the possibility of a major Eastern European crisis, this might not be the most auspicious time for a summit. Yet, as we saw in Chapters 2 and 3, Johnson would not be deterred. He was reassured by a CIA memo of 10 May which concluded that the 'Soviets will probably stop short' of military intervention: Dubcek had had a 'rough meeting' with party leaders in Moscow.[91] On 13 June, the CIA reported on the Soviet 'anxiety to find some way to avoid direct military intervention'. 'Soviet heavy-handedness' actually helped Dubcek, by increasing public sympathy for his efforts to find a viable relationship with Moscow. In the CIA's view, the Czech reformers were especially concerned that East Germany might engineer a Berlin crisis, which would naturally lead into Soviet intervention in Czechoslovakia.[92] On 11 July, Llewellyn Thompson drew Washington's attention to the delay in removing Soviet troops from close to the Czech border, following a Warsaw Pact military exercise. At this time, Thompson saw an intervention as likely, rather than inevitable. Much depended on Moscow's ability to arrest the dynamic of change: 'Soviets probably do not hope be able to turn clock back in Czechoslovakia, but they clearly making every effort stop it' [sic].[93] By early August, Thompson was predicting an invasion. Moscow could not accept Czech democratisation. Security considerations – the 'strategic location of Czechoslovakia' and 'the loss of classified information that would leak out through a Czechoslovakia friendly to the West' – also pointed to direct Soviet action. Moscow's primary concern, however, was the spread of the democratic infection, firstly to the other bloc countries, but also to the USSR itself. 'There are already numerous signs of the disaffection of intellectuals and youth, a widespread dissatisfaction with the role of the Communist Party' in the USSR, 'as well as a rising feeling of nationalism in the various Soviet republics'.[94]

During the pre-invasion period, therefore, LBJ and his advisers were receiving different messages. Not only did the Moscow Embassy's analysis differ from that offered by the CIA, it also clashed with US Ambassador Beam's view from Prague that Dubcek could make a deal with Moscow. The US Embassy in Prague welcomed Dubcek's ability to stand up to the Politburo during a meeting with Soviet party personnel at Cierna on the Czech border in July. 'Dubcek's regime can take considerable credit for saving its skin at Cierna, and for staring down the Soviet threat of force'. Beam worried, however, about the extent of concessions made by Dubcek in a subsequent meeting at Bratislava.[95]

Subsequent academic and journalistic debate on the pre-invasion period focused on the American failure to do a great deal to deter the Russians. Whether an invasion could have been deterred by some combination of American military positioning and diplomatic pressure is, of course, questionable. Some commentators have also criticised Dubcek for failing to mobilise Czech military forces.[96] Linked also to this debate about possible avenues of deterrence is the accusation – evident in the commentary by Ronald Steel quoted at the start of this chapter – of virtual superpower collusion in the invasion. Accusations of collusion were referred to by Ambassador Beam in a telegram of 22 July; the US Ambassador in Prague concluded: 'Believe Czechs are realistic in realizing limits on US action, i.e., no military support or massive economic aid'.[97] An extreme version of the 'collusion' argument would hold that the US welcomed the invasion as a tethering of the Dubcekian loose canon, seeing it as no more than a temporary setback to the détente and arms control dynamic. There certainly is evidence that senior Americans were not unaware of the positive effect of invasion on NATO cohesion. It gave Washington much greater leverage over its West European allies, damaged the appeal of Gaullist quasi-independence, and effectively quashed efforts in the US Congress to force large US troop withdrawals from Europe.[98] The most common form of the 'collusion' argument is that put forward by Steel in his September 1968 piece: that Washington somehow indicated to Moscow its unwillingness to make more than a ritual protest at the fate of the Czech reformers. Crucial to this case is the testimony of Zdanek Mlynar, a Czech reform communist, regarding a meeting with Leonid Brezhnev in Moscow on 26 August. According to Mlynar, Brezhnev indicated that he would have ordered the invasion, even at the risk of inciting war with the US. However, he had, on 18 August, been assured by LBJ that the US government still respected the division of Europe agreed in the post-World War Two meetings at Yalta and Potsdam. Washington recognised these agreements 'without reservation' in the case of Czechoslovakia and Romania, and was prepared to discuss them in the case of Yugoslavia.[99]

The researchable American archival record does not reveal evidence of pre-invasion collusion. However, the Soviets would have been well aware of the realistic limits – 'no military support or massive economic aid' (as Ambassador Beam put it) – to American backing for Prague. The possibility of a military threat was raised by the US Embassy in Bonn on 10 May:

> It is inevitable, of course, to recall the Hungarian experience. A major difference in the case of Czechoslovakia, however, is the presence of substantial US forces in Germany. This means that, contrary to the Hungarian case, we could in theory signal our support for the Czech Government by moving our troops closer to the Czech border to assist the Czechs in warding off a Soviet attack.[100]

Walt Rostow offered some detailed assessments of the nature of America's interest in the survival of Dubcek. On 10 May, Rostow wrote to Dean Rusk that a strong, diplomatic protest should be made in respect of Soviet military threats to Czechoslovakia. The American 'failure to deter the Communist takeover in Czechoslovakia in 1948 was one of the most serious mistakes of our foreign policy since the war'. The 'process of movement towards détente' was now at stake; Rostow listed the progress to détente as embracing LBJ's 7 October 1966 speech, NATO's acceptance of the Harmel Report,[101] West German *Ostpolitik*, and the real possibility of 'mutual and balanced force reductions' in Europe.[102] On 20 July, Rostow indicated that a Soviet invasion could also kill the Nonproliferation Treaty and 'probably reduce the chance for a peaceful settlement in the Middle East and Viet-Nam'. An invasion would put the US in a very difficult situation, especially if Prague called on NATO for assistance. 'Czechoslovakia', wrote Rostow, 'is surely in the Soviet sphere of influence. But that fact hardly justifies murder in broad daylight'. A Czech appeal to the United Nations would also be embarrassing: 'It would be difficult to explain why the UN Charter protects Korea against aggression, but not Czechoslovakia'. Contrary to any implication that American leaders (at least before the event) saw any benefit in invasion, Rostow argued that unimpeded Czech liberalisation was entirely in America's interest. Poland would soon follow the Czech example. East Germany would be isolated. Rostow recommended that the US 'should seriously consider the British suggestion of doing everything possible at this point to deter the Russians'.[103]

'Everything possible,' of course, did not include any serious threat of a military response. Moscow's decision to invade was taken in the near certainty that Washington would do little more than utter diplomatic protests. Oleg Kalugin, former KGB station chief in Washington, later testified that the KGB had 'stirred up fears' in the Politburo 'that Czechoslovakia could fall victim to NATO aggression or a coup unless certain actions were undertaken promptly'. Kalugin also reported, however, that 'the CIA was not involved in the developments of the Prague Spring'.[104] Moscow would have appreciated that an invasion would interrupt the détente agenda. As explained in Chapter

3, however, the Soviets were at this time not especially anxious to secure an immediate arms control agreement. They had little reason to suppose that the move to détente would be delayed in a way which would harm their interests.

Shortly before the invasion, Rusk assured Senate Minority Leader Everett Dirksen that the US had been 'stiff' with Moscow in private over Czechoslovakia. He felt, on 27 July, that the Czechs might still compromise enough 'to keep the Russians off their backs'.[105] The Secretary of State told Republican Presidential Candidate Richard Nixon on 10 August: 'We've been tough on the USSR privately, not in public'.[106] On 19 August, Rostow informed Dobrynin that 'the Soviet decisions at Cierna seemed wise to us'.[107] The following evening, at 7.06 p.m., Rostow rang LBJ to tell him that the Soviet Ambassador had an urgent message. The President asked: 'Is it Czechoslovakia?'.[108]

Invasion

LBJ, Rostow and Dobrynin assembled in the Cabinet Room at 8.15 p.m. Johnson's relaxed attitude at the meeting has reinforced the impression of American insouciance over the invasion. LBJ began the meeting by referring to a 'colour movie' of his encounter with Kosygin at Glassboro. He then discussed having his hair cut. When informed of the invasion, in Dobrynin's version of events, LBJ 'did not react at all, just thanked me for the information . . .'.[109] The recording of the meeting reveals LBJ referring to Secretary Rusk's position on Czechoslovakia, and moving immediately on to the arrangements for announcing a summit meeting in the USSR.[110]

Johnson's conduct at the meeting with Dobrynin was certainly extraordinary. He rambled on about former House Speaker Sam Rayburn's drinking habits and discussed with the Soviet Ambassador the origins of the song, 'The Yellow Rose of Texas'. Small talk was presumably LBJ's way of dealing with Dobrynin, especially when (as now) the two had glasses in their hands. The President expected to hear news of the invasion. He wished to make it clear that his main priority was the summit and arms control, rather than vain protest at what would soon become a *fait accompli*. However, the simple fact remained that, at this moment of severe international crisis, the US President treated Moscow's Ambassador to a disquisition on haircuts, public drunkenness and Texan history.

On Dobrynin's departure, LBJ convened an emergency session of the National Security Council. Johnson reported Dobrynin's statement to the effect that the Soviets 'were invading Czechoslovakia because the Czechs have asked them to come in'. (Hardliners in the Czech Communist Party, led by Slovak communist head Vasil Bil'ak had promoted the invasion. Under the 'Brezhnev Doctrine', the USSR entered Czechoslovakia, assisted by four Warsaw Pact allies, in order to assist Czech socialists against the counter-revolutionary Dubcek regime.) Johnson's main concern was still the arms control summit. He asked his advisers: 'Can we talk now after this?' Rusk suggested diplomatic protest at the UN, but also raised the spectre of Soviet action in Berlin. General Earle Wheeler advised simply: 'There is no military action we can take. We do not have the forces to do it'. For Hubert Humphrey, all the US could do was 'snort and talk'.[111]

In the ensuing weeks, Johnson and his senior advisers reassessed the prospects for a summit, worried about further Soviet action in Eastern Europe, and tried to arrive at an assessment of the precise reason for the invasion. The President took solace in the fact that the invasion would halt efforts in the US Senate to reduce American forces in Europe to 50,000. On 22 August, he remarked that Moscow's action 'may be helpful to us in not getting the troop cutbacks in Europe'.[112] At a 4 September NSC meeting, he discussed the beneficial effect of the invasion on US 'isolationism'. Clark Clifford argued that the US 'must use the crisis to prompt NATO states to improve the quality of their troops and to improve their mobilization potential'. The Germans would be pushed hard 'to increase their defense budget'.[113]

Some of LBJ's advisers saw a possibility of using the invasion as a lever not only against the Western European allies, but also against Moscow itself. According to Rusk, Moscow had 'miscalculated the political reaction in Czechoslovakia'. To the extent that the Soviets had expected a more docile reception in Czechoslovakia, and also less in the way of international protest, they might be inclined to flexibility elsewhere. Llewellyn Thompson argued that the invasion did not signal the end of détente:

> The Soviet leaders are in difficulty. They have made many bad mistakes. Although the leadership will pull itself together to face the difficulties caused by the Czech invasion, some changes in the leadership will undoubtedly be made. The effect of the Czech invasion is very great inside the Soviet Union. Our policy should be not to slam the door in their faces but to force them to pay a substantial price for their action . . .

The invasion had occurred, according to Thompson, because Moscow 'concluded Dubcek couldn't retain control of the Czech reform elements'. The contagion would have spread. At the 4 September meeting, the consensus was that the invasion was not intended as a deliberate rejection of détente. Rusk pointed out that, as Dobrynin emphasised in his contacts with the Administration, the 'Soviet Union is trying to carry on business as usual with us'.[114] As LBJ put it in an earlier meeting, the post-invasion US–USSR relationship contained 'some plusses and some minuses'.[115]

Most senior advisers concurred that the invasion was a vicious, but predictable and even rational, response to a real threat to Soviet power. Administration assessments of the invasion emphasised the remorseless, predictable exercise of Moscow's authority. There was no trace of the optimistic, 'communist diversity' language of the 1966–67 bridge-building effort. In technical military terms, according to General Wheeler, the invasion had been 'quick, efficient and effective'.[116] A State Department analysis in late September described the invasion as a 'rational act' which 'should not be seen as the first in a succession of reckless moves by the USSR which could ultimately engage NATO forces'.[117] The CIA saw the invasion as prompted by 'genuine fear' and undertaken by Moscow with 'some reluctance'.[118]

There certainly was a strong whiff of empty ritual in the American response. For example, when Rusk and Thompson discussed the refugee problem, their concern was primarily directed to doing enough to assuage international opinion. Llewellyn Thompson argued that, if the US appeared 'to be urging' Czech refugees 'to come to the United States, the Soviet Union could use this policy to argue that we are, in fact, intervening in Czechoslovakian affairs'. Rusk referred to the difficulty of registering American disapproval of the invasion in a manner that would both meet expectations in the non-communist world, and signal to Moscow that the US was prepared to accept – and indeed welcome some implications of – the invasion. Rusk reported that 'numerous activities of a good-will nature', notably the second inaugural flight to the US of a Soviet civilian airliner, had been cancelled. 'We have a difficult problem of handling the American people as well as others throughout the world who would not approve if we act as if nothing had happened'. In discussing the refugee question, Secretary Rusk also made clear his view that America had an interest in stability in Eastern Europe, even a stability imposed by Soviet force: 'We have to open our doors because if we do not, the refugees might return to Czechoslovakia and oppose the existing government. This would not be in our interest'. LBJ agreed that the US 'can accept those who desire to come to the United States but not encourage them to come'. Vice President Humphrey took the opportunity to remind him that the rather lukewarm support for the Czech refugees would be compared 'with what we did for Hungarian refugees' in 1956.[119]

It is difficult to resist the conclusion that Washington really did wish, in Rusk's phrase, to 'act as if nothing had happened'. Top-level discussions revolved around questions of managing international opinion and of keeping détente alive. Senior White House figures, including Hubert Humphrey, were alarmed by suggestions from the anti-Vietnam War movement that Czechoslovakia was 'Russia's Vietnam'. The Vice President was 'shocked to find (John Kenneth) Galbraith talking as though it was one and the same'.[120] On 31 August, Walt Rostow presented LBJ with a draft letter to Kosygin. It expressed 'deep disquiet' but urged Moscow to 'turn back towards the path we explored at Glassboro'.[121] There is no evidence that the letter was actually sent, but it encapsulated Washington's attitude. LBJ publicly condemned the invasion, but at a 27 August press conference, the issue was not even raised. (This was a special press conference, held at the LBJ Ranch to coincide with the President's sixtieth birthday. The conference was mainly concerned with the Democratic National Convention, being held in Chicago.) Johnson warned against Soviet aggression in Eastern Europe in a speech at San Antonio. On 6 September, he reported publicly that the White House had received 'some assurances', following the speech. Meanwhile, various meetings with Dobrynin affirmed that détente had not expired on 20 August. The Soviet Ambassador reassured Washington about the prospects for bilateral super-power relations, as well as about the physical safety of Alexander Dubcek.[122]

The cosiness of the US–Soviet relations at this juncture should not be over-stated. The invasion *was* a major setback for LBJ's international agenda – despite the fortuitous effect on the Senate debate on European troop levels. There was no question that the attack on Prague was, in Llewellyn Thompson's phrase, 'a brutal act of aggression'.[123] Johnson was very con-cerned about the Soviet nuclear alert which apparently accompanied the 20 August attack.[124] As Rusk told Dobrynin, Johnson would also suffer severe domestic criticism; he 'would be subject to strong criticism for his efforts in building better relations with the Soviet Union'.[125]

At least until early October, the Administration also took seriously the possibility of further invasions. On 4 September, Dean Rusk told the NSC that 'no one can be sure that the Soviets won't hit Berlin and Romania in the days ahead'.[126]

The Soviet–Romanian standoff was resolved by intra-Warsaw Pact negoti-ation, rather than by any direct intercession from Washington.[127] (Romania had refused to help the USSR in the attack on Prague.) Dean Rusk later admit-ted that a Soviet invasion of Romania would not have provoked any 'direct response' from Washington. Explicit warnings were given, however, concern-ing Yugoslavia. Any move there would, recalled Rusk 'have created a crisis of first-class proportions because the threat of the movement of Soviet armies to the Adriatic would have been of great concern to all of NATO as well as to the United States'.[128]

An attack on Yugoslavia would have endangered the European *status quo*, although a State Department assessment of September 1968 did play down Yugoslavia's strategic importance to the US.[129] A further assessment in Novem-ber concluded that the US did have 'a major stake in Yugoslavian indepen-dence'.[130] State also considered the possibility of an attack on Austria. This, of course, would have been impossible to dismiss as a rational exercise of Moscow's regional power. The State Department analysts concluded that 'any encroachment on Yugoslavia, Austria, Berlin or Germany would be of a totally different dimension' to the Czech invasion 'and would risk triggering World War III'.[131]

The Johnson Administration did not regard the US as having a major stake in Czech reform. Change within the East European satellites was welcome only to the degree that it did not upset the European strategic balance. The Czech crisis of 1968, much more than the Middle Eastern crisis of June 1967, saw the Johnson team reconnoitring the road which leads from realism to cynicism.

Notes

1 L. B. Johnson, *The Vantage Point* (London, Weidenfeld and Nicolson, 1971), p. 302.
2 Helms, Oral History, p. 34.
3 'Notes on President's meeting with Abba Eban', Meeting Notes File, box 1 (undated).
4 See Chapter 2, note 159.
5 *FRUS, 1964–1968*: Volume XVII: *Eastern Europe* (Washington DC, US Government Printing Office, 1996), p. 243.
6 Ibid., p. 252.
7 *The Economist*, 3 June 1967, p. 993.
8 Ibid., 17 June 1967, p. 1206.
9 *Time*, 16 June 1967, p. 16.
10 Ibid., 30 Aug. 1968, pp. 11–12.
11 *New York Review of Books*, 26 Sept. 1968, pp. 13–14 ('Up against the wall in Prague').
12 See D. Little, 'Nasser Delenda Est: Lyndon Johnson, the Arabs, and the 1967 Six-Day War', in H. W. Brands (ed.), *The Foreign Policies of Lyndon Johnson: Beyond Vietnam* (College Station, Texas A and M Press, 1999), pp. 145–67, at p. 149.
13 See W. I. Cohen, 'Balancing American interests in the Middle East: Lyndon Baines Johnson vs. Gamal Abdul Nasser', in W. I. Cohen and N. B. Tucker (eds.), *Lyndon Johnson Confronts the World: American Foreign Policy, 1963–1968* (Cambridge, Cambridge University Press, 1994), pp. 279–310, at p. 282.
14 Eugene Rostow, Oral History, p. 34.
15 Quoted in Little, 'Nasser Delenda Est', p. 146.
16 M. R. Beschloss (ed.), *Reaching for Glory* (New York: Simon and Schuster, 2001), p. 189 (20 Feb. 1965).
17 Quoted in Cohen, 'Balancing American interests', p. 294.
18 J. D. Glassman, *Arms for the Arabs: The Soviet Union and War in the Middle East* (Baltimore, Johns Hopkins University press, 1975), p. 37. See also M. B. Oren, *Six Days of War: June 1967 and the Making of the Modern Middle East* (New York, Oxford University Press, 2002), p. 43.
19 A. Vassiliev, *Russian Policy in the Middle East; from Messianism to Pragmatism* (Reading, Massachusetts, Ithaca Press, 1993), p. 70. Also, Oren, *Six Days of War*, pp. 54–5.
20 A. Bregman, *Israel's Wars* (London, Routledge, 2002), p. 82. See also G. Golan, *Soviet Policies in the Middle East* (Cambridge, Cambridge University Press, 1990), pp. 59–64.
21 'Record of NSC meeting, 24 May 1967', NSF: NSC Meetings File, box 2.
22 See W. B. Quandt, *Decade of Decisions: American Policy toward the Arab–Israeli Conflict, 1967–1976* (Berkeley, University of California Press, 1997), p. 40.
23 As note 21.
24 Quoted in Little, 'Nasser Delenda Est', p. 160.
25 *FRUS, 1964–1968*: Volume XIV: The Soviet Union (Washington DC, US Government Printing Office, 2001), pp. 486–7.
26 NSF: NSC Histories: Middle East Crisis, box 20. See also B. I. Kaufman, *The Arab Middle East and the United States* (New York, Twayne, 1996), ch. 4; Oren, *Six Days of War*, p. 143.
27 As note 21.
28 See H. W. Brands, *The Wages of Globalism* (New York, Oxford University Press, 1995), p. 198.

29 NSC Histories: Middle East Crisis, box 17 (26 May 1967).
30 As note 21.
31 NSC Histories: Middle East Crisis, box 19 (19 May 1967).
32 Ibid. (23 May 1967).
33 Ibid., box 17.
34 Ibid., box 18 (5 June 1967).
35 See, especially, W. B. Quandt, 'Lyndon Johnson and the June 1967 war: what color was the light?', *Middle East Journal*, 46:2 (1992) 198–288; R. B. Parker, *The Politics of Miscalculation in the Middle East* (Bloomington, Indiana University Press, 1993); R. B. Parker, *The Six Day War* (Jacksonville, University of Florida Press, 1997).
36 NSC Histories: Middle East crisis, box 19 (vol. 7).
37 *National Diplomacy: 1965–1970* (Washington DC, Congressional Quarterly, 1970), p. 93. Abba Eban in late May 1967 reported on a 'paralyzed president' (Oren, *Six Days of War*, p. 115). See also W. W. Rostow, *The Diffusion of Power* (New York, Macmillan, 1972), p. 417.
38 As note 3.
39 'The hot line exchanges', NSC Histories: The Middle East Crisis, box 19 ('vol 7', 4 Nov. 1968). The exchanges are listed ibid, Appendices G–H.
40 Ibid., box 18 ('vol 4').
41 Ibid.
42 Ibid., box 20 ('vol 8').
43 Ibid., box 18 (7 June 1967).
44 'Notes of NSC meeting, 7 June 1967', NSC Meetings File, box 1.
45 As note 3.
46 Vassiliev, *Russian Policy in the Middle East*, p. 70.
47 'Hot line letter' (sight translation), NSC Histories: The Middle East Crisis, box 19 ('vol 7').
48 As note 39.
49 'Hot line meeting June 10, 1967', NSC Histories: The Middle East Crisis, box 19 ('vol 7') (dated 22 Oct. 1968) (Saunders/Helms).
50 As note 39.
51 Helms, Oral History, pp. 33–4.
52 As note 49.
53 Oren, *Six Days of War*, p. 299; also, Brands, *The Wages of Globalism*, p. 213.
54 C. Clifford, *Counsel to the President* (New York, Random House, 1991), pp. 445–6.
55 As note 39.
56 'The hot line meetings and the Middle East in New York', NSC Histories: The Middle East Crisis, box 19 ('vol 7', 7 Nov. 1968).
57 Katzenbach, Oral History, p. 8.
58 A. Dobrynin, *In Confidence* (New York, Times Books, 1995), p. 161.
59 Roche to LBJ, 12 June 1967, NSC Histories: The Middle East Crisis, box 18.
60 Ibid., box 19 ('vol 7').
61 'Soviet role in the Middle East crisis', ibid.
62 NSF: CF: Europe and USSR: USSR, box 224, folder, 'USSR memos 26' ('Soviet party official summarizes Moscow's Middle East policy').
63 Ibid. ('USSR/Eastern Europe/Middle East', 10 Aug. 1967).
64 *FRUS, 1964–1968*: Volume XIV: *The Soviet Union* (Washington DC, US Government Printing Office, 2001), pp. 517, 523, 526.
65 Ibid., p. 527 (Presidential debriefing, 23 June 1967).
66 NSF: CF: Europe and USSR: USSR, box 230, 29 June 1967.
67 See F. A. Gerges, 'The 1967 Arab-Israeli War: US actions and Arab perceptions', in D. W. Lesch (ed.), *The Middle East and the United States* (Boulder, Westview, 1999), pp. 185–203, at p. 19.

68 Dobrynin, *In Confidence*, p. 162.

69 Anwar Sadat, *In Search of Identity: an Autobiography* (London, Collins, 1978), p. 199.

70 *FRUS, 1964–1968*: Volume XX: *Arab–Israeli Dispute, 1967–1968* (Washington DC, US Government Printing Office, 2001), p. 509 (19 Sept. 1968).

71 Ibid., p. 114 (18 Jan. 1968).

72 Ibid., pp. 523–4 (29 Sept. 1968).

73 Quoted in F. Costogliola, 'LBJ, Germany, and "the End of the Cold War"', in Cohen and Tucker (eds.), *Lyndon Johnson Confronts the World*, pp. 173–210, p. 194. See T. A. Schwartz, *Lyndon Johnson and Europe: in the Shadow of Vietnam* (Cambridge, Massachusetts, Harvard University Press, 2003).

74 *FRUS, 1964–1968*: Volume XVII: *Eastern Europe* (Washington DC, US Government Printing Office, 1996), pp. 2–3, 7–8 (27 March 1964).

75 Ibid., p. 8.

76 Rusk, Oral History, p. 24.

77 Quoted in Costigliola, 'LBJ, Germany and "the end of the Cold War"', p. 194. See also T. A. Schwartz, 'Lyndon Johnson and Europe: alliance politics, political economy, and "growing out of the Cold War"', in Brands (ed.), *The Foreign Policies of Lyndon Johnson*, pp. 19–36; R. L. Garthoff, 'Eastern Europe in the context of US–Soviet relations', in S. M. Terry (ed.), *Soviet Policy in Eastern Europe* (New Haven, Yale University Press, 1984), pp. 315–48.

78 See Chapter 2, note 93.

79 *Dept. of State Bulletin*, 2 Jan. 1967.

80 Ibid., 13 March 1967.

81 Dean Acheson to the Senate Committee on Government Operations, 27 April 1966 (quoted in Costigliola, 'LBJ, Germany . . .', p. 194).

82 As note 80.

83 *Dept. of State Bulletin*, 19 Sept. 1966.

84 *FRUS, 1964–1968*: Volume XVII: *Eastern Europe*, p. 188 (25 March 1968).

85 See C. Kennedy-Pipe, *Russia and the World, 1917–1991* (London, Arnold, 1998), p. 137.

86 *FRUS, 1964–1968*: Volume XVII: *Eastern Europe*, p. 189.

87 Ibid., p. 229 (2 Aug. 1968).

88 'NSC meeting of April 24 – Eastern Europe', NSF: NSC Meetings File, box 2.

89 Davis to Rostow, 4 June 1968, NSF: Files of W. W. Rostow, box 11, folder, 'Glassboro commencement speech'.

90 'Memorandum of conversation', NSF: CF: Europe and USSR: USSR, box 229, folder, 'Dobrynin conversations 3'.

91 Ibid., box 225, folder, 'memos xix'.

92 NSF: CF: Europe and USSR: Czechoslovakia, box 182, folder, 'Czech crisis'.

93 *FRUS, 1964–1968*: Volume XVII: *Eastern Europe*, p. 203 (11 July 1968).

94 Ibid., pp. 229–31 (22 Aug. 1968).

95 Ibid., p. 232 (4 Aug. 1968).

96 See M. Kramer, 'The Prague Spring and the Soviet invasion of Czechoslovakia' (2 parts), Cold War International History Project (available on Woodrow Wilson Center, CWIHP website).

97 *FRUS, 1964–1968*: Volume XVII: *Eastern Europe*, p. 211.

98 See Costigliola, 'LBJ, Germany . . .', p. 208.

99 Z. Mlynar, *Night Frost in Prague: The End of Humane Socialism* (London, Hurst, 1980), p. 241.

100 *FRUS, 1964–1968*: Volume XVII: *Eastern Europe*, p. 195.

101 The Harmel Report, accepted by NATO in December 1967, concluded that military security and progress towards détente were compatible.

102 *FRUS, 1964–1968*: Volume XVII: *Eastern Europe*, p. 193.

103 Ibid., pp. 206–7.
104 Kramer, 'The Prague Spring . . .' (part 2), p. 9.
105 *FRUS, 1964–1968*: Volume XVII: *Eastern Europe*, p. 219.
106 Ibid., p. 234.
107 Ibid., p. 235.
108 Johnson, *The Vantage Point*, p. 487.
109 Dobrynin, *In Confidence*, p. 180.
110 *FRUS, 1964–1968*: Volume XVII: *Eastern Europe*, pp. 236–42.
111 'Notes on emergency meeting of the National Security Council, August 20, 1968', NSC Meetings File, box 2.
112 *FRUS, 1964–1968*: Volume XVII: *Eastern Europe*, p. 249.
113 Ibid., pp. 272–8.
114 Ibid.
115 Ibid., p. 248 (22 Aug. 1968).
116 Ibid., p. 251 (23 Aug. 1968).
117 Ibid., p. 81 (undated).
118 Ibid., pp. 102–3 (7 Nov. 1968).
119 Ibid., pp. 274–5 (4 Sept. 1968).
120 Ibid., p. 249 (22 Aug. 1968).
121 Ibid., p. 264.
122 See *FRUS, 1964–1968*: Volume XIV: *The Soviet Union*, pp. 687–89 (24 Aug. 1968); *PPPUS: Lyndon B. Johnson, 1968* (Part 2) (Washington DC, US Government Printing Office, 1969), pp. 904–5; *The Johnson Presidential Press Conferences*: Volume II (London, Heyden, 1978), pp. 973–76, 982.
123 *FRUS, 1964–1968*: Volume XVII: *Eastern Europe*, p. 279 (23 Sept. 1968).
124 See ibid., p. 277 (4 Sept. 1968); also Kramer (as note 96, p. 19); B. G. Blair, *The Logic of Accidental Nuclear War* (Washington DC, Brookings Institution, 1995) p. 179.
125 *FRUS, 1964–1968*: Volume XIV: *The Soviet Union*, p. 689 (24 Aug. 1968).
126 *FRUS, 1964–1968*: Volume XVII: *Eastern Europe*, p. 276.
127 Kramer (as note 96), pp. 19–20.
128 Rusk, Oral History, pp. 25–6.
129 *FRUS, 1964–1968*: Volume XVII: *Eastern Europe*, p. 88 (undated).
130 NSF: CF: Europe and USSR: Yugoslavia, box 232, folder, 'Memos 2', 4 Nov. 1968.
131 *FRUS, 1964–1968*: Volume XVII: *Eastern Europe*, p. 86 (undated).

8

Conclusion

The intention of this concluding chapter is to direct attention, first, to President Johnson's leadership of foreign policy towards the Soviet Union, and then to consider wider questions of Cold War superpower rivalry and co-operation in the 1960s.

Johnson's leadership

The literature on Presidential foreign policy leadership exudes a host of warnings, invocations and simple assertions about the requirements for success. Presidents are advised to seek 'multiple advocacy' of different foreign policy positions, avoiding a narrow and constraining 'groupthink'.[1] They must set priorities clearly. They must find a way to express the fundamental purposes of American international engagement in a way which is clear and culturally appropriate. They must lead public opinion, energise the foreign policy bureaucracy, bargain successfully with allies, and so on. They must avoid damaging public rifts between natural enemies within the Administration – notably between the Defense and State Departments, but also (especially in the post-LBJ era) between White House and State Department advisory structures. They must find a means to share power without sacrificing the ability to lead. When framing problems, it is inevitable that Presidents will draw on prior experiences and analogies; but these analogies must be appropriate, consciously understood and capable of being modified or abandoned.[2]

As noted in Chapter 1, it is relatively easy to discard some of the commonly held myths about LBJ and foreign affairs. Homely and folksy language is not incompatible with sharp intelligence. Johnson engaged keenly with foreign policy issues and was generally well versed on international matters. He took over – indeed, he came to regret taking over – President Kennedy's advisers and advisory structures, but was not afraid to make important organisational changes. (In March 1966, LBJ adopted General Maxwell Taylor's recommendations, originally drafted in the context of counterinsurgency operations, on the need to strengthen interdepartmental co-ordination. This set up a tiered interdepartmental structure, headed by the Senior Interdepartmental Group at the State Department.)[3] Johnson's advisory structures were not redolent of narrow 'groupthink'. As David Barrett has argued, 'Lyndon Johnson had a voracious appetite for information and reached widely for diverse points of view'.[4] In judging LBJ, one also has constantly to bear in mind that this was a President who, in White House foreign affairs adviser Francis Bator's words, 'hated to be understood'. Robert Dallek quotes a Johnson aide: 'You never knew which qualities in the man were real and which were assumed. You simply couldn't tell'.[5] Johnson, the 'problem child' of the modern Presidential era, is not an easy leader to judge.

A strong case can be made for judging LBJ's leadership of Soviet policy in positive terms. 'Bridge-building', 'step-by-step' détente, 'growing out of the Cold War', the identification of appropriate areas of superpower common interest: here were at least the bones of a worthy vision for US–Soviet relations in the wake of the Cuban missile crisis. Consistent and coherent leadership, however, was not achieved. One reason for failure is obvious and really does not need to be discussed at great length. Johnson's conduct of the Vietnam War was uncertain, ineffective and lacking in long-term conceptual coherence. Aspects of his handling of the war, notably the 1965 bombing of North Vietnam (while Aleksei Kosygin was in Hanoi) and the Administration's incoherent approach to the peace process, unnecessarily harmed the development of relations with Moscow. Less obviously than his erratic conduct of the war, however, some characteristic features of LBJ's leadership style continually threatened to undermine the integrity and coherence of his personal foreign policy. These characteristics, which seemed to emanate primarily from the Johnson personality, included a dithering, 'middle way' approach to decision-making. They also included LBJ's tendency to reduce complex issues to issues of personality, even of personal hatred. Finally there is the question of Johnson's rather unstable, even schizophrenic understanding of Soviet power.

At times, Johnson was actually the very reverse of a decisional ditherer. As we saw in the previous chapter, his June 1967 decision to turn around the Sixth Fleet was taken extremely rapidly. The February 1965 decision to bomb while Kosygin was in Hanoi was taken in an extraordinarily casual manner. Sometimes Johnson simply seems to have given way to the mercurial, even irresponsible side to his nature; one thinks of the strange interview with Ambassador Dobrynin which followed the Soviet advance on Prague in August 1968. Some moments of relaxed, insouciant sureness perhaps represented an emotional release from his customary agonised and procrastinatory style of leadership. This prolonged and difficult-to-read style of decision-making, developed of course during his time as a leader in Congress, was well captured by Evans and Novak in 1966: LBJ 'did not reveal – indeed, he did not fully determine in his own mind – what his position would be until the last possible moment, when the conditions of battle were fully known to him'.[6] Dean Acheson, writing to ex-President Harry Truman in October 1966, compared

LBJ's decision-making style with that of President Franklin Roosevelt. Though superficially comparable, LBJ's mode of decisional process was always inclined to 'drift'. LBJ was 'a worse postponer of decisions' than FDR.[7]

Looking back on LBJ's decision-making as reviewed in the preceding chapters, we can see the characteristically slow weighing of options, sliding into compromise. In Chapter 3, for example, we saw the process described by Evans and Novak in operation as LBJ adjudicated between Secretary McNamara and General Wheeler on the issue of anti-ballistic missile deployment. At the key meeting at the Johnson ranch in December 1966, the President was forced to arrive at a decision. The result – deployment of the 'thin' Sentinel system – was geared more to the exigencies of bureaucratic and Congressional politics, than to the development of a clear policy on missiles. LBJ's Vietnam War escalation decisions, discussed in Chapter 4, followed a similar route of extensive gestation, succeeded by a splitting of differences. Johnson's Cuban policy, discussed in Chapter 6, involved a similar manoeuvring between accommodating Castro (as argued early in the Administration by Mac Bundy and Gordon Chase) and the aggressive approach of Thomas Mann.

What is also evident from the decisional narratives of the preceding chapters is LBJ's extreme personalisation of political debate and political issues. Clark Clifford recalled Johnson's habitual reaction to new problems and reversals of fortune: 'He reacted by thinking, *They* can't do this to Lyndon Johnson! They can't push me around this way!'[8] The rivalry with Bobby Kennedy assumed damaging proportions. We saw in Chapter 3 how a speech by RFK was the trigger to the new Presidential activism on nuclear nonproliferation. A personal row with Bobby Kennedy was, as noted in Chapter 5, a crucial factor in the undermining of the 'Phase A/Phase B' Vietnam peace initiative, involving Harold Wilson and Aleksei Kosygin. Johnson's ego was extraordinary. As Doris Kearns wrote, under this President, the 'White House machinery became the President's psyche writ large'.[9] This expansive, but vulnerable, egotism – with its constant invocation of slights and insults suffered at the hands of 'the Harvards' and 'the Fulbrights' – threatened continuously to destroy decisional and policy coherence.

Veering between a sophisticated analysis of Soviet international interests and occasional outbursts of anger at global, monolithic communist conspiracy, Johnson's view of Soviet power and intentions was unstable. LBJ saw himself as pursuing a reasonable, mature and pragmatic policy toward Moscow. He felt that 'considerable headway' had been made in the early exchanges with Khrushchev, with subsequent problems blamed on the post-1964 Kremlin regime and, as Johnson put it in 1966, the 'very regretful developments in Vietnam'.[10] LBJ saw himself as sincerely and patiently working towards understanding and identifying areas of US–Soviet 'common interest' and 'common action'.[11] 'When we have differed with the Soviet Union', he declared in 1967, 'I have tried to differ quietly and with courtesy, and without venom'.[12] In *The Vantage Point*, LBJ indicated his 'basic assumptions' about US–Soviet relations: 'that reaching agreement . . . on almost anything would take time, but that agreement could be reached if there were enough patience and understanding on both sides'.[13] In public, Johnson was always keen to portray himself as the offerer of compromise and as the opponent of harsh ideology. In October 1964, he told the Mormon Tabernacle audience in Salt Lake City that there was 'nothing to be gained from rattling our rockets or bluffing with the Soviets'.[14] Asked in a press conference in 1966 about the role of ideology in superpower relations, Johnson replied: 'I think both sides must realise that neither is going to convert the other. The United States has no interest in remaking the Soviet Union in our image. And I don't see any evidence that America will go Communist'.[15]

LBJ's public portrayal of himself as a bluff, well-intentioned pragmatist was not entirely misleading. It drew, of course, on his self-image as the successful fixer and master of the US Senate. Yet, as we have seen, Johnson also retained extraordinary views about the links between Moscow and the anti-Vietnam war movement. In some of his telephone conversations, he could all too easily slip into the language and discourse of monolithic communist conspiracy. Invocation of Johnson's pragmatism needs also to be squared with his extremely expansive understanding of his responsibilities as President. As H. W. Brands argues, this was a Presidency which embraced the tenets of American high liberalism, notably the interpenetration of domestic reform and Cold War foreign policy, and a sweeping view of Presidential power and responsibility. In January 1965 he declared that 'the state of the Union depends, in large measure, upon the state of the world'. In March 1965, he informed Congress that he wanted 'to be the President who helped to end war among the brothers of this earth'.[16] Pragmatist and visionary; conspiracy-theorist and proponent of détente; international leader and obsessive pursuer of personal quarrels; advocate of the transforming qualities of Presidential authority, and decisional ditherer: Johnson's personal contradictions destroyed the prospect of providing coherent and effective leadership.

The Cold War

At least when shorn of its wilder excesses (notably his fixation with the putative 'communism' of the anti-war movement), Johnson's ambivalence about Soviet power merely reflected the uncertainties of a generation of American leaders. The attitude of this generation was summarised in Chapter 1 as 'Munich analogy' – always stand up to dictators who wish ultimately to run the world – tempered by Cuban missile crisis: find a way of preventing disputes from spinning out of control. The ambivalence was neatly reflected in statements made by Dean Rusk in 1966 and 1967. In the earlier year, the Secretary of State spoke of the need to 'seek agreements or understandings with the Soviet Union to blunt disputes and to reduce the dangers of a great war'.[17] In the aftermath of the 1967 Glassboro summit, however, Rusk stated in public: 'There are obvious differences which are far reaching between our two countries. The basic objectives of the Soviet Union continue to be to support world revolution'.[18]

The ambivalence of LBJ and his advisers, at least to the degree that it was not permitted to degenerate into policy incoherence, to some extent reflected the essential nature of the Cold War. This was a contest which combined elements of irreconcilable ideological rivalry, pragmatic accommodation, partnership, rivalry and systemic structure. Interaction between the superpowers involved the constant testing and negotiation of positions, the exploration of a variety of points on the spectrum stretching from nuclear collision to pragmatic partnership. David Calleo described US Cold War policy as alternating 'between a hostility that stops short of genuine confrontation and a détente that stops short of genuine accommodation'.[19]

In Chapter 1, the orientation of the Johnson Administration towards détente was defined as 'aspirational' – working towards a means of coexistence which could drastically reduce the threat of nuclear conflict. Thomas Schwartz makes much of the concept of 'growing out of the Cold War', associated particularly with Francis Bator and the 1966 bridge-building initiatives.[20] Some members of the Administration may indeed have thought in terms of transcending, even ending, the Cold War. However, it is difficult to imagine figures like Dean Rusk and LBJ himself thinking in such terms. Rather aspirational détente was a way of pursuing the rivalry with Soviet communism in a way which recognised the reality of intersecting US–Soviet interests and the possibility for partnership. It recognised the mutual Washington–Moscow fear of Chinese power. However, aspirational détente was not the same as the *end* of US–Soviet rivalry. In 1968, Raymond Garthoff warned of the tendency to identify détente 'with a warm and friendly glow on the part of all concerned'. Rather, détente needed to be recognised as a strategy towards, particularly, Eastern Europe: 'to inspire, cultivate, and assist trends toward independence from Moscow'. It also, in respect of arms control, should be 'an effort to strike a mutually advantageous business deal between two sharp-eyed and coldly calculating adversaries'.[21] Garthoff's version of détente represented the prevalent view within the Johnson Administration.

Although they rarely thought in terms of transcending the Cold War, members of the Johnson Administration certainly did see the possibility for joint US–Soviet action and articulation of interest. We have encountered numerous examples: the Tashkent mediation of 1965, the recognition of common interests over nuclear non-proliferation, the various bilateral agreements, even the acceptance of Sovietisation of Cuba. The US attempted to undermine Soviet domination of Eastern Europe by bridge-building. However, as the invasion of Czechoslovakia showed, Washington was not prepared to

use military force to combat Moscow's East European ascendancy. As Eugene
Rostow remarked in 1968: 'We're not going to liberate East Germany by
force'. (He added: 'You couldn't have détente in Europe without reunification
of Germany, and you couldn't have reunification of Germany without
détente'.)[22]

The Johnson Administration certainly did see important areas of shared
interest with Moscow. The close relations between leading American figures
and Ambassador Dobrynin – to a lesser degree with Foreign Minister Andrei
Gromyko – sometimes came close to justifying the Chinese accusation of 'collusion'. The spectacle of the Soviet Ambassador giving assurances in 1964 that
the Kremlin appreciated that 'some unfortunate things occur' in election campaigns is one to treasure.[23] However, during these years, the US–Soviet relationship was still distinguished more by rivalry than by co-operation. There
was always the potential for swift, alarming confrontation, as during the Six
Day War. (The 1973 October nuclear alert, during the Middle East Yom
Kippur War, indicated that the same conditions pertained under President
Nixon.) The 'darker side' of the Cold War – from the downing of US aircraft
to institutionalised espionage – continued. In fact, rather than Washington
being too conservative in its assessment of Soviet power and intentions, a case
can be made that the Johnson team were sometimes too eager to identify areas
of common superpower interest. The Six Day War confrontation with
Kosygin, for example, was preceded by excessive American confidence in the
willingness and ability of Moscow to act as a force for moderation and mediation. In Chapter 4, we saw the degree to which the 1964–1965 Vietnam War
decisions were backed by a rather unrealistic assumption that Soviet mediation might resolve difficulties. The assumption that the Soviet 'need' for
détente would inhibit Moscow's support for North Vietnam was unreliable.
The mere conceptualisation of the Cold War as an amalgam of rivalry and
partnership was no guarantee of wise or consistent policy.

The mixture of partnership and rivalry extended into the developing world.
In South America, as we saw in Chapter 6, Moscow was reluctant to espouse
the revolutionary 'voluntarism' of the Castroites. In other areas, however, the
spillover from the Sino-Soviet split could have unpredictable effects. Again,
the US in the 1960s cannot convincingly be accused of failing adequately to
recognise the depth of the rift between the USSR and China. The communist
split was the main focus of numerous CIA analyses. As Foy Kohler acknowledged, the split was generally regarded as the 'mainspring' of Moscow's behaviour.[24] The problem was that the precise effects of the split were difficult to
assess. At one level, the Administration contemplated joint US–Soviet action
against Chinese nuclear facilities. (In Chapter 1, we even encountered a 1967
public opinion poll in which respondents envisaged the clear possibility of the
Soviet Union siding with the US against China.) However, Washington could
never be sure whether the Sino-Soviet split actually meant that Moscow felt

itself impelled to compete more aggressively with China for leadership of international communism. Part of the Administration's failure in Vietnam was attributable to the extreme difficulty of predicting the precise effect on Soviet behaviour of the break with Beijing.

To conclude, it is churlish to deny that, in very broad terms, LBJ's Soviet policy was part of 'what went right' with his Presidency. The dynamic of post-Cuban missile crisis détente was not entirely halted. The Vietnam conflict did not become a world war. Despite the 10 June 1967 confrontation with Kosygin, the world did not come desperately close to nuclear conflict. The bilateral and nonproliferation treaties were real successes. The foundations for arms control were laid, despite LBJ's unrealistic efforts to commence talks in 1968. Yet, as we have seen, the Vietnam War was not a sideshow, unfairly drawing attention away from other areas of foreign policy success. The war did not entirely destroy any possibility for success in these other areas, but certainly came close to so doing. In his memoirs, LBJ tried to make the case for foreign policy coherence and success beyond Vietnam. Yet, for much of his Presidency at least, LBJ's foreign policy *was* the war. In Johnson's own words, the war was justified by its centrality to *all* America's global purposes: 'Around the globe, from Berlin to Thailand, are people whose well-being rests, in part, on the belief that they can count on us if they are attacked. To leave Vietnam to its fate would shake the confidence of all these people in the value of an American commitment and in the value of America's word'.[25] Lyndon Johnson was an important figure in the emergence of superpower détente. However, it is in terms of 'Johnson's war', rather than 'Johnson's peace', that this Presidency deserves to stand in historical memory.

Notes

1 For some recent reflections on 'multiple advocacy', see A. L. George and E. K. Stern, 'Harnessing conflict in foreign policy making: from devil's to multiple advocacy', *Presidential Studies Quarterly*, 32:3 (2002) 484–508. Also, I. L. Janis, *Groupthink* (Boston, Houghton Mifflin, 1982).

2 See R. E. Neustadt and E. R. May, *Thinking in Time* (New York, Free Press, 1986).

3 See P. Y. Hammond, *LBJ and the Presidential Management of Foreign Relations* (Austin, University of Texas Press, 1992), p. 28.

4 D. M. Barrett, *Uncertain Warriors: Lyndon Johnson and his Vietnam Advisers* (Lawrence, University Press of Kansas, 1993), p. 172.

5 R. Dallek, 'Lyndon Johnson as a world leader', in H. W. Brands (ed.), *The Foreign Policies of Lyndon Johnson: Beyond Vietnam* (College Station, Texas A and M University Press, 1999), pp. 6–18, at p. 8.

6 R. Evans and R. Novak, *Lyndon B. Johnson: the Exercise of Power* (New York, New American Library, 1966), p. 148.

7 D. McClellan and David Acheson (eds.), *Among Friends: Personal Letters of Dean Acheson* (New York, Dodd, Mead, 1980), p. 281.

8 C. Clifford, *Counsel to the President* (New York, Random House, 1991), p. 381.

9 D. Kearns, *Lyndon Johnson and the American Dream* (New York, Harper and Row, 1976), p. 177. On 'the Bobby problem', see S. Skowronek, *The Politics Presidents Make* (Cambridge, Massachusetts, Harvard University Press, 1993), p. 349.

10 *The Johnson Presidential Press Conferences: Volume 2* (London, Heyden, 1978), p. 602 (13 Oct. 1966).

11 *PPPUS: Lyndon B. Johnson, 1967, vol. 1* (Washington DC, US Government Printing Office, 1968), p. 631 (19 June 1967).

12 Ibid., p. 10 (10 Jan. 1967).

13 L. B. Johnson, *The Vantage Point* (London, Weidenfeld and Nicolson, 1971), p. 464.

14 *PPPUS: Lyndon B. Johnson, 1964, vol. 2* (Washington DC, US Government Printing Office, 1964), p. 156 (29 Oct. 1964).

15 Ibid., *1966, vol. 2* (Washington DC, US Government Printing Office, 1967), p. 1069 (27 Sept. 1966).

16 Cited in H. W. Brands, *The Strange Death of American Liberalism* (New Haven, Yale University Press, 2001), pp. 93–5.

17 *The Outlook for Freedom* (Washington DC, Dept. of State, 1966), p. 10.

18 *The Department of State Bulletin*, 7 Aug. 1967, p. 159.

19 D. P. Calleo, *Beyond American Hegemony* (New York, Basic Books, 1987), p. 6.

20 T. A. Schwartz, 'Lyndon Johnson and Europe: alliance politics, political economy and "growing out of the Cold War"', in H. W. Brands, *The Foreign Policies of Lyndon Johnson: Beyond Vietnam* (College Station, Texas A and M University Press, 1991), pp. 37–60.

21 R. L. Garthoff, *A Journey Through the Cold War* (Washington DC, Brookings Institution, 2001), pp. 240–1.

22 E. V. Rostow, Oral History, p. 26.

23 *FRUS, 1964–1968*: Volume XIV: *The Soviet Union* (Washington DC, US Government Printing Office, 2001), p. 104.

24 Ibid., p. 361.

25 *PPPUS: Lyndon B. Johnson, 1965, vol. 1* (Washington DC, US Government Printing Office, 1966), p. 395 (7 April 1965).

Bibliographical note

Key secondary sources are cited in the chapter notes. On LBJ, special mention should be made of the work of Robert Caro. His work on Johnson's early years, and *The Years of Lyndon Johnson: The Path to Power* (New York, Knopf, 1990) was indispensable. Robert Dallek's *Flawed Giant: Lyndon Johnson and His Times, 1961–1973* is a fine biographical study of LBJ as Vice-President and President. The Johnson era also stimulated many valuable books of memoir. LBJ's own *The Vantage Point: Perspectives of the Presidency, 1963–1969* (London, Weidenfeld and Nicolson, 1971) is an underrated source. R. L. Garthoff's *A Journey Through the Cold War: a Memoir of Containment and Coexistence* (Washington DC, Brookings Institution, 2001), Walt W. Rostow's *The Diffusion of Power* (New York, Macmillan, 1972) and Jack Valenti's *A Very Human President* (New York, Norton, 1975) all provide essential insights. The literature on LBJ's foreign policy 'beyond Vietnam' is rapidly growing in size and quality. The work of H. W. Brands (notably, *The Wages of Globalism: Lyndon Johnson and the Limits of American Power* (New York, Oxford University Press, 1995)) is indispensable, as is W. I. Cohen and N. B. Tucker (eds.), *Lyndon Johnson Confronts the World: American Foreign Policy, 1963–1968* (Cambridge, Cambridge University Press, 1994). Thomas Alan Schwartz's *Lyndon Johnson and Europe: in the Shadow of Vietnam* (Cambridge, Massachusetts, Harvard University Press, 2003) is a brilliantly argued revisionist work. The best one volume study of the Cold War is Richard Crockatt's *The Fifty Years War* (London, Routledge, 1995). Particularly useful sources for *President Lyndon Johnson and Soviet Communism* were the volumes edited by Michael R. Beschloss (*Taking Charge: The Johnson White House Tapes, 1963–1964* (New York, Simon and Schuster, 1997) and *Reaching for Glory: Lyndon Johnson's Secret White House Tapes, 1964–1965* (New York, Simon and Schuster, 2001)) and Anatoly Dobrynin, *In Confidence: Moscow's Ambassador to Six Cold War Presidents* (New York, Times Books, 1995).

Index